JAPAN'S REVENGE

Håkan Hedberg

 Pitman Publishing

First published 1972

Sir Isaac Pitman and Sons Ltd.
Pitman House, Parker Street, Kingsway, London WC2B 5PB
P.O. Box 46038, Portal Street, Nairobi, Kenya

Sir Isaac Pitman (Aust.) Pty. Ltd.
Pitman House, 158 Bouverie Street, Carlton, Victoria 3053, Australia

Pitman Publishing Company S.A. Ltd.
P.O. Box 11231, Johannesburg, South Africa

ISBN: 0 273 25232 1

Reproduced and printed by photolithography and bound in
Great Britain at The Pitman Press, Bath
(G. 283:11)

Contents

Appendix:
list of statistical tables

CHAPTER ONE

The Mountain

Japan in the spring of 1972 continued her climb toward the peak of the mountain, the distant summit where victory waits, a triumph for which the climber had been waiting and fighting over the past hundred years. The winds grew ever colder in 1971; suddenly it seemed as if Japan were losing her foothold, but the rope proved stronger than anyone ever dared to believe. The struggle up the mountain-side had entered a completely new phase, but the time-keepers at the foot of the mountain only noted calmly that the quality of Japan's climbing boots was superior to that of her rivals', and that it was now only a matter of time before the Japanese would be able to swing himself up to the pinnacle and look out over the world, over all rivals, over the mountain that had been defeated.

Some people and some nations have their own private Everest: a mountain that challenges, a mountain that must be conquered. In the case of individuals, the mountains are not always the same: the targets and the mountain peaks often change as decades pass; we arrive at a new scale of values and tell ourselves that Mount X is no longer worth the struggle or that the price is too high, the sacrifices too great, the sweetness of victory perhaps too small.

For more than three years, Japan's Everest has been the GNP-per-capita mountain, the dream of becoming the richest nation in the world, as measured by the annual flow of goods and services per person. But Japan's struggle with the mountain has been eternal, because before the Japanese shouldered the per-capita challenge they had considered themselves duty bound to win other frosty peaks: first to avoid the fate of China, swallowed by the Western colonial powers; then to achieve naval parity with the leading powers of the West, and fulful the dream of ruling Asia, solving forever their raw material problems; a dream that ended with the snapping of the rope, and a plunge to the bottom of the abyss of defeat in World War II. It was a humbled and beaten climber who in 1945 started looking up towards the new dream mountain: to regain, somehow, Japan's prewar standard of living. This target seemed a shifting mirage, because Japan had lost everything: the rope, the ice pick, the boots. The area of her empire had shrunk to half. But in 1951 industrial production overtook the pre-war peak level, and in 1955 the dream came true: a real standard of living as high as before the war. In 1960 a new mountain was spotted through the binoculars: the possibility of surpassing West Germany — No. 3 on world GNP charts — in total economic power. When this peak too had been conquered (1969), and Japan had swung herself up to the No. 20 position in world rankings of GNP per capita, then the clouds lifted and suddenly the Japanese saw an incredibly beautiful mountain with a peak glistening as if it were carved of gold: No. 1 in GNP per person! The field marshals of statistics scrutinized the slopes of the mountain and made their pronouncement: we should be able to climb abreast of the Americans by 1984, and by 1988-92, at the very latest, we should have defeated all competitors and be at the peak. Then we shall have succeeded in realizing the ambitions that first began to stir at the dawn of the Meiji Era in 1868. Then we will have proved definitely that the Japanese are the equals of any Western people.

Does the dream still exist? Has the rope been frayed, is the Japanese climber as hypnotically bound to the victory dream now — in 1972 — as three years ago?

My renewed meeting with the Japanese climber and the wild swings of his mountain pick presented a new picture as I studied Japan's pattern of economic behaviour in the June, 1968—August, 1969 period, and I did not hesitate to sketch a very negative image of Japan in *The Japanese Challenge* (Bonniers, Sweden, November, 1969). The country that I had come to know in 1953-64 had changed, was on the road to becoming 'a second USA', a nation elbowing so sharply for success that I ventured to make two short-range predictions: firstly, that Japan would be slammed against the wall within eighteen months, secondly that Japan, within two years, would be forced by outside pressure to revalue the yen upwards by 15-20 per cent, two forecasts that became realities.

I returned to Japan in December 1970, and in this book I have tried to describe the new acts, the new conditions in Japan's mountaineering drama, the new stage directions, and the new strategy for victory. My range of vision is deliberately as limited as my previous book: a piece of the future, the macro-economic frames; the strategy; trend evaluation and changes in world economic power balance. These limitations have their roots in personal interests and shortcomings: as I am not a psychologist or sociologist, the 'soul of Japan' must remain an unwritten page in this book, with the exception of the national characteristics that determine and influence the outcome of the climb up the mountain.

In some sections of this book, I present my own calculations, but the main purpose this time is also to describe how the Japanese themselves look at their own economic future and their role in the world, and particularly the Japanese economists who dominate the public discussion. They are the map readers, constantly studying the mountain, who are plotting a course as straight as possible to the summit, one as free as possible from unsuspected obstacles or disastrous plunges.

It was fairly easy to sit looking into the crystal ball in the summer of 1969 and glance toward 1985. Now, in the spring of 1972, it is considerably more difficult to discern a solid pattern, because the attitudes within Japan have undergone such a drastic change; but the gap between an attitude change and a policy change has always been very wide in Japan. People with sane and safe professions — such as professors — would probably elect to refrain from making any definite evaluation of trends as based on Japan's 1972 situation: 'Too many factors of uncertainty; the misty picture must become more clear.' An economic journalist does not have this free choice: it is his duty to report his 'of-the-minute material' as fast as possible because otherwise he becomes a past tense writer, devoting himself to economic history instead of economic journalism.

One more reservation: my selection of facts is subjective, because I have to decide for myself what facts I consider interesting and essential. When I wrote *The Japanese Challenge* I had become tired of the Western cliché view of Japan: 'The miracle machine; the explosion of affluence.' So I held up a number of fragments toward the light, a mosaic of very limited size, and found that too much of Japan's newly created society contradicted my own value norms and my own demands of the shape a society should take, how a society should function. An express train on the road to its own special Hell, or, at least, towards environmental destruction. An express train without a conductor, a train where the passengers had no chance of getting off or influencing its course. My hope was that the Western reader would continue his search, go to other books, other sources, and there partake of other fragments, a balancing mosaic.

In this book I have chosen to include also some facets of strength in the economic development of the Japanese people. This does not mean that my own values have changed or that the negative fragments that I held up to the light in 1969 have diminished in any way. The positive factors have been included because otherwise the reader would be tempted to draw an erroneous conclusion concerning Japan's economic future, being unable to judge whether or not the rope will be strong enough.

The quality of the rope will influence the future of both Americans and Europeans, will to a great extent determine our own living conditions and our own freedom to determine our economic policies: that is, our nominal right to choose weapons, our nominal right to decide by ourselves whether we shall pursue a policy of strengthening the international competitive power of our industry or a policy that further strengthens our welfare machinery.

The United States has accepted the Japanese challenge: In 1971, President Richard M. Nixon declared repeatedly and with ever more fervour, 'We shall remain No 1!' That is, the United States is firmly determined to remain standing at the peak of the mountain of mirage, does not want to lose the illusion of being 'the world's most affluent nation.'

In Europe it might be tempting to shrug one's shoulders and say: 'Let the Japanese keep on running up their Everest; we, however, are tired of mountain climbing, we have arrived at a new scale of values...We must make clear to the Japanese that we do not consider ourselves involved in any kind of competition with them, that they are welcome to keep on running alone and in isolation — and then they may give up. So let us close our eyes to the results of Japan's mountaineering operations, let us calmly ignore the figures pouring forth from Japan's forecasting machinery. And, at the very worst, we can postpone the decision whether or not to compete for another decade or so, because has not Herman Kahn proclaimed that the Japanese will overtake the US by 1990 in GNP per capita, and then around Year 2000 in total production?'

But the problem we face is not a problem of the 1980's. It is the 1970's that will prove to be Japan's fateful decade, its make-or-break decade. We shall know already within this decade whether Japan can 'win' or not.

These are some of the definite trends (and they are not just the result of mechanically lengthening or extrapolating past growth curves):

1. Japan has *already* defeated the United States in annual total fixed investments per capita, i.e. in total effort, including manufacturing industry investments per capita and public investments per capita; this development will further accelerate

2. Though Japan's current GNP per capita is only 50 per cent of the US current figure, Japan's own leading economists agree that Japan will overtake the US in GNP per capita by 1980 at the latest. My own forecast is that this milestone in world economic history willbe reached by as early as 1978, after only six years

3. The hourly wage of Japan's industrial employee is only half of the West German figure — but in 1980, Suzuki-san will be earning 15 per cent more than his German colleague, and will even earn more than the Swedes, who now lead Europe's high-pay league

4. Despite this there will be a further strengthening of Japan's competitive power in 1980 as compared with

1972, because of a much faster rise in productivity than
any other country

5. A change of course: by 1977 Suzuki-san will have
dethroned the Swede as world champion in annual
public investments per capita

6. Conclusion: the 'challenge' is already a phase of the
past, Japan's growth has entered the phase of revenge,
and now it is only a question of time — and ethics —
when the revenge will come and *how* we in the West will
interpret Japan's frenzied enthusiasm in taking the very
last steps to the mountain peak.

Shall we interpret Japan's strategy for the 1970's — a
strategy outlined in this book — as an athlete's challenge, as a
friendly, battle-eager boxing-glove that will never deal
another dirty blow, as a shot no more lethal than that of a
starting pistol; 'We lost militarily in 1945, but now we shall
try to prove that we have other qualities, which will give us
an economic revenge.' Or will the outside world — Peking, for
example — interpret Japan's competition signals as the first
act of a drama of economic revenge, a first act that must
necessarily be followed by a second act: attempts at military
revenge? The key question: How will people in the United
States look at Japan's victorious surges, the success of an
allied power that each month becomes more of a threat to the
US economic front sectors throughout the world?

For more than three decades, the Japanese people have
patiently shouldered all burdens in the conquest of each new
target, forced to sacrifice too much of themselves on the altar
of growth in both industry and business. When Prime
Minister Eisaku Sato retires in the summer of 1972, thus
ending the seven and a half year Sato era, will he then be
replaced by a man who might encourage revenge for the
Japanese people, against industry, against the system of
allocating national resources?

The questions mount up as Japan grows, coming ever
nearer to closing the gap between itself and the front runner
of world economy, the US.

All of us — in London, Hamburg, Stockholm, Chicago —
will of necessity have to follow the climb of the Japanese; we
shall be able to see how he sometimes slips on the icy

crevices, how his hold on the rope sometimes seems dangerously weak — and how the struggle continues, the climber's struggle with himself and with the ever more cruel mountain. It is no spectacular pleasure to watch an elite athlete in practice to see how he punishes his own body in order to win Olympic gold. As for Japan, we shall be watching Japan's struggle in our living rooms: via TV we are already watching, and will be watching, ever more documentaries showing how the skies over Japan turn more and more yellow, how the victims cry out in desperate protest. Via TV we watch the powerful Group of Ten discuss the value of currencies, including the yen. We see thousands of Japanese police encircle wildly firing students, groups of activists who want to blast apart the establishment, to cut the rope on the whole mountain climbing operation. None of us can escape the sight of Japan's victories and defeats, her sufferings and her triumphs.

Our very method of watching the painful struggle may gradually become more and more Japanese: TV sets made in Japan. When the shipping executives of London and Gothenburg appear on TV and speak of bad times, they are really saying that there is a recession in Japan, that freight demand in traffic between Japan and the raw material countries is too weak. When Asea and Siemens and SKF and Olympia and Facit publish deteriorating financial accounts, it is often a direct result of the hectic speed in Japan's rush up the mountain slopes.

There should be a limit to human ambitions and the ambitions of nations. Where this limit is, we never know — until it is too late. For two centuries it has been our cultural heritage to try to do our best, to burst out of the frames, to look beyond what seems the possible.

As Japan in the spring of 1972 looks up towards the mountain, many people will have difficulty in breathing the air of the street below, so many that it already seems appropriate to ask this question: when Japan takes the final step, will the victorious message from the peak be a choking death-rattle, 'We made it! We won! Sayonara?'

The risk of national suicide is hot on the heels of the mountain climber, and is thus a part of Japan's strategy for victory. The Japanese — that is the ruling Establishment — are now fully aware that it is more important to survive than to win.

CHAPTER TWO

August,1945

> *'Boys, be ambitious!'* William S.
> Clark, American teacher, in a
> farewell speech to Japan's
> schoolboys, in 1877; three
> words still quoted in all Japanese
> schools, and in management
> speeches to each annual crop of
> new employees: 'Shonen-yo,
> taishi o idake!'

The war is over. All efforts have been in vain. Emperor Hirohito, 44, ruler of Japan for the past nineteen years and the Son of Heaven, leans nervously towards the microphone and begins to address his defeated people: The war has 'not necessarily' developed to Japan's advantage. The enemy has started using 'a new and extremely cruel bomb,' and if Japan were to continue the struggle, this would not only mean the collapse and extinction of the Japanese nation, but would 'also lead to the total extermination of human civilization.' Thus this decision to end the war, to accept the Potsdam Declaration of the Allied Powers; unconditional surrender.

It is noon on August 15, 1945, and the recording which the Emperor had made late the previous night is played over the state radio network, via loudspeakers hastily installed in all factories, schools, ministries, military barracks and offices. For the first time the people listen to the voice of the Emperor. For the first time, many realise that Japan is not invincible. Millions stand at attention, even more millions burst into tears. Everywhere the same scene: husband, wife, children, embrace each other, cry together in despair.

The rope has snapped. The atomic bombs over Hiroshima and Nagasaki on August 6 and August 9 have snapped the last strand of the ambitions which grew and grew, dreams born of the desperation of 1853 — when the gunboats of American Commodore Matthew Perry anchored and opened up by force a completely unprotected country, which had for centuries isolated itself from the world and from the industrial revolution. Perry kindled a thirst for knowledge and racial equality. 'Knowledge shall be sought in all parts of the world,' declared the sixteen-year-old Emperor Meiji in April 1868, when the inner circle close to him had toppled the Shogunate and restored, after a lapse of 800 years, the power of the Imperial System. Out and into the world streamed groups of Japanese, hunting for the most modern technology of the time: the steam engine, the gas lamp, telegrams, lightning conductors, properties of different metals. They also learned how to open and run a bank, a workshop, an industry, and foreign advisers were employed inside Japan to show them how to create an Army, a Navy.

Japan learned Western patterns of thought fast, too fast: war against China in 1894, and Japan wins; war against Russia in 1904, and Japan wins again. An insignificant but profitable role as an ally of Great Britain during World War I. There are strong liberal currents in the 1920's, even jazz music, and now 95 per cent of the people can read and write. But the grip of the generals on the power machine is hardening. Invasion of Manchuria in 1931, total war against China in July 1936, and between these two dates the State Budget share of the Navy and the Army grows from 31 to 47 per cent. The generals and the financial-industrial leaders discover that they share the same interests: to further 'secure' the supply of war material. The ambitions grow: a Greater East Asia Co-Prosperity Sphere, a life line of steel and military might between Japan and the raw material sources in Indonesia, Malaya, and the Philippines. Between 1930 and 1941, Japan's annual production of aircraft jumps from 400 to 5,000, and the iron fist is strengthened by the world's largest battleships.

Japan feels herself encircled, halted in her search for security by the containment policy of the A-B-C-D Powers (Americans, British, Chinese, Dutch). The man in the street feels that the Western powers want to put a rope around the Japanese neck, to deprive the country of the essential materials that are so badly needed. In Europe, Adolf Hitler is starting to silence some of those who would strangle Japan. War breaks out in 1939, France falls in June 1940, and with the friendly approval of the quisling Vichy Government, Japan marches into Indo-China in July 1941, one month after the German armies have started rolling into the Soviet Union. The United States is still neutral; isolationists dominate Congress. President Franklin D Roosevelt, however, is seeking war in order to save Great Britain, but finds no opportunity.

June and July, 1941: the US halts all oil shipments to Japan, which had been taking 80 per cent of her oil imports from America. The US stops all trade with Japan, freezes all Japanese assets in America, closes all US harbours to Japanese ships. The White House gives an ultimatum: not one drop of oil until all Japanese acts of war have ceased in China and Indo-China. August: Japan presents a compromise proposal; it expresses willingness to come to a halt in Indo-China and make no more conquests; willingness, indeed, to evacuate Indo-China if Japan's raw material interests there are respected and if the US helps achieve an agreement with China favourable to Japan, a treaty aimed at giving Japan more or less a free hand in China. America rejects all compromise overtures.

September, 1941: The Nazi armies inside Russia are meeting ever stiffer resistance, are becoming bogged down, but Tokyo does not know this and signs an alliance with Hitler. September 6: decision to go to war against the US if no agreement is reached before the end of October.

As early as January, 1941, America's ambassador to Tokyo, Joseph C Grew, reported rumours in the Japanese capital that Japan might strike without any warning against Pearl Harbor, the world's strongest navy base. Washington's wise analysts shrug their shoulders: the thought is unthinkable, utterly impossible. September 24: the US intercepts a Japanese message ordering intensified espionage operations in Pearl Harbor, and in October the US Navy Chief of Staff warns his admiral colleague in Pearl Harbor that a Japanese attack can be expected. That same month, the Konoye Cabinet falls, and General Hideki Tojo becomes Prime Minister.

November, 1971: the White House rejects two more compromise proposals, and Japan submits on November 20 a 'definite' proposal. As each day passes, Japan's precious oil is dripping away.

December 8, Tokyo time (December 7, US time), the code words are flashed from Tokyo:

'Climb Niitaka Mountain!' ('Nitakayama Nobore')

The signals are received by the Japanese commander of the greatest air strike force ever gathered by any navy for an attack against a single target: 353 planes that fly in over Pearl Harbor, and in a few hours virtually crush America's Pacific Navy. Five battleships are sunk, three badly damaged, and 2,400 American soldiers and sailors are killed in the raid. The sneak attack, without any declaration of war, has given a rich yield: America's military presence in the waters of Asia has been virtually eliminated. But within three days, the US is at war not only with Japan but also with Germany and Italy. Japan's 'Operation Z' has helped President Roosevelt awaken the American nation. (After the war, Admiral Chuichi Hara, commander of the aircraft carriers whose aircraft wiped out Pearl Harbor: 'Roosevelt should have given us a medal')

American war historians agreed as early as in 1948 on these findings:

1. The war planners in Tokyo never felt there was any possibility of Japan defeating America
2. Their aim was to win a great, introductory victory; and with a total lack of insight into the psychology of the American people, they thought that an initial victory would make the US sit down and negotiate, then accept the compromises that had been offered by Japan
3. Staff analysis in Tokyo showed clearly that Japan did not have the economic or industrial power needed in order to win a protracted, several years' war with the US
4. Japan should never again be put into a situation in which the Japanese feel themselves encircled, isolated, victims of discrimination, met everywhere by strangling ropes, barriers.

During the initial war years, Japan's war propaganda succeeded in making most of Japan's 70 million people believe that Japan's military forces truly were invincible, and that there was a realistic foundation for the slogan: 'All eight corners of the world under one roof' (ie, the Japanese roof), because there was no free press to analyse the illusions. The Japanese have always been skilled analysts, at all levels, and often extremely unskilled in arriving at sensible decisions based on these analyses.

Let us pause a while to look at Japan's economic strength in 1940 and the war years, facts mainly found in Professor Jerome B Cohen's monumental work of 1949, *Japan's Economy in War and Reconstruction,* but with the author's interpretation of the facts.

1940: Japan is still basically an agrarian nation, with 42 per cent of her labour force engaged in farming. Seventy per cent of the farmers rent their land, they have between them a grand total of only 90 tractors, and the saying is: 'A farmer can neither die nor live.'

Between 1930 and 1940 there has been a second industrial revolution: light industry, mainly textiles, has been reduced from 62 to 27 per cent of industry's total production value, with heavy industry advancing from 38 to 73 per cent. Now there is strength to produce great volumes of steel, cannons, battleships, military electronics. But the quality is uneven. Japan is able to develop a military fighter plane, Mitsubishi's 'A6M Zero', which for two years is a nightmare to American pilots. But Japanese trucks are stalled in China; the only ones rolling efficiently are those equipped with Ford engines. The steel is not good enough, the casting technique inferior, and there is no system for achieving either long production runs or consistently reliable quality.

Production: In 1940, it takes almost 200 man-hours for a Japanese to make a ton of dynamite, only ten for the American worker. Coal: the Japanese is able to mine only half of his British colleague's annual total, one-twelfth of the American's. Steel: the Japanese is able to make, in 1941, about 54 tons per year, the German 81 tons; but by 1944, the Japanese level has shrunk to forty per cent of this and the German's to sixty-five per cent.

Not even during one war year is Japan able to produce more than 10 per cent of America's total ammunition output, and the same is true for coal and steel: about one-thirteenth.

The total economy: Between 1940 and 1944, Japan is able, through desperate efforts, to increase her total production (GNP) by one-fourth — the US by two-thirds. The base of Japan's economy is too weak.

In the peak year of 1944, Japan was able to produce the following, as compared to the United States: aircraft engines 14 per cent, tanks four per cent, cargo and supply ships 17 per cent, war ships 11 per cent. The average: ten per cent. Germany and Great Britain, too, out-produce Asia's leading industrial state. Trucks and passenger cars: Japan's level is only 18 per cent of Germany's and 20 per cent of Britain's. Machine tools are too few in number, too poor in quality. In Japan's aircraft industry, which at one time employed about two million workers, one-third of them women, there are 6.1 workers per machine tool as compared to 4.2 in Germany.

Aircraft: Japan is almost able to catch up with Germany and Britain in annual production, but is outclassed by the US.

Table 1: A 4 — 1 Defeat In Aircraft Production

	1941	1944	Totals, four years
Japan	5,088	28,180	58,822
Germany	11,766	39,807	92,656
Great Britain	20,100	26,500	96,400
United States	19,433	100,752	261,826

Source: Cohen

Oil: The United States is producing 700 times as much. When the war starts, Japan's oil stock is expected to last about one year. In 1944, the number of practice hours for a pilot is cut to thirty, half of what had been considered the minimum, and all practice navigation flights cease. One of the major factors behind the creation of the 'Kamikaze' corps — suicide pilots who crashed their planes on to the decks of American warships — was that oil was need only for the flight to the target, never back.

By the end of the war, 60 Japanese cities have been devastated by American bombers; ashes cover two-thirds of Tokyo, Osaka, Nagoya. In Germany, about 15 per cent of all housing was destroyed, in Japan 24 per cent. But while the rain of bombs over Germany covered a three-year period, and thus offered some opportunity for rebuilding, most of Japan's destruction came within a seven-month period, in 1945. In eighteen months, between 1944 and August, 1945, a total of 22 million Japanese, or one-third of the population, fled from their homes.

The Japanese had sown a wind, and had to reap the whirlwind.

'The Japanese civilian was punished more heavily by the war than the civilian population in Germany or Britain,' notes Professor Cohen and mentions particularly the years and years of under-nourishment.

By 1937, Japan's real standard of living began to decline. In 1941, the calorie content of the Japanese diet is only six per cent over what is considered the absolute minimum for survival. Between 1940 and 1944, consumption expenditures for goods and services drop 30 per cent in Japan, 22 per cent in Germany — but rise in the United States. In the city of Kyoto a weight loss of at least ten kilograms is suffered by 65 per cent of all adults.

At the end of the war, the physicians are unanimous in their verdict: 'Under-nourishment, extreme tiredness, loss of weight, rapid advance of tuberculosis.'

Two problems are in the forefront of all thoughts during the weeks that follow the Emperor's proclamation to his people that the war had 'not necessarily' developed to the advantage of Japan:

- Under-nourishment and the consequent tiredness: how could this people be expected to have the strength to build a new nation?
- Japan must get new leaders with a new scale of values.

CHAPTER THREE

The secret document

'. . . I do believe we have laid a foundation on which we can try to catch up with America and perhaps even outstrip it.'
Takeo Fukuda, 1969
Then Japan's Finance Minister, now Foreign Minister and leading candidate for the premiership race in the summer of 1972.

The financial and industrial rulers of Japan's new economic empire are all present. The session can begin. The doors are closed. It is 2 p.m. For the next two hours, the sixteen council members will discuss Japan's strategy for the 1970's, will come to a decision.

The Tokyo air is muggy this Tuesday, May 25, 1971. In the street outside the building where the decision-makers are meeting, there is a constant roar of traffic, a constant staccato beat of hurrying feet, for this is the very heart of New Japan, the centre of the world's most dynamic economy.

The newspapers and the nine million colour-TV sets are out with the news of the last few hours: the Home Minister injured in a traffic accident; temperature right now 28.8 degrees; Okubo-san, the rapist-killer, says that he has buried 'only' eight girl victims; Prime Minister Sato declares that Japan does not intend to revalue the yen; the mercury content in people's hair has been found to be dangerously high and for a report on this, over to our staff reporters in Kumamoto-ken; the Crown Prince and the Crown Princess will visit Afghanistan in the beginning of June, and the Chisso annual corporation meeting has just opened at Osaka, marked by 400 guards beating up 400 people crippled by the so-called Minamata environmental disease. The world outside Japan: a new report of America's dwindling gold reserves; a spokesman for the US State Department firmly denies that the US is applying pressure in any way to make Japan revalue. ('These reports are absolutely without any foundation of any kind,' UPI quotes Charles Bray as saying); and President Nixon has declared in a speech in Birmingham, Alabama, that as the war in Vietnam is being phased out, everybody can look forward to 'an era of peace.' Japan's ambassador in Washington tells a dinner party that 'myths' about Japan's trade policies are threatening to 'poison' Japanese-American trade relations. Finally: do not forget to watch tonight's hour-long NKH colour-TV programme about Japan's educational system in the years 1990 and 2000.

At the time of Emperor Meiji the Japanese were already used to thinking twenty to thirty years ahead, and they are still the same this day in May.

Citizens of the New Japan are hurrying along in the street outside the sixteen rulers' smoky room. They are a young people, with as many as 21 per cent in the age group 16 to 24 compared to 16 per cent in the US. Half the population belongs to the postwar generation. It is a dissatisfied generation.

On the table in front of the sixteen is a 173-page document, which they must now approve or reject. The theme of this document: the war against poverty and for material affluence has 'not necessarily' developed to the advantage of the Japanese people. It is a document of self-criticism and soul-searching, a ruthless description of failures behind the facades of the Miracle, an official dissection that could never be imagined in any other country. It is a document where both words and figures demand a new course, with man and not business now at the helm. Both the strategy and the document are the result of eighteen months' hard work by a group of 50 MITI (Ministry for International Trade and Industry) civil servants. The council now in session, the 'Industrial Structure Council' (Sangyo kozou shingikai) is being asked to give the green light — or flatly reject the '1980 vision.'

MITI has arrived at new patterns of thought, particularly the group of young elite officials who drafted the document, and now the young bureaucrats are asking the sixteen gentlemen at the table to accept the new thoughts.

But there is a certain age gap between the overwhelming majority of the people in Young Japan, and the sixteen rulers who now are thumbing through the document while key officials from MITI outline the new strategy.

The combined age of the sixteen: 1,068 years, an average of 67, or twelve years more than Japan's official retirement age. All except one were born during the reign of Emperor Meiji, 1868-1912. Five of those who are to decide the shape of Japan) in 1980 are more than 73 years old.

Eight of the sixteen have committed 'amakudari' — 'descent from Heaven'; first civil servants for many years, then over to the finance and business world. Thirteen have graduated from Todai, the eye-of-the-needle university, for generations the chief training ground for all Japanese intellectuals.

There, presiding at the table, we find Kogoro Uemura, 78, known as the premier of the business world, President, since 1968, of the powerful Keidanren, Japan's industrial federation. He is expected to resign, at the very earliest, in 1974. Mr Uemura has many, many memories; he remembers how Admiral Togo, 'the Nelson of Japan,' utterly destroyed the Russian fleet and captured Port Arthur at the turn of the century. Today's youngsters cannot even remember America's military occupation of Japan half a centry later, from 1945-51. A civil servant between 1918 and 1940, in the MITI of that time, finally vice minister's rank, and a wartime role as a sort of Japanese Albert Speer of the coal industry. After the war, he is one of 2,000 purged businessmen but step by step he works his way up again; is elected board chairman of Japan Air Lines in 1963, serves for many years as Keidanren Vice-President under Taizo Ishizaka (who surrenders the presidency when he is 82, to organize the Osaka World Expo of 1970), and then at the age of 75 — twenty years after the normal retirement age — Uemura is given the responsibility of sitting in the chief's chair and beginning to influence the future structure of Japan's industry.

At this table — in New Japan — we also find Mr Uemura's vice-president, Teizou Horikoshi, 73, member of a long series of boards and also, somehow, a cousin of Tokyo's Marxist governor, Ryokichi Minobe. And look: there sits a 76-year old professor of economics, Hiromi Arisawa, member of the Atomic Power Council, the Space Development Council, etc etc, plus the Fabian Society. Mr Arisawa, too, has emerged from the ranks of the purged — but from the other side of the fence. Contrary to Mr Uemura, Arisawa fought against the war effort, entered the so-called professors' group in the 1930's, a group that firmly denounced militarism, and was forced to resign from his university in 1938. The board room of 'Japan, (1971) Inc,' however, has no time for old quarrels.

The junior member of this table is the outrageously young Eiji Kageyama, 55, who took his Todai University degree in 1940, was a civil servant and a vice-minister before being elected president of the Japan Chamber of Commerce and Industry and of the organization's Tokyo body.

Next, a man feared by his rivals all over the world: Toshio Doko, 75, the supertanker pioneer, formerly president of Ishikawajima-Harima (IHI), now chairman of the board of Toshiba, a man who gets up at 4 every morning, is at his desk before any other employee arrives, and keeps his door open to any visitor bewteen 7.30 and 8.30 am; a man who thoroughly dislikes night-clubs and is generally regarded as a one-man dictator. His belief: that Japan's consensus system functions perfectly well as long as he is allowed to make all important decisions. When Doko-san, about a dozen years ago, accepted the offer to leave the shipyard and go in and 'clean up,' re-vitalize Toshiba, everybody expected that the factory floors would be the scene of the first swings of his rationalization hatchet. They were wrong: first to go were all management cars. During his years as a powerful shipyard company boss, Doko was to be seen standing in a bus queue every morning, even when it rained, just like the workers from whom he demanded miracles.

Over there a completely different man, the thin figure of

Yoshizane Iwasa, 66, chairman of the board of Fuji Bank, as of this year Japan's largest bank; also chairman of the Japan Bank Federation; also vice-president of Keidanren. Mr Iwasa is one of the key men who decides which competing 'cyclists' are to be kept alive and which will pass away, among the under-financed companies that so easily lose balance when the speed of growth slows down. Since industry's total debt burden has reached a sum of 390 billion dollars, most executives tend to listen very carefully when Mr Iwasa speaks.

And there's the representative of the House of Mitsui, Tetsuzo Mizukami, 68, director, who at the age of 58 became president of Mitsui Bussan, the trading house which every year handles more business than some 80 of the world's nations and which is a part of the Mitsui Zaibatsu that was broken up by the occupation authorities – but rapidly rose again, a trading house whose sales climbed from 4.2 to 10.4 billion dollars between 1965 and 1970, an annual growth of 19.7 per cent. Mr. Mizukami has many, many positions, even that of vice-chairman of the Japan Athletic Federation.

A man who does not handle billions of dollars but whose newspaper influences the thought pattern of Japan's business world is: Jiro Enjoji, 65, since 1965 president of *Nihon Keizai Shimbun,* Japan's *Wall Street Journal* (by 1985, people may refer to WSJ as America's *Nihon Keizai*). This daily financial newspaper has lifted its circulation since 1951 from 400,000 to 1,400,000 copies, making it larger than either the *Financial Times* or the WSJ, and 'Nikkei' also has more economic reporters than any rival on this earth. Mr Enjoji took the long road to the corridors of power: a Nikkei foreign correspondent before and during the war, in Germany, Spain, Portugal; Managing Editor in the early 1950's, editor-in-chief in 1960, and now a member of Tokyo's Stock Exchange Board and of the councils and committees through which Japan is run, such as the Rice Price Council and the Total Energy Council, and also chairman of two special committees of the council in session today, with one committee handling questions relating to the location of industries – a hot potato, as more and more communities throughout Japan have started to say, 'no, thanks' — and the other a committee charged with measures to halt industrial environment destruction. Enjoji-san is also chairman of the Transportation Ministry's private advisory board. He is deeply respected in his own newspaper house. One reason is that he is an art fanatic but considers the private ownership of art a mortal sin; every painting, every piece of pottery must be available to the public. This is why Nikkei's own columns are full of four-colour photos of art, and why Nikkei sponsors more public art exhibitions than any other daily in the world. Nikkei's readers get their newspaper twice a day — which is the case also with the general newspapers — a morning and an evening edition, an achievement not matched by any other economic daily outside Japan.

Then there are two young brothers: Kaneo Ishihara, 60, president of the National Japan Development Bank (Nihon Kaihatsu Ginko), formerly deputy finance minister; still writes poetry between the budget account sheets. His speciality: 'haiku,' the almost brutally precise poetry that limits itself to seventeen syllables. His brother, Takeo Ishihara, 63, just by chance, it seems, also a former vice-minister, but at MITI, now a leader of industry, electric power, atomic energy.

And look: another former MITI vice-minister, Koushichi Ueno, 65, now in the electric power industry. Over there, a tough-looking man, Toshio Eguchi, 59, Tokyo's police chief in 1963-65, now a businessman. Yes, one more ex-MITI vice-minister, Hisatsugu Tokunaga, 63, now one of the key directors of Nippon Steel (Shin Nittetsu), the world's biggest steel company. The last trio at the table: 76-year old Yoshimichi Hori, a chemist and power expert, Hajime Takagi, 63, whose various organizations run most of Japan's smaller business enterprises, and finally, Michikazu Kono, 63, deputy head of the Bank of Japan.

The group of sixteen at the table of power know that they are old, and they know why the press writes so brutally: 'There is a need now, as in 1946, for a second purge at the top of the power groups. They know that the former purge, which had political purposes, cleaned out most of Japan's white-haired executives, pushing into power such young men as the 49-year old shipyard man Doko, men who could create and follow new patterns of thought and who could turn Japan's war-oriented industry to peacetime profit.

Still, it comes as a slap in the face when the men of power lower their aged heads and in the document on the table read that 'one who stands on a hill and yet has the wisdom of an ant crawling up a slope is not fit for leadership in a new era.' Several hearts beat nervously in protest at the sight of another sentence: that industry '. . . must, above all, put an end to the simple-minded thinking and behaviour that have allowed it to produce both goods and environmental hazards at the same time.'

The sixteen have discussed the complex of problems thoroughly at a number of sessions over the past six months, have arrived at a common outlook in shaping the 1970's, but the acid has not been spared by the MITI officials who wrote the final report that is now in front of the group, a report summarizing the views of the Council and scheduled to be given to the waiting press at the end of this session. Expressions such as the 'narrow peep-holes' of earlier policies, and the necessity to abolish now 'obsolete privileges' — aren't they a bit too strong?

As the MITI officials continue to explain the work ahead in the 1970's, several of the rulers let their thoughts wander, let them float back in time: Isn't Japan, Inc a pretty good business when compared to conditions in the autumn of hunger and defeat 26 years ago?

Remember, back in 1937 Japan's total GNP was only 65 per cent of Great Britain's, 85 per cent of Germany's — but both of these countries have now been overtaken, haven't they? We now make twenty times as much steel as our average for the years of 1934-36. Just a month ago, President Nixon claimed that Japan would probably defeat the US steel industry in total output within two years, and our steel workers now produce more per man-hour than the Americans or the Germans. We can afford to import 100 times as much oil as in 1934-36, and we make *3,000 times* as many passenger cars. Our shipyards turn out a tonnage 30 times greater than America's, and compared to the prewar level, our people are now consuming 12 times as much meat, 17 times as much milk. We have even defeated the USA in the production of colour-TV sets. At the end of this fiscal year, there will be a colour-TV in every second household, while Europe's richest countries enjoy a level of only 10-15 per cent. The earlier income gap between rural households and urban wage-earner households has been eliminated completely. Our total production capacity is 12.4 times as large as before the war — isn't that so? We have tried harder than any other people on this earth, and just a few weeks ago, Dr Hisao Kanamori — yes, a very promising lad, only 49 — said that if we keep on trying hard, we shall defeat the American in GNP per capita by as early as 1982. So could it really be said that we, we of Emperor Meiji's generation, have completely failed?

Such are the thoughts of the sixteen at the table of power. But they do know that as in the case of the generals of the 1930's, they too have sown a wind and will now have to reap the whirlwind. They have sown success, yes, a dramatic rise in the purchasing power of the people, and in the people's life-span and physique — in height and weight — but the ruling Establishment has also helped plant poison in the air, poison in the rivers and poison in the oceans along the coasts of Japan. They have sown wide dissatisfaction within the young generation that has never known hunger, never experienced war. It is not a working class that has started to condemn the aged power elite, because every new opinion poll gives the same reassuring answer: 90 per cent of all respondents make a cross in the right spot, confirm that they consider themselves as belonging to the middle-class, with even industrial labour families claiming this identity. It is an army of young housewives, aged 35, who have risen in protest — against unrestrained economic growth, against the lack of balance between private and public investments. They are demanding a different content in the pattern of growth, are voicing their rights to clean air. These demands are supported by the press, which thunders the message, twice a day.

The 16 know that a new era has arrived, that Japan will never be quite the same again, as a result of the public debate which has raged across the nation for the last year. Several of them cannot understand why, but they understand that new methods will be needed if their ambitions for 1980 are to be realized. The clouds over Japan are many and thick; hence this document, hence this bitter medicine of self-criticism.

Meanwhile, outside Japan, no more applause, ever more denunciations. The German Mark started floating two weeks ago, and they are saying in all capitals that the yen also must be revalued because Japan's trade surpluses have grown so large. The pace of Japan's removal of her own trade barriers is denounced as unbearably slow. *Time* magazine recently had a long cover article in which a member of the Nixon Cabinet, not identified, uttered these strange words: "The Japanese are still fighting the war, but it is no longer a shooting war but an economic war. Their immediate aim is to try to dominate the Pacific, and after that, perhaps the whole world.' The magazine had suddenly discovered that Japan was growing into a 'superpower' and that the protectionists of Japan were so firmly entrenched that the only way of making them negotiate was to 'club them over the head.' These tough sentences are reprinted in every daily newspaper, alongside furious leader colums demanding that Japan quickly liberalize her import trade. Now it is probably so, the gentlemen around the table muse. Japan would probably be wise to revalue the yen six per cent or so, in a year or two, but every new monthly report on Japan's foreign trade results makes the hearts beat faster and faster: over-success in exports — up 90 per cent for cars, up 30 per cent for steel. Synthetic fibres: Japan now has a 21 per cent share of world production, and the export increase rate is probably too fast, an increase of about 300 per cent for synthetic yarns alone in the first half of 1971. The current trend is a trade balance surplus of 6-8 billion dollars this year, but if the home market recovers from the recession that began late in the summer of 1970 — yes, in calendar 1970, real GNP growth was only 11,2 per cent — then the surplus will shrink, since we shall be importing more raw materials and machinery.

Within Japan, the past year has been a taxing one for the country's rulers. None of the sixteen can tell exactly when the starting pistol was fired, when the avalanche of criticism began to engulf the whole country. One finger on the trigger was a series of eighteen articles in the *Asahi Shimbun,* a national daily newspaper, in the spring of 1970. The eighteen contributors, most of them economists, wrote on one theme: 'Kutabare GNP!' ('To hell with GNP!'). The backbone of the criticism was that industry and business had harvested the fruits of economic growth, while the people had had to pay the price — they might be on the road toward nominal affluence but were in the meantime lacking welfare and lacking real quality in living and life. The writers questioned not only the berserk fury that had marked industry's fixed investments over the past five years, with annual leaps of more than 20 per cent, but also the quality of 25 years of postwar work. Worst of all, there was a general questioning of the principles that had been guiding the country for more than 100 years, since the Meiji Restoration: to increase production, at any price. These principles aimed at 'a rich country, a strong army,' and though Japan's army was now small and weak, who could tell, the second element of the Meiji slogan might become true again; thus the need to arrest a trend that could lead towards full-scale rearmament. The titles of the articles were whiplashes: *The Life of the Pulling Horse* (how the common man works two months more per year than an employee in the West); *The Export Animal; He Who Saves, Loses* (inflation); *The Crazy Flowers of the Night* (with business spending on entertainment, including night-club visits, more than three billion dollars a year); *The Great Strategy for Waste* (advertising).

The overall judgement: beautiful clean factories and a social infra-structure — housing, sewerage, streets, play-grounds, etc — worthy of an under-developed country. Nature itself was being destroyed, with the smoke of factory chimneys and factory drainage poisoning both the environment and the people.

Mid-July, 1971: a group of school-children suddenly collapse on the ground, while doing exercises — blue in the face, gasping for air, choking. The photo-chemical fog has struck. The children are taken to hospital, their lives saved. But now all the mass media are joining the campaign: we shall all of us, within ten years, have to wear gas-masks. Japan's editorial writers have always criticized the ruling

Establishment — the Government party, the bureaucracy, the business group organizations — and have done so ever since 1945, but the criticism now gushing forth has completely new dimensions. All the younger members of the power apparatus start thinking — and thinking aloud: where, where is Japan really heading? We must try to steer our economic growth into a more sensible course. If it had been a group of old people who were knocked out by the smog, reaction would probably have been less violent, but those involved were a group of tomorrow's consumers, tomorrow's leaders.

As of this hour, ten months have passed since the children fell to the ground, and the sixteen members of the Industrial Structure Council know that even if they should want to arrest this groping toward a new course, it is already too late. The last blow — and perhaps the heaviest: a few weeks ago (April 14), one of the country's most powerful men stood up and declared that Japan no longer had any alternative but to strive for 'harmonic and balanced growth aimed at the creation of a new welfare state.' The speaker: Kazutaka Kikawada, 65, since 1960 head of one of the four dominant business organizations, 'Keizai Doyukai' (Committee for Economic Development); the other three power groups: Keidanren, the Chamber of Commerce and Industry, and the Employers Federation (Nikkeiren). Kikawada, who spoke before the general assembly of his organization, said that through her aggressive performance in overseas markets, Japan was 'provoking criticism and revulsion in other countries.' New thinking was needed at home, too: 'Japan has for too long over-emphasized technological and material development, and as a result of selecting the wrong techniques our country now faces increasing environmental destruction and increasing threats to the lives of the people, two things that contradict the very basic principles of human welfare and mankind's progress.'

Just the day before the Council meeting came another blow from Kikawada-san, a speech in which he called for a course towards a 'welfare state' with the rapid creation of a social infrastructure, plus 'drastic' liberalization of imports and a definite farewell to the old principle of giving priority to production.

Several of the sixteen glance once again through the opening paragraphs of the document in front of them; first a reference to the situation in 1945:

Our first and foremost desire was to get rid of hunger and cold. And when that desire was satisfied, we wanted to be able to enjoy a better standard of living and realize our aspiration to catch up with the Western countries — an aspiration which has been with us for over 100 years since the dawn of the Mieji Era. The first goal was largely reached ten years or so after the war. Then our efforts were directed to the attainment of the second goal and there occurred what the Westerners called a 'miracle' of the Japanese economy.

Although a full understanding of the 'miracle' requires further studies, we can be reasonably proud of what we have so far achieved.

Now a nod from the powerful men, that little of their pride should be saved, allowed to survive; they also agree with a pronouncement in the next sentence that the people of Japan 'have persevered and saved.'

And now we look back with mixed feelings of joy and sorrow at an era which is ending. It is not merely the end of the postwar era but the end of the century which began in Meiji. Japan, once awakened to the modern world by the appearance of Commodore Perry's 'black ships,' has become the world's largest 'black ship' exporter. Things that the people of Meiji never even dreamed of have become commonplace today.

Another solemn nod by the fifteen Meiji men; only one of the group was born in the era of Emperor Taisho, none in the Showa era that began when Hirohito mounted the Throne in 1926.

An era which ends ushers in a new one. The new era is called forth by the achievements of the preceding era as well as by contradictions and rigidities accumulated behind the achievement.

Until today, we have been climbing a steep and narrow uphill path, not bothering to look around us but only gazing into the bright clouds above the slope as ideals to be realized. After that effort, the Japanese economy stands on a pass of the road overlooking the vast expanse of the world.

Now that their basic requirements are fulfilled, the people begin to demand more with happy abandon: not just the fulfilment of material needs but something more beautiful: clean water and air, cities more comfortable to live in, a country more considerate of their wishes, a more care-free life, enjoyment of work, etc.

And so the ruthless sentences, the whiplash:

The Industry, therefore, is called upon to answer the great variety of requirements by drawing upon all its resources. It must, above all, end the simple-minded thinking and behaviour that have allowed it to produce both goods and environment hazards at the same time.

So to a pessimistic — and realistic — evaluation of Japan's international role:

The international position of the Japanese economy is also undergoing a change. It is no longer an ant going uphill but has grown so large that every aspect of its conduct invariably influences the world economy to no small extent.

For good or for evil, there are influences in both directions.

It is now possible that a change in the world economy could annihilate the Japanese economy. That our economy, which has grown to a world giant inseparably entwined with the world economy, is a historical development that we have never experienced in the past.

Under these circumstances, it would be possible for us either to play a new world role or to walk the path to decline.

Industrial corporations should realize that the 'simple-minded pursuit of greater capacity is rapidly becoming obsolete.'

As for government organizations, there are too many people looking out through 'narrow peepholes.' And new forces are emerging: consumers and local residents of different regions, 'and there is a need for a new adjustment mechanism to assure an equilibrium of all forces.'

Gone is the age when it sufficed for atomistic enterprises to play pantomime, directed by divine and invisible hands.

Looking at international society, we find that the age of linear thought — when the nation was bent only on building up its international competitive power — has ended.

In the new age of pluralism, a nation, if it is to attain its own prosperity, must be deeply conscious not only of its own enterprises and consumers but also of the conditions of its partner countries, their industries and workers.

One may think that we can live through such an era if we arm ourselves with huge material facilities.

That is wrong.

Both in management of enterprises and national administration, we must rack our brains and seek every possible means to create a world where individuals and all peoples can live more humanly.

This means a new industrial structure, measures to help the so-called knowledge industries, the brain-intensive branches, to increase their share of total production value, and thus gradually replace these sectors where most employees are engaged in excusively simple work operations. There is a need to develop new technology to bring about this change-over, but this time there must be measures to 'control and administer' the new technology-flow, in order not to harm the interests of the people and society as a whole.

New situations and problems call in a new era.

The 1970's are not just the new leaf in the calendar; they represent an era which is totally different from the '50's and '60's or from the whole period of 100 years from the Meiji Restoration.

It is for that reason that new policies must be conceived for the trade and industry of the 1970's.

A different era calls for new ways of thought, behaviour, policies and organization.

He who stands on a hill and yet has the wisdom of an ant crawling up a slope is not fit for leadership in the new era.

Conventional ideas and behaviour are left behind or lose their influence, and instead a variety of new concepts of value and complex relations become established.

The 1970's will be the years of change and mobility and

will consequently provide new opportunities.

The new age offers Japan the choice of either fading away or making a great leap forward.

To be successful in the test, the vigour and creativeness of the people must be regenerated.

We should be prepared to part with conventional ideas, existing structures and privileges which have. become obsolete and build up new ideals.

The reality behind these Japanese-language sentences is crystal clear: they reflect thousands and thousands of hours of savage debate within the state machinery about the course to be pursued, with the 'progressives' having won agreement to their view: a new attitude towards the world, new policies inside Japan. A groping to create a 'new national heart,' a decent society – and as evidence of this groping and struggle, I consider the MITI document being quoted to be one of the milestones in the development of Japanese thought.

The document then mentions the need to quantify the Japanese economy of the 1970's. It would be good if 'national goals' could be set before deciding the industrial and economic goals. It is difficult to reach agreement on national goals for coming years when the 'people's wants and standards of values will become diversified. A national goal tends to be abstract in nature if it is to win a wide consensus.'

In spite of these 'it-cannot-be-done' pronouncements, the document's authors outline these 'three national goals for the 1970's' (in the author's abridged version):

1. *Ensure a humanly bountiful life for everyone*
   Particular efforts will be made to ensure a sustained improvement in the standard of living; to create an excellent environment with due attention to the relationship between human activities and social and natural environs – and further to create 'a beautiful land to be loved by all people.'

2. *Contribute positively to the peace and progress of the international society*
   Japan should play a responsible role and make the contributions expected of a major economic power, while earnestly keeping its status as a peaceful nation.

3. *Maintain and promote the creativeness and vigour of the*

people which provide the basis for achieving the above two goals

Particular efforts are to be made so that such creativeness and vigour may be demonstrated by all strata of people, young and old, on the strength of affluence of their life and provide circumstances where people will feel that life is worth living.

A surprise: the 'national goals' no longer include the determination to catch up with and outrun the countries of the Western world.

The document adds that in today's highly industrialized society it is the responsibility of the industrial sector to make sure that national goals are achieved. Thus, the goals for industry and the economy must be set in such a way that national goals can be realized; hence these five goals for the two sectors in the 1970's:

1. Maintain the overall growth potential of industry and improve the basic conditions of industrial development
2. Improve the quality of the people's life
3. Secure favourable social and natural environments and create a beautiful land
4. Increase such jobs as will make people feel that their life is more significant, and secure safe and comfortable working conditions
5. Contribute to a growth of the Japanese economy in harmony with international economic society.

Earlier, the document notes, Japan was racing only for growth and quantitative expansion. Now the nation must start making the most of economic growth to attain the listed goals. Thus a change in emphasis: 'a shift from "growth pursuance" to "growth utilization".'

So a walk on to slippery ice, with bold steps. There has been a discussion of a 'trade-off' relationship between economic growth and a number of undesirable effects, such as deterioration of the environment, international trade friction, traffic congestion. It is noted that 'these undesirable effects begin to increase sharply when the economic growth has passed a *critical point.*'

Until the critical point is reached, it is possible to realize a higher economic growth with less ill effects by directing increased flow of production towards eliminating the undesirable consequences of economic growth.

Although it is difficult to foresee the critical point in the 1970's, it is worth noting that there will be two opposing possibilities:

1. The fact that during the processes of the past economic expansion, there was an increasing imbalance between the social capital stock (accumulated public investments) and the annual flow of economic activities in this country, and that the Japanese economy has already grown big in terms of international economy — this fact indicated a lowering of the critical point

2. On the other hand, the fact that Japan's economy has steadily increased its growth potential over the past score of years, suggests a possibility that the critical point is still *far away*. The possibility will become reality when part of the growing economy is utilized to augment the stock of social capital and promote international cooperation.

No need to worry about the critical point, then. So the time has come to disclose a number of goals in 'quantitative terms':

- A real annual GNP growth rate of 'about 10 per cent'
- This would mean that Japan's total GNP in 1980 'will nearly equal that of the six EEC countries combined or that of the Soviet Union, and Japan's per capita income will approximate to that of the US'
- A total economy of the size of EEC or the USSR requires proportionately large research and development (R & D) investment, and thus Japan's annual R & D expenditure should rise from an annual level of 0.8 trillion yen in 1970 to 5 trillion yen in 1980, in constant 1965 prices (new parity conversion: a rise from 2.6 to 16.2 billion dollars, a six-fold leap)
- To set the levels of the US, EEC and USSR as targets in various sectors; in the case of working conditions, for example, to catch up with the American level by slashing working hours in the 1970's by twelve per cent, compared to a reduction of only five per cent in the

1960's. Efforts will be made to 'generalize a five-day week and to increase paid holidays'

- The American levels must also be reached in such sectors as social capital stock (accumulated public investments and private housing) and education — with social capital investments of 584 billion dollars in the 1970's, compared to 149 billion dollars in the 1960's, both in the 1965 constant prices
- Education: the number of pupils now advancing from nine school years to higher education is at present 82 per cent of all pupils — this figure must be raised to 95 per cent. As for enrolment at universities and other higher academic institutions, the present number is 17 per cent of all members of the age group 19-22 years — and this percentage must be raised to 46 per cent. Therefore, Government expenditure on education must go up four times, from two to nine trillion yen (from 6.5 to a 1980 annual figure of 29.2 billion dollars)
- Environmental destruction: industries that are particularly liable to cause pollution are directed to spend nine per cent of their total investments on preventing environmental disruption, while the average for other industries is set at seven per cent.
- Japan's relations with the world: aid to developing countries should be raised from the present annual sum of 1.3 billion dollars to about 7.5 billion dollars in 1980. (Author's note: including direct investments, export credits). 'In addition, Japan should cooperate with other advanced countries in the field of technology and with the Communist bloc nations with a view to solving East-West problems.'

The Council's aged Meiji-ans note with great satisfaction that the 1970 work programme is not completely free from ambitions of a magnitude that would have pleased the decision-makers of 1870 and they nod their heads as they read the conclusion of the document:

When and if these goals are realized, Japan will have entirely closed the gap with Western countries and will henceforth enter into a truly new phase of her history.

It is 3.59 pm and with the strength of a 78-year old, Mr

Uemura lets his chairman's gavel swing and hit the table. The document had noted that 'due to lack of time,' the Council had not had the opportunity to discuss Japan's 'urgent' foreign relations problems, but things will probably work out all right. For two hours, the sixteen men of power had looked into the year 1980 and found the situation there very good. They raise themselves from the table of heavy decisions, and march out to their big, black cars, some of them equipped with lace curtains — motorized palanquins of the 1970's.

The New Era has begun.

A few days later I am sitting in front of the chief architect of MITI's 1980 document, Naohiro Amaya, the ministry's planning chief and key economic strategist, only 48 years old, and equipped with — to quote those who know him — 'one of the nation's best brains.' We are sitting in his office, and the milieu is about as luxurious as a Swedish military barracks of the 1930's — walls bare of wallpaper, uncarpeted floors, endlessly long corridors without a single touch of decoration. MITI may be a power centre but none of the power is visible. Mr Amaya is short, even for a Japanese, has warm laughing eyes, and after six years abroad speaks better English than most Englishmen. He receives me in a very friendly manner and I seem to spot an extra touch of friendliness in his eyes. Perhaps he enjoyed reading the suggestion in my 'challenge' book that MITI should be smashed to pieces.

I draw my sword right away. The new course: is it not a bit strange that MITI, which has for generations battled for the interests of industry, the producers, should suddenly come up with a strategy for the country's consumers, for large public investments?

'MITI has changed,' he says. 'The MITI of 1971 is not the same MITI as that of 1969, though they still won't believe this out in the city!'

It is not only those in the group of 50 who drafted the 1980 document who have changed their way of thinking? Mr.

Amaya is a little hesitant in describing the situation but this emerges: yes, there are some who are resisting, who find it difficult to understand the new course, but they are officials at a lower level. He guesses that the whole career cadre, about 2,000 of the Ministry's 20,000-odd officials, have fully realized the seriousness of the situation, the necessity to build a different Japan, with a different set of values, and these 2,000 men are young. They are the ones who will participate in and help direct the creation of tomorrow's Japan. The others? Those who would rather move their hands in exactly the same way year after year, hold the same rubber stamp for a life-span, they are now trying to understand the vision of 1980 — 'but it is rather like what happens when somebody buys a manual on how to play golf; the hands are willing but the body does not move. But they will learn; don't worry!'

You yourself presented the work programme to the sixteen-man Council. No protests?

'No. But this programme would have been impossible two years ago. Then they would have said: look, MITI has its head in the clouds, this is mere day-dreaming . . .

'We simply haven't got any free choice any longer; we just have to change Japan's course. We must switch from an era of raw material waste to an era where we use as few raw materials as possible. We must enter the knowledge industries. We know the current situation and the frightening trend: at present Japan consumes about 10 per cent of the world's raw material resources, by 1980 it will be roughly 30 per cent and in the year 2000, everything!'

There are two possibilities open to us, adds Mr Amaya, either to lower the economic growth rate or to change the country's industrial structure.

'Let me give you just one example of why we must change our structure. We are exporting more than 20 million tons of steel, and this means that we are exporting our environment, because every ton of steel requires, among other things, a lot of water, and we are short of water — we are already tapping so much underground water that the islands of Japan are steadily sinking — and each ton of steel also means consumption of fresh air. Why export steel at a price of 100 dollars per ton, when we should be aiming at a price of one million dollars per ton, for example high-quality steel for aircraft engines? So we wish to reduce our export volume, lessen our raw material needs, and make other products, goods made mainly through intellectual work as a main component, not physical raw sweat.

The public investment programme, including support for the private housing sector? 'Our present situation is not worthy of a human being. Our homes are so small and so full of gadgets that it is not too much of an exaggeration to say that we shall soon be sleeping on top of our refrigerators. We must increase the share of our national resources going into public investment to something more than 10 per cent'. (This would be roughly three times the US effort, and on a par with the world champion, Sweden.)

Is this sufficient? Will the investments accumulated during the 1970's become large enough for the Japan of 1980 to be described as a country fit for people?

'We do not know, but we do know that we must re-make the Japanese islands, turn Japan into a Switzerland or a Sweden.'

There will be 'drastic' changes in a number of fields, adds Mr Amaya. He mentions the health sector (the majority of Japan's 100,000 physicians are in private practice); education, and the apartment construction industry. 'Though our technique has improved over the past two years, our methods are not too different from those of the Tokugawa Era' (The era that immediately preceded the Meiji Era). (Here the author guesses that MITI would enjoy absorbing the Construction Ministry, turning it into a section of MITI, and letting tough MITI hands subject the construction sector to the same hard squeezes that turn other industrial sectors, such as steel, into world leaders.)

Of all your headaches, which one is the worst?

'The fact that we must abandon the market mechanism, the price, within a number of sectors. We have been rather successful in handling the price factor, in letting prices decide market changes and direct the general development, but we must now tackle a great number of fields where this market mechanism does not function: health, education, the public sector, congested cities, environmental disruption, the right of workers to a safe, accident-free job environment, etc. We who have been able to handle the price factor are now entering areas where we lack experience, but where you in Sweden, for example, have been pioneers; and it would be helpful if we could learn from your experience.'

He adds: 'We must learn how to make public goods and services, and this means a new way of thinking at all levels. As for the private sector, here we must give the market mechanism full elbow-room — we must end the government intervention which keeps on protecting low-productive Japanese enterprises from international competition. Here the market mechanism must function in such a way that we achieve an optimal distribution and the most efficient use of our resources and of technological innovation.'

The Japanese are work addicts — how long will this continue?

'At least another 30 years! It normally takes that sort of time before basic attitudes towards work are changed. This is probably your experience in Europe, and I hope this will also prove true in Japan, because the work tasks in front of us are huge, really huge.'

This spring is Japan's last spring of illusions.

Between the Council meeting on May 25 and President Nixon's 'I-shall-visit-China' move seven weeks later — a move that makes the ground shake under the feet of the Japanese people — the rain-heavy skies over Japan keep on thickening, assume threatening dimensions. This does not prevent 104 million Japanese from enjoying the pleasures of summer, though the average number of summer vacation days is less than a week. And the country's numerous forecasters are looking into the future with shining eyes. In June, the Sanwa Bank publishes a ten-year forecast. Though Europe got the five-day week in the mid-1950's, the Sanwa forecaster plays it safe: predicts bravely that by 1980 the Japanese can expect a free Saturday every second week — and in that year, Japan will be fourth in GNP per capita. Also: the Japanese rush to visit foreign countries will be '19 times as hectic as in 1965' and there will be a five-fold increase in total leisure expenditure.

I put that forecast aside on my desk, because I am still busy trying to understand MITI's 1980 programme. Several essential pieces of the puzzle are missing, though I, as well as Japan's own journalists, have received MITI's 173-page Japanese-language document. The *Nihon Keizai,* for example, publishes excerpts from the document for seven days in a row, but I do not find in any newspaper the answer to two questions: firstly, MITI's real growth rate of 'about 10 per cent,' and this in a country where no figure is ever produced without at least one decimal; secondly, the failure to reveal the GNE-structure for 1980, so that one can see clearly the difference between the expenditure pattern in 1970 and in 1980, changes in consumption and investment ratios.

Does 'about 10 per cent' mean perhaps 9 per cent? Why only the accumulated figure for public fixed investments? Why not also for private fixed investments? The total GNP figure for a certain year as such is of minor importance, but this is not true for the relationship of the components, because the GNE structure reveals clearly both the volume of the weight-lifting effort and the presence or absence of balance in a nation's expenditure pattern.

One day I stretch out my curious hand an extra ten centimetres for a supplementary, uncirculated document, and look – yes, it *is* MITI's GNE structure for 1980! Now the puzzle is complete, the missing pieces are there, and the fog vanishes.

The tables of this secret document explain the vague words about the need to 'mobilize all resources.' The GNE structure points the way: total economic mobilization. Japan goes to war against itself and does it by allocating her resources just as in war-time, by reducing the share for private consumption to the lowest possible level, to a ratio of GNE comparable to the World War II level in Great Britain and Germany.

Between the years 1970 and 1980, there will be these structural changes in GNE expenditure:

Private consumption: In constant price, ie volume, a fall from 49.8% to 44.5%, in nominal prices from 51.1% to 48.9%

Total fixed investments, excluding inventory investments: a rise from 38.1% to 45.8% in constant prices — in nominal prices up from 36.1% to 39.6%

Investment components: Private business fixed investments, a sector where price increases are almost negligible: up in volume from 22.5% to 26.0%; in nominal prices a reduction from 20.2% to 17.5%

Public investments: in volume a rise from 9.1% to 11.8%, in nominal prices up from 8.7% to 10.8%.

Private housing: in volume up from 6.5% to 8.0%, in nominal prices up from 7.2% to 11.3% (meaning high price increases in apartment construction).

Foreign transactions surplus (Exports and other income from abroad minus imports and other payments): in volume a rise from 1.0% to 1.4%, in nominal price a reduction — because of a minimal rise in export prices — from 1.1% to 0.75%.

The real growth rate: 10.6 per cent. In nominal prices: 15.4 per cent.

This mobilization of the nation's resources, the strategy to get the people who have 'persevered and saved' to save even more and endure even more, would lift Japan's annual GNP — in nominal prices — from 72.4 trillion yen to 303.2 trillion yen, or from 235 billion dollars to 984 billion dollars (at new parity of 308). In real terms: a 1980 GNP of 520 billion dollars, in 1965 prices, which means that by 1980 Japan's economy would have already passed the ambitious 1985 target set officially in the spring of 1969, the programme which I at that time described as 'the greatest challenge' ever presented to the world.

The MITI growth rate of 10.6 per cent is 34 per cent more than the annual pace of 7.9 per cent staked out in 1969 — a figure which was considered not too under-ambitious, as it was roughly double the normal Western growth rates.

Since the cake is growing so large, private consumption, too, will be huge in 1980, climbing at an annual real rate of 9.4 per cent, faster than in any other country — but in the era of 'new thinking,' the new era when the leaders of the ants are expected to act differently, the ants should have been told the truth: that private business fixed investments are assumed to be speeding ahead at an annual real clip of 12.3 per cent, sixteen per cent faster than the growth rate of the total economy.

The document in front of the rulers had warned that the Japanese could not survive the new era simply by 'arming ourselves with huge materialist facilities. That is wrong.'

The idea may be wrong but I do not think there was any great cause for alarm among the sixteen decision makers. A few minutes with my electronic calculator — made in Japan — show the truth: while public and housing investments during the decade are allocated an accumulated ten-year-figure of 584 billion dollars (in 1965 prices), private business fixed investments will zoom to an accumulation of 850' billion dollars.

Such are my thoughts this summer as ever more disturbing reports keep coming in about the situation in a rival ant-hill on the other side of the Pacific.

President Nixon speaks in July in Kansas City. He says the US is facing 'a challenge that we could not even dream of twenty-five years ago.' Within the next five to twenty years, the US will be faced with four other 'power centres': Western Europe, Japan, the Soviet Union and China.

'This is no bad thing,' the President adds, and then the Japanese breathe a little easier, interpreting the President's words as something of an encouragement, an echo of the American teacher William C Clark's farewell speech to the schoolboys of Japan in 1877: 'Boys, be ambitious!'

CHAPTER FOUR

Nixon's Pearl Harbor

> *'I was sitting in the barber's
> chair, and I almost fell out.'*
> Armin H Meyer
> US Ambassador to Japan in the
> summer of 1971

'Sell! Sell! Sell!'

The screams on the floors of the stock exchange in Japan's eight major cities echo the despair and shock.

It is a few minutes past ten on the morning of Monday, August 16, 1971. The President of the United States has struck. Richard M Nixon has just started talking via TV to the American people — Sunday night, Washington time — and for each new minute of the eighteen-minute speech increasingly frenzied signals are being flashed from the brokers' head offices which are in direct private radio communication with some 600 floor representatives on the floor of Tokyo's so-called 'First List' alone. At this hour, other world stock exchanges are closed, because of the time difference, and they refuse to open their doors; the White House has given even Prime Minister Eisaku Sato only ten minutes' advance warning before the President begins his speech.

Billions of dollars disappear for each new minute of the speech, as the hysterical sell orders grow in strength with every new minute at the exchange in Tokyo, Osaka, Nagoya, Hiroshima, Kyoto, Fukuoka, Niigata and Sapporo. This is one of history's most expensive speeches.

Japan is experiencing 'Nikson shokku' No 2, for only one month earlier Nixon shocked Japan, and the world, by announcing his decision to visit China. Throughout the post-war period, the US has forced Japan — her main ally in

Asia — to participate in her containment policy towards China. When the Nixon-Kissinger axis decides to throw this policy overboard, then Japan is given only three minutes' notice. In that week of July, most Japanese felt as if the earth was shaking under their feet, because Japan's protector nation was no longer interested in Japan's views. When Nixon strikes this second blow, it is as if a trap door is opened. And through this hole billions of dollars disappear in a few hours, in many cases the family savings of several years. Something else goes down the drain — and this is more important — the last of Japan's illusions about the safety and the stability of the United States as a market for Japanese export products in the 1970's.

Nixon is announcing 'temporary' measures: in addition to a divorce between gold and the dollar, and a wage and price freeze, there is to be an extra import duty of 10 per cent in order to force an international adjustment of 'unfair' currency exchange rates. But there is nothing temporary in Nixon's words that the US, in the 1970's, must find employment for another twenty million Americans, or in Nixon's interpretation of America's competitive situation: 'There is no longer any need for the United States to compete with one arm tied behind her back.'

The answer from Tokyo is immediate; not from Prime Minister Sato, who had noted Nixon's China move by commenting 'I never want to see that man's face again,' but from one of the heavy-weights of Japan's business world. 'This is a declaration of war,' exclaims Shigeo Nagano, chairman of Japan's Chamber of Commerce and Industry, and Chairman of the board of Nippon Steel (Shin Nittetsu), the world's largest steel company. But Japan's immediate answer is being given on the floors of the exchanges, where everybody knows that in the first half of 1971, the US market swallowed 31.6 per cent of Japan's total exports; the floors, where everybody realizes that Nixon's words will flatten completely the upward trend in the business cycle that had just been spotted. It was this home market lull, since July, 1970, that brought about Japan's intensified export efforts. In 1970, the increase in imports had been greater than the increase in the exports jump, mainly due to enormous purchases of raw materials, but in 1971 the nation has been digesting this huge stock of raw materials and exports have begun a death-or-glory surge upwards: month after month exports zoom 25 per cent, imports only 5 per cent — there is even a drop in purchases from the US — and month after month, Japan's five-star products — including cars and colour-TV sets — are rushing forward at an annual pace of 70–90 per cent, a trend that more than doubles the US deficit in merchandise trade with Japan to about three billion dollars.

Nixon's words threaten to wreck the victorious export trend, smashing the atmosphere of peace and calm that had reigned in Japan on the previous day, when millions of Japanese lowered their heads to pay respect to the memory of the war's end twenty-six years ago. On August 9, even 'Tensei Jingo,' the chronically pessimistic columnist of the daily *Asahi Shimbun,* had been swayed to smile a little, recollecting how much the young post-war generation had grown physically compared to the pre-war generation, and the hungry people who had walked the ruined streets in the autumn of defeat: 'Now tall Japanese walk through the same streets dressed as if for the beach. The long legs of the girls are beautiful. We feel: "Ah, peace is wonderful!" '

But on this morning of August 16, none of the panic-stricken floor men has any chance to reflect on the increasing beauty of Japanese girls' legs: now it is a matter of saving the shirt, selling out. Now everybody will believe that the miracle of Japan has been smashed to pieces and the floor men must sell while they can still get anything for the shares.

'This is New York 1929!' echo the shouts in the corridors of four giant firms of stockbrokers, Nomura, Nikko, Daiwa and Yamaichi (Daiwa alone, for example, has 6,000 employees), the so-called Big Four among 83 brokerage firms; four giants with the right to station 30 men each on the floor of Tokyo's First List alone. This list covers a total of about 800 shares, the nation's strongest corporations, and transactions here amount to about 75 per cent of all stock exchange business, and 90 per cent of the value of all shares throughout Japan. (The 225 strongest corporations of the First List are listed in an average price index known as

Tokyo's Dow-Jones Index.)

The parallel with the New York crash, on this 'Black Monday' for Japan, is no exaggeration; for a week the Tokyo Stock Exchange seems to be bleeding to death. It is a bloodbath in which the Sato Cabinet tries to play the role of a completely disinterested and non-alarmed observer; like France, Japan does not intend to surrender before Nixon's rate adjustment demands and does not intend to let the yen float. It is only after the gnomes – in this case Japan's own giant banks – have crushed the capacity of the Bank of Japan to buy dollars that the Government finally throws in the towel, late on Friday, August 27, and the yen starts floating on the following day.

The convulsions of Japan's stock exchanges during the week following the Nixon shock are worth reporting, at least the main features, and this for two reasons: 1. It would be surprising if Japan were not hit by more shocks in the 1970's. 2. The 1971 selling wave reflected the emotional and irrational actions of the Japenese when thrown into a crisis situation, particularly when they have the feeling that Japan has been brutally slammed against a wall; at such times they see almost no possibility of survival for even the nation's strongest corporations. 3. A growing number of foreign stock funds are putting larger and larger sums into Japanese stocks, and the co-owners of these mutual funds would be well warned to remember that the Tokyo Exchange is not only a fascinating lottery of giant profits, where the investor can rapidly multiply his fortune, but also a terrifying suicide exchange, a helter-skelter that can knock the stuffing out of any incompetent stock buyer.

At the moment Nixon starts speaking ('My fellow Americans' – though he means, to an equally great extent, now hear this, you who are sitting over there in Tokyo), the number of Japanese stock owners amounts to between six and eighteen million. The lower figure is probably more correct, assuming that the average owner has shares in at least three different companies in his portfolio. About 39 per cent of the 120 billion shares – most with a face value, parity, as low as 50 yen, or 6p, just about the value of the stock certificate's paper cost – are owned by private individuals, another 31 per cent by financial institutions, including banks, 3 per cent by foreign corporations, 23 per cent by Japanese corporations, mostly industrial firms, 1 per cent by the brokerage firms, 0.3 per cent by the Government and by public corporations, and finally 0.2 per cent by foreign individuals. The number of foreign individual owners: about 40,000 in March of 1971, with a total of three billion shares – and probably 50,000 at the moment when Nixon assures his listeners that 'our best days are ahead of us.'

While Nixon's face is being made up for TV, the mountain of Japanese stocks is worth about 80 billion dollars (at the 1972 exchange rate). Much of the berserk fury that marked Japan's GNP growth has also been reflected in the growth of share values at the eight stock exchanges.

Table 2: Before Mr. Nixon Spoke: $80 Billion

Billions of Dollars

	All Japan (8 exchanges)	Tokyo's First List	Daily volume (millions of shares)	Annual volume (billions of shares)
1966	31·6	28·3		(7·6)
1967	31·3	27·9		(6.3)
1968	42·6	37·8	(149)	(11·7)
1969	61·8	54·2	(162)	(18·7)
1970	54·6	49·0	(138)	(12·0)
July 31, 1971	76·4	69·3	(195)	(July: 2·1)
August 14, 1971		72·1		

Japan's stock exchanges are open between 9 and 11 am and between 1 and 3 pm, but there is only a morning session on Saturdays and those two hours were not long enough on August 14, when all the indexes rose very strongly: the First List index to 2,740. When the gates open on Monday morning, there are purchase orders that must be acted upon. Between 9.00 and 9.15 am, the index rises four points, because the order book is made up of 51 million shares for sale and 91 million purchasing bids. Up to 10 am, the index drops only one point, but at 9.30 – the moment when US Secretary of State William P Rogers first tries to get through on the telephone to Prime Minister Sato – the brokers already know that Nixon is to give an important, and negative, speech half an hour later, and they are starting to get in touch with some of their major clients. The overwhelming majority of Japan's executives, however, are at this moment, as always, en route to their offices by car. When Rogers's telephone call is switched to the Prime Minister's residence, the answer is Japan's traditional answer in a crisis: 'Chotto matte, kudasai,' please wait, we must try to find somebody who understands English. It is not until 9.50 am that we find Mr Sato sitting in his office, surrounded by Foreign Office interpreters who have been running over at olympic speed, and by his chief Cabinet secretary and other assistants. Sato is listening in shocked silence to the telephone, as he receives a simultaneous translation of Rogers's devastating words. After twenty minutes, at 10.10, Mr Sato hangs up his receiver. But all hell has already broken loose two kilometres away from the Premier's residence, because Kabutocho, Japan's Wall Street district, has received the news faster via bulletins flashed from the international news agencies. At 10.05 the first massive selling signals appear: the back of the hand plus a number of furiously working fingers is being rapidly switched to display the hand's front, and within 55 minutes the First List alone has lost almost two billion dollars. The sum is equal to Japan's annual defence budget, or three months' exports to the United States.

When the exchange opens again after a two-hour lunch break, which provides a change to meditate and calmly analyze the situation, the result is evident: at 1 pm 428 million stocks are for sale — and no one on the floor wants to buy. The hour between 1 and 2 pm costs the stock owners another billon dollars. And ever more floor representatives are rushing to posts No 10 and No 11, where electronics and cars, the backbone of Japan's export offensive, are traded. These are the country's most competitive sectors. The hands all speak the same language: Sell!

Of the First List's 824 shares, all drop with the exception of about 20. Toyota, the first day, an insignificant drop from 3,400 to 3,380, but Matsushita Denki of the 'National' and

'Panasonic' brands — falls heavily, by 25 per cent, to 470 yen.

When the Tokyo Exchange doors are closed at 3 pm, the First List alone has lost 3.6 billion dollars on this initial day, and the 225 bluechip shares in the Dow-Jones index have fallen 8 per cent, an index loss of 210 points. When Stalin died in 1953, and when Bernie Cornfield's IOS was breaking hearts all over the world in the spring of 1971, the Tokyo index did drop a bit more, in per cent, but the analysts behind the nation's sorobans all agree: this is the worst monetary loss ever suffered in Japan's stock exchange history.

On this first day, Nixon's eighteen-minute speech has cost Japan's stock savers about 200 million dollars per minute. A share value equal to half the value of the Stockholm Stock Exchange has been wiped out. But those who later in the evening sit and watch the dramatic colour-TV scenes from Monday's four chaotic hours suspect that the Nixon bill may prove to be even more expensive.

In New York, too, there are convulsions at the stock exchange, but it is a panic of happiness — 'this is a new ball game' — and the exchange sets new records for every new hour. Thirty-two million shares are traded this day, two million more than the old record. The Dow-Jones average makes a record leap of 33 points to 889. The floor traders toss paper up in the air, and cheer lustily. 'You stood a good chance of getting trampled if you weren't careful,' reports UPI.

At least one American supports the view of steel man Nagano. Professor Edwin O Reischauer, a former Ambassador to Japan, tells an AP reporter in the US that if Nixon has once again failed to inform Prime Minister Sato in advance, 'it is another diplomatic "boo boo" (mistake) — almost a declaration of trade war.'

When the little man — who in all countries buys at the top and sells at the bottom — opens his morning newspaper a few hours before Tuesday's trading starts, he reads that the Emperor's forthcoming trip to Europe will cost half a million dollars, a sum that looks rather small this morning, and he notes that the police have now dissolved their investigating force in the Okubo rape-killer case, after an input of '18,721 man-days,' and at a cost, for the taxpayer, of about 300,000 dollars. Traffic policemen have been able to finish counting the bodies from Saturday's road accidents: 78 dead, a new daily record, because Japan has already defeated the US in the number of automobiles per square kilometre. Next Friday, the British Council has invited guests to a day-long course: 'How to make tea, British-style, instructed by English specialists.' On the next page Suzuki-san, our little man, finds the wise and responsible words that always guide the people when a crisis strikes or heads to its climax: first, a statement from the four Opposition parties that Japan should not revalue; secondly, a hastily manufactured disaster forecast by MITI, predicting a loss in Japan's exports to the US of two billion dollars, meaning that the 30 per cent jump over the 1970 figure of 5.9 billion dollars, a jump generally expected, will not materialize. The reason: Nixon's 10 per cent import duty. Suzuki-san keeps on reading. In Europe, the banks do not engage in money exchange, because the dollar is now a leper, but the Bank of Japan on Monday acted in quite the opposite way. It threw in 600 million dollars in support purchases to prop up the dollar rate, and the trend is crystal clear: in the days to follow, the Bank of Japan is determined to fight as bravely and as stubbornly as at Guadalcanal and Midway and Bataan; to fight until the last bag of dollars has been filled. Suzuki-san sighs and calls his broker.

Tuesday, August 17: Between 9 and 11 am, the Bank of Japan buys another 400 million dollars, at an hourly pace of two hundred million, but the Stock Exchange's First List is crashing downwards at a speed three times as fast: hourly losses of 700 million dollars. The index for the 225 bluechips falls only 89 points today, compared to the 210 drop of the previous day, and some support buying is noted: the confused little man has started acting. Index comparisons, to remember when the next crisis strikes Japan: (*see table next page*)

Table 3: The Index Slide

	Monday, August 16	Tuesday, August 17
9.15 a.m.	+ 4	− 20
10.00 a.m.	− 1	− 76
11.00 a.m.	− 95	− 131
13.15 p.m.	− 139	− 104
14.00 p.m.	− 195	− 102
15.00 p.m.	− 210	− 89

The trend between 9 and 11 points towards a definite crash. The Cabinet's economic ministers are in session, and I — and the millions of people who own stocks — am awaiting, nervously, the calm statesman-like words that are usually solemnly uttered whenever there is thunder over the islands of Japan. MITI Minister Kakuei Tanaka, one of the three major candidates for the premiership, lives up to all expectations. He emerges from this meeting to tell the waiting press that the forecasters of MITI have now revised their loss forecasts — upwards: it would be wise to expect, during the seven months left of this fiscal year, a total export loss of 'between 2.5 and 3.0 billion dollars,' about ten per cent below the earlier target of 23-24 billion dollars. (The ultimate result, as announced in a communiqué dated in mid-April, 1972: about 25 billion dollars).

But the Shinto Gods who always keep a guarding and protective eye open for the Japanese people — and their stock exchanges — intervene in the disaster symphony being played by the MITI orchestra. Stock Exchange rules are sacred until the minute they are changed, and the Board announces two changes this Tuesday: the lowering of the cash margin from 50 to 40 per cent, and a reduction to half for the level of fluctuation any single stock is allowed before trading in this stock is automatically stopped. A stock worth 1,500 yen has previously been allowed to go up or down 200 yen in one day, but is now allowed to rise or fall only 100 yen. People attacking a stock will thus have to wait until next day before they can unleash another charge, and on this day most analysts fear that the next day will be even worse. They are correct.

Wednesday, August 18: The First List index goes up during the early morning hours, because Suzuki-san believes that the bottom has been reached. Now he wants to buy and make a little money on the rise that is certain to follow. His illusions are crushed between 1 and 3 pm when the index plunges 112 points, a two-hour loss of 2.4 billion dollars, compared to the previous day's loss of 2.9 billion spread over a four-hour period. Thus far, Nixon's speech has caused the First List alone a three-day loss of nine billion dollars, a sum 50 per cent greater than Japan's 1970 exports to the US. Will this suffering never end? When will the 'sharks' move in? There must surely be a bottom, somewhere?

The sharks refuse to make a move, because they are not so sure where the bottom is either. Their traditional pattern of behaviour: they buy a stock at, for example, 80; when a slide downward starts at the level of 100, they usually succeed in selling for 99, then cash Profit A. They move in again to buy when the stock costs only 70, and then hold the stock for four months, sell it for 110, cash Profit B.

The Exchange's neighbour, the Bank of Japan, displays as much drama: the yen must not be allowed to float. In the spring of 1945, the generals of Okinawa were prepared to fight until the last schoolgirl, and the strategists of the Bank of Japan indicate that the taxpayer's money is sufficient to buy up any number of billions of dollars, at 360 yen per dollar, compared to an unwanted floating rate of 320–340.

Thursday, August 19: it is officially announced that Emperor Hirohito will on the next day receive Finance Minister Mikio Mizuta and listen to a lecture on 'the international monetary crisis,' a lecture of 'one hour and 45 minutes; 20 minutes longer than originally scheduled,' but the fact that Mr Mizuta will have to inform the Emperor that the dollar crisis has 'not necessarily' developed to Japan's advantage does not succeed in pacifying the Stock Exchange. On the contrary: the First List index drops another 138 points, and another 2.3 billion dollars vanishes.

Is this the bottom?

In four days, or 16 trading hours, the eight exchanges have lost a total of 14 billion dollars. The Hiroshima index has fallen to 81.8 per cent with the value of all First List stocks down to 84.4 per cent of the August 14 level. Osaka's First List has fallen less, is at the 88.8 per cent level. What happens if MITI issues another forecast?! The exchange analysts wipe their sweaty brows, because it is the best stocks, the strongest corporations, which have taken the worst beating, a total vote of no confidence.

Five examples of the Thursday value, as compared with the August 14 level, (and with the company's five-year sales development 1966-70 brackets):

Toyota: 73.9 %, still an improvement compared to the previous day's 71.6% (Japan's largest industrial company in 1970, with annual sales of 2.3 billion dollars after an annual growth rate of 27.6% for five years)

Matsushita Denki: 70.4% compared to Wednesday's 62% (No. 5 in size: 2.0 billion dollars, annual growth rate 29.4%)

Tokyo Marine: 67.2% (marine insurance; 369 million dollars, annual growth rate 28.6%)

Sony: 72% (354 million dollars, ranked 57th in size but 14th as an exporter, an annual growth rate of 34.4%)

TDK: 55% (Japan's largest maker of electronic components; 87 million dollars, annual growth rate 40%).

No, this is not the bottom, not yet, even though Friday's trading indicates this: index up 94 points, First List value up 298 million dollars. The market drops slightly on the following day (minus 178 million dollars), but plunges heavily on Monday, August 23, a fall of 115 index points costing the First List 2.3 billion dollars, mainly because of rumours — later denied — that IMF analysts had suggested a revaluation rate for the yen of 17—25 per cent. *This* is the bottom, and the market refuses to crash — or to react — when the yen starts floating. But by this time, Tokyo's First List has lost 13.7 billion dollars, all exchanges a total of 16 billion. The losses suffered by the speculators and the small savers equal the cost of France's nuclear arms programme over the last decade, plus another 30 per cent.

Mrs Suzuki, the widow, cannot afford to put her money in a bank at an interest rate of 3—5 per cent while the consumer price index rises at an annual pace of 6-7 per cent, and she does not have the large sums needed to put her money into land and in that way earn interest of 15-18 per cent per year.

So she owns some stocks, she and banker Watanabe and the 'sharks,' and all of them, the big and the small savers, are in these dark August days licking their wounds.

President Nixon's people are generous in the moment of victory. Even normally sane analysts, such as Edwin L Dale, Jr of the *New York Times,* push the knife in an extra inch in their comments. The opinion of Mr Dale on August 24, also reprinted in Japan:

> What is entirely clear is that the United States in a single dramatic stroke has shown the world exactly how powerful it still is, despite all the talk about a 'weak' dollar. In breaking the link between the dollar and gold and imposing a 10 per cent import tax, the US has shown who is Gulliver and who are the Lilliputians.

Mr Dale also names the Lilliputians: 'West Germany, Japan, Britain and the other leading industrial nations.'

Well, well, I tell myself in this month of August: the Japanese Lilliputians will prove much tougher than Gulliver could ever imagine.

Journalistically, it would be nice if I could now add that 'this bitter autumn, the Japanese clenched their fists in fury and swore an oath between their teeth: "We shall repay. Mr Nixon is going to get this bill in return. We shall take our revenge." '

The truth is just the opposite. This autumn the Japanese are attacking themselves: we have certainly misbehaved; we never realized fully that America's economic situation was that desperate, we swear never again to act in such a way that other nations turn in rage against us. These declarations of self-criticism are heard in public speeches, in editorial columns, in man-to-man conversations in the streets. 'We must liberalize ourselves; we must try to understand the problems of other countries.'

For several months, there is a heavy blanket of mourning over the islands of Japan: what people mourned was the belief that the United States harboured friendly feelings towards Japan. For decades the Japanese had declared their — to quote the *Asahi* daily — 'unrequited love' toward the US. Year after year America has topped all Japanese opinion polls as the most popular country, while Japan — according to polls by the *Yomiuri* newspaper — has steadily fallen in favour in the American people's ranking list of most trust-worthy nations: Japan now down to 16th place, a reduction in votes from 12 to 8 per cent between 1969 and 1971.

This is a cruel autumn for Japan: an autumn of loneliness, in which Japan experiences a feeling of being expelled from the community of nations, this time for having been too successful in peaceful competition.

(Words of military aggressiveness are absent in Japan, but not on the other side of the Pacific. In mid-October, two months after Nixon's second, 'shock,' US Treasury Secretary John Connally announces that the US has entered into 'a war of competition and an economic war' with nations with which the US is trading.)

In Japan, mourning and feelings of loneliness do not mean passivity. This autumn the Japanese look each other in the eye and say: Let us get going again, let us try a little bit harder — and then see what happens.

About 31 years ago, Japan had committed the worst mistake in her history: by striking against Pearl Harbor, without warning, Japan helped Roosevelt awaken the American people. In August 1971, Nixon committed the same mistake; he deeply shocked an allied people, and in October he goes one step further, gives an ultimatum and forces Japan to scrap the 'voluntary' textile exports agreement concluded in the summer of 1971, pushing the Government of Japan into signing a formal textile treaty, though textile imports from Japan amount to only about two per cent of the total US consumption.

This autumn, Mr Nixon is successful in making the Japanese people arrive at this unspoken concensus:

- Now we had better save and strengthen the industry which we have been denouncing for more than a year
- Because industry is our daily bread — or rice bowl
- We thought, at one time, that we could build a welfare state rapidly, look forward toward working less hard, be satisfied with a lower growth rate
- Now we know that we cannot trust any other protector nation but ourselves: we must grow rapidly so that we can afford both an internationally competitive industry and a welfare state.

This awareness could be seen emerging in October and November, 1971. Officially, the Japanese continued to see dark clouds and difficulties everywhere, but members of the inner circles noted calmly: merely a slight dent in our upward growth curve.

Once again, the Japanese sit down to study MITI's 1980 programme, the 1985 programme of Dr Hisao Kanamori: the most ambitious growth programmes ever presented to a people.

Foreign analysts visiting Japan this autumn fail to discover the changes of attitude, the new tone, the new emphasis. They see only the heavy rain, the lightning striking through the thunder clouds, and they rush to their typewriters: 'The Miracle is over, the miracle is over, over over . . .' They are being deceived by forecasters who have always been proved wrong in the past, who with the stubbornness of an automaton keep proclaiming the end of the miracle every fourth year (As one example, take an interview statement by Professor Shigeto Tsuru in *Dagens Nyheter* of March 28, 1972, made to a visiting *Dagens Nyheter* guest writer: from now on a growth rate as low as '4-6 per cent'). But they are most of all led astray by the professional pessimists: the editorial writers of Japan's leading national dailies, men who at each new recession — 1954, 1958, 1962, 1965 and again in 1970-71 — always display the same pattern of action: they fall to the ground, tear at the carpet in despair: in July 1971 a department store sales growth of only 15 per cent; this December probably only 10 per cent: dear me, the sky is falling! I have listened to these songs of doom for eighteen years, off and on, and I have learned that in evaluating Japan's future growth rate, one is wise to pay a visit to other sources, other analysts.

The ultimate fate of Japan's stock exchanges? About what could have been expected:

- At the end of December 1971, all indexes caught up with the record level registered on August 14
- On April 8, 1972, the total value of all stocks was 86

billion dollars — about six billion more than on August 14

- Index for Tokyo's First List: 3,255, a rise of 18 per cent over the level just before Mr Nixon began his speech.

Many of the Japanese who lost heavily from their savings during the week of shock and panic are not to be found among those who have made a profit on the latest market rise. They were scared away — they do not want to experience more Pearl Harbors in reverse.

CHAPTER FIVE

Timetable for victory

*'Too often Administration
spokesmen have talked as if the
US has an inalienable right to be
No 1 in world economic power,
and that other nations have a
duty to help it maintain that
position.'*
Time Magazine, Jan. 24, 1972

The year is 1851, and the journalist at the *Economist's*
editorial office in London walks to the window. He looks
down at the busy street below, noting the hansom cabs
whose numbers appear to be increasing almost daily, because
the economy of the British Empire is beating with an ever
faster pulse. He walks back to his desk, slowly and
thoughtfully fondles his bushy beard, takes up his pen once
again and writes — now with fast and determined strokes —
that 'it is as certain as the next eclipse' that the United States
of America, within the not too distant future, will overtake
Great Britain in total annual production.

His choice of words is as precise and free of doubt as the
authoritative statements that are to characterize the language
of future-probing economic journalists a century later, and
the verdict pronounced over this first villain of the species is
short, sharp and cruel. 'It just can't happen, old chap!'
proclaim the wise men in every London pub, because they
are sitting in the very heart of the world's first industrial
state, where the industrialization process had begun at the
end of the 18th century. The result: virtual world dominance
for the British economy for almost the whole of the 19th
century. Two decades after the eclipse forecast, people are
still musing in the London pubs. By now Great Britain has

one-fourth of all world trade, one-third of world industrial production, is making more pig iron than the rest of the world combined, owns forty per cent of world merchant tonnage, and London is the centre of world finance. But the eclipse process is in full swing: a low British growth rate while the Unites States continues to leap forward — and the British Era is definitely over by 1913; a year when Great Britain is still the world's leading exporter but now produces only one-third of˜ America's pig iron volume, and Great Britain's one-third of world industrial production has shrunk to one-seventh. About ten per cent of Britain's national income is devoted to overseas investments, and no other country can afford that, but now there is grudging agreement in the pubs: a new nation is on the throne, the American is now No 1 in annual production of goods and services per year, and the competitive power of British industry compared to America's is only a beautiful memory.

The American Era of overwhelming dominance was not as long; a period of 55 years, 1914-69, with these five patterns:

- *A First Chapter* of about three decades when America's potential industrial rivals — Britain, Germany, France, USSR, China and Japan — were busy beating each other to death or recovering from war wounds
- *A Second Chapter,* 1945-60, with America holding a hand of five aces, and superiority factors rolling across the earth: industrial efficiency; capital; technology; management knowledge and control systems; marketing techniques
- *A Third Chapter,* 1961-69: Other countries absorb the American lessons, and the US fails in her half-hearted attempts to break the trend of the 1950's with too low productivity increases. Out and across the world stream a flock of companies no longer satisfied with the profit development within the United States; and at the same pace as the competitive power of America's home-based industries withers away, the US also loses the merchandise trade surpluses she needs to finance her military adventures and her overseas direct investments
- *A Fourth Chapter:* the virtual capitulation of the dollar in August, 1971, after Japanese and other foreign

companies have begun to chew up ever larger pieces of the American market as if it were candy-floss. In 1971, the US also suffers her first annual merchandise trade deficit since the 1880's. In 1971, too, the US steel industry is dethroned by the Soviet Union, in total production, for the first time since the 1880's

- *The Fifth Chapter* is Japan's reveng , 1972-80, America's defeat in annual production per capita, and the inability of US industry to compete with the Japanese in free competition. Some pages of the revenge chapter have already been written, some as early as in 1969 and 1970. The indicators now present, which show mercilessly that Japan's per-capita-revenge cannot be prevented, are far stronger than the burden of evidence on the desk of my *Economist* colleague in 1851.

The only factor of uncertainty is the mood of the American, his mental balance, the temptation to stick out a leg in the path of the hurtling Japanese. This risk did not exist when the Englishman stepped aside at the top of the mountain (Why make a fuss about it? It wouldn't be cricket), and the American swung himself up. The risk of a national shock is probably zero in a nation where 'business' has never been really close to the people's hearts — business is just a pause between the foxhunting and the race meeting which is why it is so very pleasant to visit Britain, and will be at least until the day her standard of living slips to that of Greece. The American, however, is success-oriented from the day when, as a very small boy, he starts a newspaper round and earns his first dollar; his success as an adult is measured in dollars, and despite all the crises within the US in the last decades — race riots, urban collapse — Joe Brown has always had one sweetener left to chew on: We are the world's most efficient people. Our system is the world's most efficient, because as measured in annual production of goods and services per person, we are far ahead of other countries — Yes, Sir, that's free enterprise!'

Now even that sweetener is floating away, in the direction of Suzuki-san's open mouth. Everything indicates that America's per-capita defeat is the bitter pill that must be swallowed during the presidential term that begins in January, 1977. The Japanese victory will probably be proclaimed in the last quarter of 1978, and this means that the US counter-offensive must start rolling effectively during President Nixon's second term, 1973-76. Examples: the 'America, Inc' complex, with its cooperation between private business and the State, that was being sketched in 1971 in order better to compete with 'Japan, Inc'; the hints of a softening of America's anti-trust laws, which would mean that the big American wolves are let loose in the battle with the wildly galloping Japanese samurais. It will be a fight in vain — Japan holds the stronger cards.

The strength and intensity of the growth of the Japanese economy have been described in my earlier book, mainly in comparisons with the Soviet Union and West Germany. A few examples of a different nature: it took seven decades for the superpower of the 19the century, Britain, to increase her exports six times; Japan achieved a six-fold leap in one decade (1961-70). It took the US seventeen years (1927-1944) to take the stride from 100 to 200 billion dollars in annual GNP, in nominal prices; Japan did it in only five (1966-70). It took the US eleven years to lift her exports from 7 to 20 billion dollars (1945-56). Japan managed to do it in seven (1965-71).

In 1953, the annual per capita production of Britain, one of the victorious Allies, was four times that of the defeated Japanese — 940 dollars versus 230. In 1965 the Japanese reached the half-as-good-level, overtaking the British in 1970, with 2,217 dollars versus, 2,207.

History is ruthless to countries that do not keep up with the pace, particularly in the real income tables, as the cosmetics of inflation often falsify or to a great extent distort tables showing nominal prices. When Japan's 'Victory' is announced in 1978, a figure in nominal prices will be given — Japan's GNP per capita in 1978 prices, compared to America's figure for the same year — and it is hardly likely that the American public will listen to objections from the professors: 'Well, but wait, is this in 1953 prices or 1960 prices?' In that year, the American will have money in his pocket that purchases at 1978 prices, as a result of wages paid at the 1978 price level — a basic reality, and any constant-prices comparisons are unlikely to weaken the shock when it is announced that Japan's annual production of goods and services per man, woman and child has now overtaken that of the US.

Here is a revealing nominal prices table comparing the GNP per capita development for Britain and Japan, 1953-70, in dollars (at the 1970 exchange rate, followed by these revaluation percentages: Japan plus 16.88 per cent and Britain plus 8.57 per cent).

Table 4: How Britain Lost the Per Capita Race

Dollars

	Japan	Great Britain	Comparison in %	The gap in dollars
1953	230	940	24·5	710
1955	270	1,050	25·7	780
1960	460	1,380	33·3	920
1965	900	1,840	48·9	940
1969	1,630	1,970	82·7	340
1970	1,987	2,033	93·3	136
New 1972 parities:				
1969	1,905	2,139	89·1	234
1970	2,217	2,207	100·4	+ 10

Source: author; OECD's per capita sums

The table shatters a generally accepted myth: for twelve years, the gap or distance as measured in dollars grew, though the Japanese kept eating up the British lead. It may be wise to recall the illusory 'yes, but the gap is growing' arguments that marked the growth debate in the United States following the launching of Russia's first Sputnik in 1957, because the gap illusion will now be taken out of the closet again, in comparisons with Japan's per capita leaps. In 1971, the US per capita figure increased by about 250 dollars, Japan's by only about 210 dollars, ie the gap widened though Japan's percentage ratio of the American level changed from 46.8 per cent in 1970 to about 48.5 per cent in 1971, and crossed the half-as-good level in 1972, in spite of the fact that 1972 promises to be a unique high-growth year in American postwar history.

In five years, Britain's we-are-twice-as-productive position towards Japan vanished. Can the Japanese repeat this performance in the race with the US in the six years of 1973-78?

This has been the per capita development:

Table 5: How Rapidly is Japan Approaching the US?

	US GNP per capita in dollars	Year when Japan reached or reaches that level	"Lag" in number of years
1909	349	1958	49 years
1929	858	1965	36 years
1933	442		
1945	1,520	1968	23 years
1955	2,430	1971	16 years
1960	2,788	1972	12 years
1970	4,740	(1975)	5 years

Note: Current Prices.

Source: author

The table in nominal prices above discloses nothing about real purchasing power development, giving the impression that a 1909 dollar may be compared to a 1958 dollar in Japan. Despite these shortcomings, the table does indicate the income explosion: in three years, 1966-68, the Japanese per capita sum escalated as much as the equivalent sum did in the US over a 16-year period, 1930-45. In another three years, 1969-71, the Japanese caught up with the US effort in the whole decade of 1946-55. It took the Japanese six years, 1966-71, to match America's twenty-five-year gain from 1930-55.

No sane analyst expects Japan to be able to repeat the growth offensive of 1966-70, when the total GNP scored an annual real increase of 12.5 per cent and about 17 per cent in nominal prices. One arrives at the per capita figure by deducting from the total GNP growth percentage the year's population growth, which in Japan was 1.1 per cent per year in the 1960's (but 1.2 per cent per year in the 1970's) as compared to America's 1.3 per cent in both the 1960's and 1970's. But America's slow growth, compared to Japan's, is an old historical trend:

Table 6: America's Slow Growth is an Old, Old Story

	GNP, ANNUAL REAL GROWTH IN %			SAME, IN CURRENT PRICES		
	1913–38	1951–60	1961–70	1953–70	1961–65	1966–70
Japan	4·0	8·8	11·1	14·4	14·4	17·1
US	2·0	3·3	4·1	6·0	6·1	7·1
USA's pace versus Japan's	50%	37·5%	36·9%	41·7%	42·4%	41·5%
Britain		2·6	(2·8)	6·4		
West Germany		7·5	4·8	9·3	8·8	6·4

Source: author; official statistics; Stanley H. Cohen for 1913–38.

Can the United States break this historical trend? 'No', answer Japan's economists, with a sad shake of their heads; partly because the struggle would be more interesting if the competitor were also able to run reasonably fast, partly because they realize that Japan's victories in various fields in the 1970's also carry the seeds of defeat — the risk that the competitor will once again over-react in response to Japan's over-success.

The strongest fortresses in America's defensive front have already collapsed.

If a private individual wants to become richer than his neighbours, both in annual and in accumulated riches, he must save more than his neighbours and invest more and in a more growth-rewarding way. The same is true for a country's economy. There are six major components in the Gross National Expenditure account (GNE = GNP's expenditure side): two consumption components and four 'effort' components, including three investment sectors and finally the overseas transactions net (exports and other factors of income from abroad, minus the same import figures), a net which reflects both an effort and a country's competitive power.

It is a shock to discover that though the per capita resources of the Japanese are only half his American counterpart's, he has already overtaken his rival in total effort, not only relatively — as a percentage of total resources — but also in absolute per capita figures.

My conclusion is based on an analysis of the total final results for 1970 (for Japan fiscal year, US calendar year). In this year, the US total GNP amounted to 974.1 billion dollars, Japan's to 236.9 billion dollars (at the new parity rate of 308 yen per dollar, with a US population of 205.4 million and a Japanese population of 103.9 million, or 50.6 per cent of the US population level, with the total GNP sum 24.3 per cent of America's.

The per capita comparison results in an index that I should like to refer to as an 'index of revenge' or 'index of defeat.'

Table 7: The Index Points the Way: Ultimate Defeat

	Share of GNP in per cent (%)		GNP per capita in dollars (1970)		"Index of defeat" GNP per capita structure (US = 100)
	JAPAN	US	JAPAN	US	JAPAN
GNP per capita	(100)	(100)	2,281	4,742	48·1
Total consumption	58·7	82·5	1,339	3,912	34·2
(a) private	50·5	63·2	1,152	2,997	38·4
(b) public	8·2	19·3	187	915	20·4
The total effort					
(fixed investments)	35·6	16·8	811	797	102
(a) private gross					
fixed investment	20·7	10·5	472	497	95
(b) private housing					
investment	6·9	3·1	157	148	106
(c) public investment	8·0	3·2	182	152	120
To be added:					
(a) overseas net	1·1	0·3	25	14	178
(b) inventory investment					
change (of no					
importance;					
cyclical)	4·6	0·2	105	9·5	—

Note: These estimates were based on the preliminary fiscal 1970 results for Japan, with the result and structure slightly revised in March, 1972, but without any basic changes. For an estimate of the 1972 neck-and-neck race in fixed investments, see table 30a in Chapter 9 ('The Revolution').

The March 1972 revisions gave Japan a 1970 per capita figure of 2,287 dollars, and a "total effort" of 804 dollars, which would lower Japan's index point to 101 (public investments 193 dollars or 8·45% of GNP; private fixed investments 460 dollars and 20.1%; private housing investments 151 dollars and 6·6% of GNP, a total effort of 35.15%.

According to preliminary results, Japan's total 'effort' in the recession year of fiscal 1971 (which ended March 31, 1972) amounted to 857 dollars or 34·33% of GNP, with private fixed investments dropping to 18·3%, private housing investments falling slightly, from 6·6% to 6.55% and public investments rising strongly from 8·45% to 9·45%. GNP per capita in fiscal 1971: 2,496 dollars.

Source: author's estimates

Elements of the revenge picture that are already present:

1. **The Lift** In 1953, US total fixed investments per capita were 6.5 times as large as those of the Japanese. In 1970 the Japanese raced ahead
2. **The Pace** The Japanese were able to do this by running almost six times as fast, in the investment race, measured in constant price, that is 13.3 per cent versus 2.3 per cent per year, and about three times as fast when using nominal prices; 16.4 versus 4.7 per cent, all in the 1954-68 period
3. **Production** Suzuki-san has already defeated Joe Brown in per capita production in 9 out of 12 major production groups, including steel, ships, synthetic fibres, TV sets, passenger cars, newsprint and ethylene (*See* Appendix tables)
4. **Industry's Muscles** The American is still just ahead in 'total private business fixed investments,' in nominal prices, a sector which also includes the non-manufacturing facilities, department stores, office buildings, etc. But there is in the total sum one item of particular interest, reflecting international competitive power, namely the investments of manufacturing industry. Here the Japanese was able to spend only half of Mr Brown's sum in 1965, but had by 1970 out-classed his rival, taking a 30-per cent lead: 201 dollars per year for Suzuki-san, 155 for Mr Brown. Total national sums: 20.8 billion dollars for Japan, 31.9 billion for the US
5. **Steel** In total national steel investments, Japan was able to spend 86 per cent of the US sum in 1969, but in the following year, Japan had seized a 27-per cent lead (2.2 billion versus 1.7 billion dollars). This was a

primary reason why Japan was able in 1971 to increase her global steel exports by 34 per cent, to about 24 million tons

6. **Productivity**
- The US steel industry requires 7.31 man-hours to make a ton of steel, at an employment cost of 5.68 dollars per man-hour. In Japan: 5.7 man-hours at an hourly cost of 1.80 dollars (And then one wonders in what sort of world America's trade negotiators are that 'the Japanese must, somehow, be persuaded to start importing American steel'!)
- A Japanese steel worker turns out 277 tons per year, the American 222, a West German 158. Personnel cost per steel worker per year: 10,005 dollars in the US, for Japan about one-third of that figure or 3,033 dollars, according to 1968 Japanese statistics and at the old exchange rate. The Japanese cost was reported as being half the West German level
- Within the whole of manufacturing industry, Japanese productivity — production per man-hour — rose 3.6 times as fast as in the United States in the 1961-70 period, annual increase rates of 11.1 versus 3.1 per cent — and *seven times as fast* in the four-year period of 1966-69 (rates of 14.7 versus 2.1 per cent), and, finally, a twelve-fold difference in the year of 1970 (13.9 per cent and 1.1 per cent). The annual increase in wages, 1961-70: three times as fast as in the US (Details: *See* Appendix tables)

7. **Machine Tools** — the work horses of industry. As late as 1967, the US had a one-third share of total world production. By 1971 America had slipped to a share of 10 per cent, trailing the Soviet Union, West Germany and Japan

8. **Exports per Capita** In 1960, Brown's annual result was twice as good as Suzuki's (113 versus 44 dollars).In 1970, the US lead had shrunk to 11 per cent and in the following year Suzuki had the same lead, 232 versus 209 dollars; according to customs statistics (With import figures of 190 for Japan, cif, and 219, fob, for the US.)

9. **Total Exports** In 1971, Japan reached 55 per cent of the US level, with 24 billion dollars against America's 43.5 billion — 'But we shall have overtaken the US by 1980, at the latest,' announced Japan's MITI in a forecast dated January, 1972.

10. **Trade Balance** When the American Empire was at the peak of its power — in 1964, for example, the year before the bombing of North Vietnam began and also the year before the five-year period that saw US productivity increases shrink almost to nothing, when most of the US GNP growth was thin air, inflation — a new record was set by the US in its global merchandise trade surplus: an annual surplus of 7.8 billion dollars (with both exports and imports in fob prices, excluding freight and insurance costs). In that year, the US export value increased by 3.2 billion dollars, also a new record.
In 1971 Japan smashed both of these records, with a trade balance surplus of 7.9 billion dollars and an increase in exports of 3.9 billion dollars

11. **Prestige of Size** Just one example. In 1967, US Steel was the world's No 1 steel producer, with 29 million tons in that year, followed by Bethlehem and Republic, also American companies. In fourth and fifth places were Japan's Yawata and Fuji, with a combined production of 17 million tons or 58 per cent of US Steel's level. In 1970, Yawata and Fuji merged to become Nippon Steel (in Japan, however, the company is known as Shin Nittetsu), and was immediately the world leader, a position claimed again in 1971, with 30.5 million tons, while US Steel was able to make only 85 per cent of its rival's output

12. **Savings** All Japan's small investors have already succeeded in defeating the US in annual household savings per capita ('Personal savings' — though the wage level within the manufacturing industry, for example, is only one-third of the US level.) It is all these 'little people' who via the banks lend their money to the business world, including Nippon Steel,

so that Japan's industry will continue to be able to run three to six times faster than world rivals.

The development in annual household savings (by households and non-profit institutions);

Table 8: Suzuki-San has a Twenty per cent Lead

In New Personal Savings per Year

	Totals billions of dollars		Per Capita dollars	
	Japan	US	Japan	US
1955	2·8	15·8	31	95
1965	12·7	28·4	129	146
1970	30·5	50·2	294	244
Annual growth rate	1956-65		15·3%	4·4%
	1966-70		17·9%	
	1956-70		16·2%	6·5%

Source: author; Bank of Japan

What saved America's face a little in the series above was a 34 per cent savings jump in the US in the year of 1970 (from 37.6 to 50.2 billion dollars), a year of apprehension when US real GNP decreased 0.7 per cent and fear of unemployment soared. Normally, the US savings ratio of disposable income (after tax) is six per cent, as compared to accelerating efforts by Suzuki-san: 13.4 per cent in 1955 and 20.4 per cent in 1970, and seven per cent for the Briton and 14-16 per cent for the West German. Only God is able to interpret Sweden's savings statistics, but an official of the Bank of Japan points in triumph with his econometric forefinger to a table which indicates that the Swedish ratio was 9.8 per cent in 1968, meaning 200 dollars per capita, meaning that the Swede also has been defeated, and it is only a question of time before even the compulsive savers of West Germany (about 300 dollars) will find themselves overtaken too, probably in 1972 to 1973.

Now Japan's consumer price index rose at an annual pace of 59 per cent between 1961 and 1970, but that is pretty weak consolation for a social-democratic heart, when studying the acceleration table above. The real growth in savings stands at 10 per cent and rose to 12 per cent in the 1966-70 period, as the CPI rose only 5.5 per cent per year in the latter period.

America's savers have been defeated, Suzuki-san is 20 per cent ahead. Some of his other statistical triumphs in the pursuit of riches will be discussed in later chapters.

After this long parade of evidence, back to the main question: can the Japanese really defeat the Americans in annual GNP per capita, and if so, what is the likely timetable?

Let me retreat in time. It is the spring of 1969, and I am sitting opposite Professor Osamu Shimomura, the strategist behind the investment and growth offensive of the 1960's. There is a strong note of optimism in Japan this spring because industrial production is advancing at an annual rate of 17 per cent, exports at 23 per cent, real GNP at 12.1 per cent, and the outside world is still applauding the Japanese miracle; except that the Americans have started to make noises about something called 'the textile issue.' Shimomura predicts that Japan will overtake the USSR in total GNP in 1985, at the very latest, but he emphasizes that the chances of defeating the US in total GNP are 'nil.' But perhaps per capita? The professor answers by giving me a set of figures (See *The Japanese Challenge*) indicating that Japan's per capita figure, in the best of two alternatives, would be 89 per cent of the US sum by 1988, (or 8,100 dollars for Suzuki, 9,100 or 11,000 dollars for Brown).

After 1988? 'Perhaps a 20 per cent chance of catching up with the US in per capita GNP.'

Two and a half years later, October, 1971, and the autumn rain is falling heavily outside the professor's windows. This year industrial production is rising only about four per cent, real GNP only 6.1 per cent, because Japan has been suffering from a recession since July, 1970. Worst of all: the Nixon 'shocks.' Most Japanese have been sighing unhappily this autumn, and even nature itself is turning against the nation: autumn leaves are turning yellow and red five days earlier than usual, a sign of a long and difficult winter to come. The

Tokyo correspondent of the *New York Times* has just reported, poetically, that the Japanese 'have begun a voyage towards uncharted seas, and not even their leaders can be certain of where the voyage will take them.' So I am a bit nervous as I await an answer from the professor, an economist who has proved correct in his forecasts, in all essential aspects, over the past fifteen years. Could it be that the 20 per cent chance has been halved? A shipwreck in uncharted seas?

The professor puts his cup of coffee aside, says quietly and calmly, this time with a hundred per cent confidence in his voice:

'We shall catch up with the American per capita figure in 1980.'

A few months later, in February 1972, I am sitting opposite another economist, Dr Hisao Kanamori, twelve years younger than the 60-year old professor and his leading rival as the nation's dominant forecaster. In front of me I have Kanamori's prediction dated April 1971: per capita victory as early as in 1982. That was about four months before the thunder struck; perhaps a revision?

Dr Kanamori looks merrily at me, takes his pipe out of his mouth (a pipe that looks as if it has survived many bites, probably beginning with his two years at Oxford in the mid-1950's).

'We shall pass the US per capita figure in 1980, at the latest. That is, after eight years.'

The two economists disagree on most questions of Japan's development in the 1970s — a conflict of critical importance, as will be seen in the next chapter. But they do agree on two subjects: firstly, Japan's economic growth must now enter a quality phase, an era giving priority to people and not to machines; secondly, that Japan, despite any change of course, will dethrone the Americans.

Each new revaluation of the Japanese yen will raise its value against the dollar, and thus result in one or more 'extra' or free-ride lifts upward, in the 1970's. But only those who insist on remaining blind can afford to keep on believing that Japan's triumphs will be mere statistical victories.

Table 9: Timetable for America's Defeat in GNP Per Capita

| | JAPAN | | | | | USA | |
| | Kana-mori | Shimo-mura | Yamaichi Shoken | Nomura Institute | Author | Shimomura | Kanamori |
	(Jan. 1972)	(Aug. 1971)	(March 1972)	(March 1972)	(March 1972)	(1971)	(1972)
			R = new revaluation				
	Annual Per Capita Growth, in Current Prices, in Per Cent, 1971—80						
	12·6	12·1	13·5	13·5	12·5	3·1	5·7
	But the Figures Below also Include the Effects of Revaluation rate 360 =						
1970		(308)	2,287	2,287	2,287	4,740	4,740
1971					2,496		5,010
1972					2,800		5,296
1973				3,145 + R3,165 = 3,460			5,598
1974					3,575 + R = 3,933		5,917
1975	4,140	3,770 (4,406)	4,213 + R = 4,634		4,445	5,522	6,254
1976				5,387	5,020	5,693	6,610
1977				—	5,675	5,868	6,987
1978	5,910 (6,501)	5,210 (6,090)	6,850	—	6,412 + R = 7,053	6,052	7,385
1979	6,654 (7,320)	5,660 (6,615)	7,800	—	7,970	6,237	7,807
1980	8,240 (8,240)	6,040 (7,060)	8,880	—	9,005	6,400	8,217

Note: Dr. Kanamori, a civil servant, predicts a revaluation by 10 per cent by 1980. The author, being more free to speculate, anticipates two revaluations, one in 1974 and another one in 1978, each lifting the yen by ten per cent against the dollar. Nomura expects the next revaluation to take place in 1973; Yamaichi says 1974. As for the US growth, America is at present following Kanamori's trend line.

The author expects a real growth rate for Japan of 8·5%, plus a GNP implicit deflator (general price increase) of 5·2%, giving a total nominal growth rate of 13·7% and a per capita growth of 12·5%.

Yamaichi expects an annual real growth rate of 9·3% in 1971—80, while Nomura predicts an average of 8·9% for the 1971—76 period. Using the 1972 parity of 308 yen per dollar, Yamaichi expects a nominal GNP in 1980 of 935 billion dollars, with exports, etc, in that year of 89·2 billion dollars, and imports of 78 billion dollars. Yamaichi expects private business fixed investments to grow at an annual nominal rate of 13·2%, Government fixed investments at a rate of 19·4%.

My forecast of two sizeable revaluations is not over-ambitious, in view of two facts: (1) Japan's fast labour productivity growth, so fast that any new revaluation handicap is quickly eaten up by new productivity leaps· (2) West Germany's revaluations in the past, a combined jump of 30% over an 11-year period. The value of the D Mark was raised by 5% in March 1961, by another 9.3% in October, 1969, and by another 13·57% in December, 1971. On this last date, the yen's value was raised 16·88% against the dollar but only 7·66% against gold, compared to the D Mark's rise of 4·61% against gold. Thus, Japan's 1971 revaluation toward the dollar was tough but this was not the case for the yen versus European currencies.

In his inaugural address in January 1969, President Nixon declared: 'The American dream does not come to those who fall asleep.' He emphasized: 'We will press urgently forward.' In the three-year period that followed that daring speech, 1969-71, the US GNP per capita rose a total of 17 per cent, in nominal prices. Most of the increase was air: real increase during the whole three-year period was 0.9 per cent per capita, meaning 95 per cent air, inflation.

During President Nixon's first three years in power, Suzuki-san ran 33 times as fast, as measured in constant prices. This trend is temporary: the era of overwhelming superiority in speed will enter a calmer phase, but all the factors indicate that while it took six decades before my *Economist* colleague's forecast came true, the world will see the 'eclipse' of the Americans six years from now, in 1978.

CHAPTER SIX

The Brain Power Index

> *'Japan's future had been the*
> *subject of highly speculative*
> *predictions even before Haakan*
> *Hedberg and Herman Kahn*
> *startled an unsuspecting public*
> *with the announcement that*
> *Japan would become an*
> *economic superpower.*
> *... But there always remains*
> *the possibility that some time*
> *around 1975, the yen may have*
> *to be revalued.'*
> Kuranosuke Saito
> Director of Research Depart-
> ment, Fuji Bank, in the
> *Euromoney* magazine of March,
> 1971.

Mysteries should be confronted at night, not in the early morning hours. As I wake up one morning in Tokyo and start the working day by thumbing through the *Nihon Keizai* economic daily, my eyes collide with a 1985 diagram. Two bold curves shooting two arrows straight towards the sky — up, up, up. One of the arrows is marked 'GNP', the other one identified merely as 'BPI', and even this arrow is climbing at a dizzying pace, is assumed to reach 313.1 index points in 1985. But *what* is BPI? I ask my Japanese wife, but she shakes her head sadly. As I am a rather typical Swedish gentleman and husband, I ask politely: 'Why did I ever marry you? You don't even know what BPI is!' My wife, corrupted by post-war ideals about democracy and equal rights for women, escorts me just as politely to the door, and says: 'You'd better go and see your friends at Keizai Kikakucho.'

I race for a taxi, hurry downtown, but the first person I meet at the Economic Planning Agency (Japan's planning ministry) just shakes his head, answering in a low voice: 'I am sorry but I just can't tell you what BPI is.' Suddenly I am struck by the thought, the suspicion that he probably *does* know but is not at liberty to disclose the truth; the newspaper may — by mistake — have got hold of a state secret. Such things do happen in Japan. A few minutes later, however, I am introduced to a young man, aged about 28, who will probably be one of the nation's leading economists in the 1990's, and he looks at me as if I am a visitor from a strange planet, unable to understand the alphabet of earth-men:

'BPI, Mr. Hedberg? BPI means Brain Power Index, and this index here shows very clearly that the brain-power of the Japanese people in the year of 1985 will be at a level of 313.1 points, compared to 100 in the base year of 1955.'

At this very moment I realize the futility of ever again doubting a glorious economic future for Japan. Increased education, ever more accumulated school years, do mean increased brain-power, of course, but only in Japan would they have the audacity to sit down and make an index of its development, and this with an exactness of one decimal: 313 point 1.

Just an anecdote? No, the brain-power curve is Japan's index of fate, the factor that will determine whether Japan is also going to win in total GNP. It is Japan's most crucial make-or-break factor in the decade of the 1970's.

It is the quality of Japan's brainpower that will decide whether Japan really has the economic potential to create, by 1985, another four or nine 'new Japans', additional Japans — that is, a GNP power or total production power five or ten times as great as the Japan of 1965 (base year) in Japan for all constant prices comparisons, the base year when Japan's GNP was 88.1 billion dollars, at the old exchange rate of 360, but 102.9 billion at the new rate of 308. Real GNP in the calendar year of 1970, new rate: 182.8 billion dollars — meaning that in five years, Japan's productive power grew 78 per cent, compared to Britain's 10 per cent, West Germany's 25 per cent, America's 17 per cent. In five years, the

Japanese created a new Great Britain in productive power).

Let us for a while ignore the question of whether Japan's land and atmosphere can endure an ever higher economic density — the question now is the *potential,* what it is possible to achieve, strictly from the point of view of growth.

These are the targets that have been staked out, in constant 1965 prices; and in billions of dollars, at the rate of 308 yen per dollar:

Table 10: How Many New Japans?

Forecaster for 1985	Date of forecast	GNP result in 1965 (real GNP)	Annual real growth %	Target figure for 1985	1985 vs 1965 (fold)	Number of 'new' Japans
Economic Planning Agency (EPA)	May 1969	103	7·9%	450	4·4	3·4
Kanamori Group (JERC)	April 1971	103	9·9%	784	7·6	6·6
Professor Hiroya Ueno in macro-economic model for EPA	June 1971	103	11%	932	9·0	8·0
Ministry of Construction	Sept. 1971	103	9·6	649	6·3	5·3
Forecaster for 1980				**1980 target (real)**	**1980 GNP in nominal price**	
MITI	May 1971	103	10·6	519	984 (rate 308)	
Yamaichi Shoken	March 1972	103	9·3	455	935 (rate 308)	
Kanamori Group (JERC)	Jan. 1972	—	—	—	870 (rate 308) 956 (rate 280)	
Katsumi Mitani	Aug. 1971	—	—	—	844 (rate 308)	
Professor Osamu Shimomura	Aug. 1971	—	—	—	700 (rate 360) 818 (rate 308)	

Note: In billions of dollars (Exchange rate: 308 unless noted otherwise)

The table illuminates the truth: accelerating ambitions since 1969. Professor Ueno's 1985 figure means a GNP roughly equal to three EECs of the bloc's strength in 1965, or eight times West Germany's GNP.

Is Japan's brain power of a sufficiently impressive volume for her to maintain the growth rate of the 1956-70 period over the next fifteen years?

'No', answers Professor Osamu Shimomura; the brain-power is not good enough to make real GNP grow at an annual rate of 9-10 per cent.

'Yes,' answers Dr Hisao Kanamori just as firmly; Japan does have the brain-power — or, rather the technological development power, the innovative force — that is required for her to grow as fast in 1971-85 as in 1956-70.

This is a conflict between two giants, two men who do not sit and mumble silently in their studies, as is often the case in the West — they quarrel on an open stage: in daily newspapers, in lectures, in meetings with power groups which have to make the crucial investment decisions. The quarrel centres on the engine, or rather one of the two main engines generating economic growth.

What is economic growth? What is it that makes total production increase, and what makes the components grow at different rates? Two explanations, both equally true:

- We can, in a purely mechanical way, purely monetarily, measure the growth in GNP in a certain year. In the fiscal year that ended in Japan on March 31, 1972, real GNP probably grew by 5.9 per cent or about 11 billion dollars (to 197.7 billion dollars). As private consumption normally takes half of the national expenditure (GNE), the contribution of this sector to GNP growth is also, normally, half of the increase. But this was a recession year, so the contribution from private business fixed investment was only two per cent compared to 27 per cent in the previous year, and the contribution of private consumption as much as 62 per cent compared to 41 per cent in the previous year, and the contribution from 'exports, etc' as much as 36 per cent — or four billion dollars — versus 22 per cent in the previous year; but 'exports etc' should contribute only four per cent in fiscal 1972-73, assuming that home market business conditions have improved by the autumn of 1972.

- But what is it that makes consumption grow, what makes a business man invest in a new machine or machine tool, makes him rapidly increase his equipment investments? It is the so-called 'technological factor' — innovation. If no one invents a new and better machine, no businessman can buy this non-existent machine. And if no one thinks up a new gadget, for example, a video-tape recorder for home use, then the private consumer cannot buy it, no one makes it and nobody can invest in the equipment to manufacture this VTR. The technological factor is one of the five hidden causes behind economic growth. This factor has been responsible for about 45 per cent of Japan's past GNP growth (meaning that if real GNP in one year grew by 10 per cent, then the technological factor contributed with almost half or 4.3 percentage points). This factor is a part of the general brain-power of a people, and Japan has to a great extent bought this factor from abroad — in the form of about 16,000 patent and licence agreements.

Table 11: The Five Hidden Causes of Growth

	1956-70 (15 years)	1971-85 (15 years)
Capital increase	43	54
Labour force increase	9	3
Working time	−1	−4
Rate of operation	2	—
Technological progress	45	47
Source: Kanamori	100	100

Professor Shimomura bases his pessimism (ie he believes in a future with a considerably reduced contribution, pulling help, from the technological factor) on four arguments:

1. Japan has already bought so much technology that there is not much left to buy; the foreign shelves are almost bare
2. America's economic growth will be weak, so weak that the US economy cannot be expected to generate enough new technology or new innovations to satisfy Japan's enormous hunger for innovation
3. Even if Japan's own research and development efforts were to increase very rapidly, this would not offset, nor balance, the reduction in flow of foreign technology to Japan

4. And even if there should be a wide, wide flow of new technology both foreign and domestic, the effect of this — the contribution to increase — would be considerably lower than in earlier years. The effect or impact was tremendous when Japan's economy could be likened to that of a young boy, but now our economy is that of a mature, adult man, and thus the impact will be less.

'Wrong' answers Dr. Kanamori; there is no statistical evidence of any reduction in the flow into Japan of foreign technology.

(According to an official announcement dated March, 1972, Japan's payments for imports of foreign technology climbed by 17.7 per cent in fiscal year 1970 to an annual sum of 506 million dollars, a sum covering royalty payments for both old and new agreements. Japan's own royalty receipts: only 68.8 million dollars or 13.6 per cent of the outflow as compared to West Germany's 39 per cent. Still, Japan's receipts rose by 27.7 per cent in 1970).

Dr Kanamori's arguments are not completely waterproof: the flow may very well grow in volume but the number of break-through technologies may go down. A patent for a new rat trap, for example, does not raise the GNP as much as a patent for a new steel process; one million rat traps times an added value of one dollar is considerably less than the purchase by twenty steel companies of a new, license-manufactured steel furnace with an added value of one million dollars.

'But most important of all,' adds Dr Kanamori (and here the MITI forecasters nod approvingly), 'Japan will become the world's leading research and development country. We shall overtake the United States in annual R & D investments as a share of GNP!'

Dr Kanamori and his colleagues at JERC expect roughly a twenty-fold leap in technological brain-power expenditure between 1970 and 1985.

This is his view of what will happen — an annual R & D investment trust of 75 billion dollars in the year of 1985: (The figure for 1970 is the author's estimate):

Table 12: Japan's Technological Drive in the Future

R & D expenditure, annually, in billions of dollars

	1969	1970	1975	1980	1985
Domestic technology	3·0	(3·7)	11·2	30	75
Payments for imported technology	0·3	(0·5)	1·0	1·9	3·1
Total, in % of GNP	1·71	(1·8%)	2·46%	3·16%	3·95%

US R & D expenditures are believed to have dropped from a high of about three per cent of GNP to a current level of 2.5 per cent, which in 1972 would mean about 28 billion dollars (a sum that is two-thirds financed by the state: eg military research, aero space). Japan's almost completely peace-oriented, down-to-earth R & D expenditure should in 1972 amount to 2.2 per cent of the annual GNP (of 297 billion dollars), or 6.5 billion. The difference between Japan's 6.5 billion and America's 28 billion is roughly 1-4, but research salaries are probably three times as high in the US and quality of research about on par.

In 1962, Japan's R & D expenditure per capita: about 10 dollars compared to 94 dollars for the American (a 1-10 ratio), 34 dollars for the Briton. In 1972: probably 60 dollars for Suzuki-san, 140 for Joe Brown (the lag has shrunk to 40 per cent), but Japan gets more per invested dollar and the analysts who sit in Washington and shed tears over their trade statistics do not complain about the quality of Japan's technology.

With only half of America's population, Japan has 70 per cent more researchers in the civilian sector, it was noted by an economist of the US Trade Department, Michael Boretsky, in the April 1972 issue of *Fortune*. He gave as one explanation that Japan does not suffer from the phenomenon so common in the US: the military sector outbidding and buying up ever more civilian researchers.

Back to the technological factor quarrel:

Professor Shimomura, arguing that the impact must be smaller on an adult economy than on a young one, points to how Japan has been racing so far in GNP per capita:

Table 13: Shimomura: We Are Approaching the Ceiling

GNP per capita	Japan	US
1950	1	14-fold
1955	1	9-fold
1960	1	6-fold
1965	1	3.8-fold
1970	1	2.45-fold
1980	1	1 (parity)

Input of technology affected output very much when the ratio was 1-14 but cannot be expected to provide the same 'lift' in the 1-2 and 1-1 era. Thus there will be fewer 'rings on the water' effects.

Therefore, Kanamori and Shimomura also disagree violently as to future growth of sectors that are directly dependent on the technology factor, for example, private business fixed investments (excluding private housing investment); per year and in billions of dollars:

Table 14: A Disagreement of 5-1 for 1985

Gross private fixed investments, in billions of dollars

	1970	1975	1980	1985
Shimomura says:	48	63	82	82
Kanamori says:	48	104	207	399

The 1980 figure suggested by Dr Kanamori would be more than double the equivalent US figure for 1972:

Shimomura, meanwhile, contends that though these investments increased five times in the 1960's, the increase in the whole decade of the 1970's will be only 71 per cent, or an annual growth rate as low as 5.7 per cent. Kanamori: a decade boost of 331 per cent, an annual pace of 15.8 per cent. Shimomura: oh, no, less innovation, reduced innovation eagerness, because there will be very little new to invest in.

Shimomura says there will be a revolutionary change in Japan's GNE expenditure structure. Not at all, answers Kanamori, 'private business fixed investments will stay at the same 20 per cent of the GNE level.' Shimomura: No, a plunge to half that level:

Table 15: Share of Gross National Expenditure

In %, nominal prices

	1970	1975	1980	1985
Shimomura says:	20·4	13·0	10·1	7·5
Kanamori says:	20·4	20·9	20·5	20·0

By 1980, according to Shimomura's thinking, Japan will have slipped down to the ambition level of the United States in the private investment sector, but Kanamori says no, he sees a mountain of new technology ahead. The nation's numerous economists seem to be split in two: half supporting Kanamori, half the professor.

Shimomura: In the future, public fixed investments must lead, must pull our economy forwards, be the pace-setters, here replacing the private equipment sector − and thus he forecasts accumulated public fixed investments of 760 billion dollars in the 1970's, while Kanamori is a bit more tight-fisted, wants to spend 'only' 654 billions.

As for total production, GNP, the two forecasters agree, on the whole, as far as 1980 − when the US per capita has fallen and after that: a very low growth rate, says Shimomura. Oh, no, says Kanamori − a sum of about two trillion per year by 1985 (double the US level of 1970).

Table 16: Race or Crawl Between 1980 and 1985?

Total GNP, in billions of dollars (rate 308), fiscal years, in nominal prices

	1970	1975	1980	1985	1988
Shimomura, Apr. 1969	216	409	662	991	1,193
Aug. 1971	234	484	818	1,107	1,214
Kanamori, Apr. 1971	239	497	1,007	1,992	−
Jan. 1972		463	870	−	−

To sum up: Shimomura is more optimistic now than in the spring of 1969 − when he gave me figures bold enough to scare most Western analysts out of their chairs. Kanamori has reduced his GNP growth rate about one per cent, following the Nixon shock of 1971.

The table indicates that Nixon's eighteen-minute speech will cost Japan about 500 billion dollars in the 1970's — in accumulated GNP loss (my estimate) based on the assumption that Kanamori was predicting the correct growth trend in April of 1971 and that he was as correct in his forecast of January 1972; if so, a Nixon bill of 137 billion dollars for the year 1980 alone. The dramatic rise in President Nixon's personal Brain Power Index in that week of August would thus cost Japan more — in GNP loss — than seven American annual defence budgets, or roughly three times the US costs in the Vietnam War.

Professor Shimomura made his forecast on August 11, five days before Nixon lifted his hammer. 'I find no reason to revise my forecast,' Shimomura now says.

Japan's economists see in Nixon a factor of irritation; they consider the technological factor far more important. The different judgements of technological trends are best seen in this table comparing how the two forecasters look at annual GNP growth and annual growth in private business fixed investments, still in nominal prices:

Table 17: From Leaps of 20% to Zero Growth?

Gross private fixed investments, annual growth

	Gross National Product Shimomura Kanamori		Gross private investment Shimomaura Kanamori		Kanamori, Jan. 1972 GNP growth, exclusive of revaluation lifts	
1967-70	17·3%	17·3%	23·5%	—	1961-70	15·9%
1971-75	15·7	15·7	5·8	16·0	1968-75	14·5%
1976-80	11·1	15·2	5·6	14·8	1976-80	13·4%
1981-85	6·2	14·6	0 (!)	14·0		
1986-88	3·1	—	0 (!)	—		

Note: all in nominal prices

How soon will we know the truth — when will the fog surrounding the technological factor vanish? When shall we know whether Japan is going to follow Kanamori's trend line for private business fixed investments — plus 15 per cent per year — or Shimomura's trend line of 5 per cent annually? I posed this question in separate interviews with the two forecasters:

'Within two years,' says Professor Shimomura, calmly sipping his tea.

'Within two years,' says Dr Kanamori and takes a hard bite into his pipe.

If Dr Kanamori proves correct, then Japan will also defeat the US in total GNP in the mid-1990's, measured in nominal prices. If he is wrong, well, Japan will then have to be content with becoming the richest nation in the world in annual GNP flow per capita.

The problem is fateful not only for Japan. It is of importance also to Swedish, British and American industry. If Kanamori is correct, then you would be wise in urging your children to start learning Japanese, because we shall then be living in a world that will become more and more Japan-oriented. Because then it will be in Japan that we buy most of our technology, no longer in the US to the same great extent. Then it will be the Japanese who crash through the technological barriers – in fields such as energy, ocean development, transportation technology, biochemistry, new metals. And Japan will become the world's largest import market.

Can the countdown start? Twenty-four months, 23–22–21 . . . soon, soon comes the Word . . . ?

No. The science of a nation's economy, macro-economics, is not an exact science, where the molecules behave as they should behave, in a fixed pattern. In spite of all econometric equations and mumbo-jumbo, economic trends are often a question of Faith: We may believe that we know how Suzuki-san, Svensson and Smith will behave in their purchasing patterns this autumn or in 1975, but Svensson is a funny man; he may change his mind. This element of faith makes it possible, too, for the economic journalist to disagree with the experts, particularly if other experts share his doubts. I believe that it may take four years before we know for certain; that Japan may very well follow Shimomura's trend line for four years (1971-74), and after that switch to the 15 per cent track of Kanamori.

I believe that Japan has entered a cycle of 'lull' of the same type as in 1962-65, that is lull for private business fixed investments, not for the total economy – the lull that always comes between typhoons.

Three times Japan has been forced by external reasons to push hard on the brakes: 1954, 1958, 1962, because of balance of payment reasons, dwindling foreign reserves. (The recessions of 1965 and 1970-71 had a different origin: weak demand, weak investments).

When the 'external' brake disappeared for ever in 1968 and Japan entered a condition of permanent surplus, a new situation was created, a new era begun. Therefore, or perhaps very much because of the disappearance of the brake, Kanamori in 1970 presented a startling 'acceleration theory.' (For an English-language analysis, see the 1971 Winter Issue of *Japan Interpreter,* a Kanamori article titled 'The economics of growth rate acceleration').

Kanamori saw a clear acceleration trend, giving this series for real GNP growth, in per cent, per year:

Table 18: Faster and Faster!

Kanamori's acceleration theory

Worth remembering: Japan regained her prewar industrial production level in 1951, her real income level per capita in about 1955		
	1951-55	8·6
	1956-60	9·1
	1961-65	9·7
	1966-70	13·1
	1951-60	8·8
	1961-70	11·4

Note: Annual real GNP growth in per cent. The 1966-70 series was preliminary, based on the assumption that the fiscal 1970 growth rate would be 12·3%. The final 1970 figure: (·5%. (All years fiscal years).

Despite this apparent acceleration, Dr Kanamori is forecasting ever lower growth rates per five-year period up to 1985.

A Western businessman interested in selling investment goods, such as industrial equipment, to Japan, would be wise to use a different way of separating the years from Kanamori's, for example my own grouping of the years — see table below — which I think gives two very clear signals: first, the typhoon character of Japan's economy, and secondly, that a period of weak investments for three or four years says nothing about the technological factor; another two years of weak equipment investments will not necessarily prove that Shimomura is correct.

Table 19: When Will The Next Typhoon Strike?

Calendar years

		A GNP, real growth per year in %		B Total gross fixed investment		C Prof. Miyohei Shinohara:
		Per year	Period average	Per year	Period average	wage cost per produced unit; annually
1959	typhoon	9·2		14·6		
1960		14·1	12·9	31·7	24·6	-0·9 (1958-61)
1961		15·6		28·2		
1962	lull	6·4		10·8		
1963		10·6	8·6	9·9	9·9	+5·1 (1962-65)
1964		13·3		17·1		
1965		4·4		2·2		
1966	typhoon	10·0		11·8		
1967		13·2		18·1		
1968		14·4	12·2	22·1	16·7	+2·5 (1966-69)
1969		12·1		17·5		
1970		11·2		14·4		

Source: Author's estimates; excluding 'C'

Forecast Dated March 22, 1972, By Nomura Institute

Fiscal years; GNP in constant price; nominal for gross fixed investments

1971	lull		
1972		6·5	4·2
1973			
1974	typhoon		
1975		11·3	23·5
1976			

Note: See also appendix of tables; table showing slowdown of manufacturing industry investments, a virtual standstill in the four-year period of 1962-65.

America's scientific attaché in Tokyo proclaimed in a *Business Week* article in 1971 that one could predict 'an awful crash' for the Japanese economy some time in the 1970's — because the Japanese had for too long, in his opinion, been walking along the primrose path: they had neglected basic research. This bill must one day be paid, he argued. 'I do not share that opinion,' says Sweden's scientific attaché in Tokyo, Nils Hornmark, a former engineer. 'I strongly believe in Japan's technological future, and I foresee no reduction in Japan's imports of quality-rich technology.'

I remember the many American economists who visited Japan in the 1950's and the first half of the 1960's. They, too, were always expecting a crash, just around the corner, for Japan's economy — 'a dismally low self-financing ratio' and lack of efficiency in systems.' Thus, I find it rather hard to believe that there can have been any more drastic improvement in the analytical power index of persons attached to the US Embassy or in the vicinity of that influence.

I believe that Dr Kanamori will prove correct in his opinion about the pulling power of the technological factor. A primary reason for this belief is that the Japanese have already succeeded in giving 'technology' new dimensions. The earlier image is one of association: a balding researcher with a high, high forehead, deep in thought; suddenly Eureka! And a new world product: the steam engine, the Aga beacon towers for ships, ballbearings. The Japanese have extended the boundaries of the technological process to cover a long series of fronts:

- Basic interest in technology among the people, among employees
- The world's most efficient hunt for new technology. Japanese R & D tentacles are to be found all over the world, both hunters sent out on more permanent watching assignments, and the flocks of technological missions that are seen queuing up every day, every hour at the Haneda Airport departure gates
- Ability to apply the imported technology very quickly, without running into barriers of resistance on the factory floor or in the office
- A feverish eagerness to take one more step, improve on the technology that has been bought. Just one example: the Wankel rotary engine was developed in West Germany. The Toyo Kogyo automobile company of Hiroshima bought the licence about ten years ago. Who

is now selling the most rotary-engine-powered cars in the US market? Toyo Kogyo. Who is now far ahead in this technology? The Japanese.

- Two daily industrial newspapers (*Nikkan Kogyo* and *Nihon Kogyo*) both giving depth-coverage to the 'new products' sector, a fast and very active what's-available-now journalism that helps speed up structural changes within the economy and daily reminds company executives to search for new methods, new solutions.

In the West, it often happens that the head of a company, (a company which he himself probably founded) wants to keep on improving and changing the firm's product. This works rather well for some time, but the company grows, starts employing cost analysts, and the chief's interference, his eagerness to make 'small changes,' begin to be treated with more and more scepticism and hostility. 'Keep the old man away from the shop floor; we must wait several more years before making any changes — we must have a long and profitable production run.' Finally, some influential members of the Board give the signal: Away with the old man, he disturbs production, he is a threat to the continued stability and survival of the company.

In Japan, there are plenty of 'old men,' aged 20 and more, who constantly advance suggestions for rapid changes in the product. Just one example: electronic calculators, where the Japanese developed four 'generations' of calculating machine in four years, were constantly going back to the assembly line and undergoing changes. Profits were low, yes, but in five years the Japanese had captured 80 per cent of the world market. Facit of Sweden fell to its knees, Olympia of Germany staggered. 'The Japanese are too fast, we just cannot keep pace with them.'

It is late in March, 1972, and I am a little worried, as I sit behind my typewriter. I have just looked back at the earlier estimate that Nixon's August move may cost Japan as much as 500 billion dollars this decade. That sum divided by 105 million Japanese plus myself? A personal loss of 4,762 dollars, answers my electronic calculator, made in Japan. Just imagine if the real loss turns out to be twice as high! Kanamori and Shimomura are government civil servants; perhaps one should talk to somebody from the world of private business, someone directly attached to the reality of the cash flow; a sane and sensible banker, for example, preferably a young banker with new values, who may no longer consider high economic growth terribly important? All right, let us head for a bank, one of the private banks which now have a combined deposit balance of 100 billion dollars.

I approach the gates of Japan's largest bank, the Dai-Ichi Kangyo Ginko, ranked sixth in the world, after the 1971 merger between one bank which enjoyed an annual net profit growth of 20.6 per cent in the 1966-70 period, and another which had been climbing at an annual rate of 25.4 per cent. With profits like those, *that's* where I shall find the realists. And the bank's deposit balance is very realistic: almost 15 billion dollars.

I am lucky: I am received by Yutaka Kawata, 36, and Hiroshi Kashiwagi, 37, both economists and both bearing the title of assistant manager of the bank's economic research department. Their clear eyes give testimony of both realism and brain power.

Do you happen to have a new forecast for the future?

'Yes, Mr. Hedberg, we have just worked out a new forecast for the three-year term that begins with the new fiscal year in a few days, and ends in March, 1975.'

A minute later, he is back, weighed down with an armful of forecasting documents, and he is almost staggering on his way to the low table where we are sitting. As Professor Shimomura, the civil servant, usually holds only a small scrap or two of paper when he talks to me, I immediately notice the realism of bankers, the volume of work and sweat behind their new forecast.

'At the end of December, 1971, just after the revaluation agreement, we at the bank worked out a three-year forecast for the period that was to start three months later. At that time we had reason to believe that the real increase in Japan's GNP in the fiscal year 1972-73 would amount to 8.7 per cent,' says Mr. Kawata.

(Very optimistic, I reflect to myself, in view of the fact that in January of 1972 Shimomura predicted plus five per cent and Kanamori plus nine per cent).

'In the last few days we have revised the figure for the new fiscal year . . .'

(Well, well, I tell myself, now for the shock, now my share of the half-a-trillion dollar loss will zoom)

'. . . and the new figure is 9.1 per cent!'

As I try to catch my breath, Mr. Kawata adds that they are not yet completely ready with the revision of the December forecast, but some figures are ready. They must keep on revising because two components have proved stronger than they thought just before Christmas: first, the volume of public expenditure presented in January, and secondly, strong export growth.

Gentlemen, what annual average did you predict last December for the next three fiscal years, 1972-74?

'An average of between 10.3 and 10.4 per cent!'

But Japan has been squeezed by the Nixon shock. Doesn't this have any measurable effect?

'The Japanese people have now completely recovered from that shock, which was of a psychological nature and had no macro-economic effect. The upswing in domestic business conditions is now under way.'

But are we not supposed to face a deep and prolonged dent in private business investments? Some people blame this on the technological factor, others blame earlier over-investment?

'Ha? What dent?'

I clarify, and then Mr Kawata and Mr Kashiwagi write the following table in my note-book, to clarify their surprise at my question: (see table next page)

'Industrial fixed investments will be weak in 1972, but there will be a great boost upwards for other sectors, mainly the non-manufacturing sector's building activities and purchase of equipment. The question marks mean that we are not yet completely ready with the new figures.'

'Gentlemen, you are not only economists and bankers, you are also human beings, and as human beings perhaps you are happy about the fact that there will be a standstill of several

Table 20: The Four Question Marks

Gross private fixed investment — annual increase in per cent; (Excluded: private housing investments)			
	1972	1973	1974
Total	6·8	19	16
(a) manufacturing industry investment.	3-4	?	?
(b) other sectors (non-manufacturing)	17	?	?

years in manufacturing investment, meaning a chance for public investment — tree-lined pavements, etc — to advance? As young people I expect you welcome the industrial investment standstill?

'Ha? What standstill?'

I clarify, and then the two bank economists emphasize that they do not necessarily believe in weak industrial investment in 1973 and 1974; the figures are not ready yet, the forecast is being revised — upwards! 'We believe in rapid structural changes over the next few years.'

The trade balance?

The December forecast was a surplus of 8.3 billion dollars in Fiscal 1972, now a new figure is available: 9.0 billion.

I do believe in that figure. I interrupt, my guess would be as much as ten billion. Now the bank economists look at me with increased respect, because so far I have only asked very odd questions. 'So perhaps we could discuss revaluation? Off the record?' We do so, and I do not think that I am disclosing a state secret if I mention that the two do not believe there will be any revaluation within the next year and would be very unhappy if there is another one in the 1970's.

The realism of the bankers has shocked me, and I am looking in vain for an opening in their bulwark of optimism.

Let us return for a moment to the Nixon shock. He did after all force you to revalue? We have the five classical GNP growth factors: capital, technology, labour force, working time, rate of operation. In the future, we may have to add perhaps a sixth factor affecting Japan's potential. Shall we call it the Nixon Factor?

'Your questions are very interesting, Mr Hedberg,' says Mr Kashiwagi.

His colleague shakes his head, says that he cannot comprehend how such a sixth factor could be put into the macro-economic pattern. (He was probably thinking of the difficulty of evaluating such a factor's coefficient, or possible multiplier effect distortions).

Mr Kashiwagi: 'I see what you mean! I do not think that such a sixth factor could be allocated the same importance as the other five factors, but it is true that reaction abroad to Japan's export successes could have effects on our economy which would be difficult to measure.'

Mr Kawata: 'The effect would be rather small, as exports make up only about ten per cent of our GNP compared to about twenty per cent in Sweden. Perhaps the Nixon shock had wider repercussions in Sweden?'

The two economists recall that it was comparatively easy to break the 1965 recession, because during the five-year period that followed, there were two pace-setters: the automobile industry and the colour-TV industry, both pulling other sectors upwards. Right now no front runner can be spotted, but the so-called future industries are on their way. 'We cannot say exactly when they will arrive, whether in 1973 or 1975, but Japan's banks will support these new industries, help them grow fast.'

A new attempt to cause confusion: What about all this talk of the end of the world? Wise men are saying that we are pursuing a course heading straight for doomsday: soon no natural resources or raw materials left, maybe total environmental destruction? You two are young people with a new scale of values — don't you experience an inner conflict when you spend your days forecasting super-growth and helping to find the money required for super-growth? Doesn't it give you sleepless nights?

Happy laughter.

'We don't have time to worry! You do ask interesting questions!'

Mr Kashiwagi adds, now very seriously: 'We Japanese have no alternative. We have only one course open to us: we must do our best. We must work as efficiently as possible.'

But suppose it were established in thirty years' time that it was no good that you did your best?

'We Japanese must do our best.'

There are about ten highly qualified economists at this bank. Are there perhaps times when you all sit discussing the end of mankind and the world?

This is theoretically possible, answers Mr Kashiwagi — 'but not during office hours!' I reply that we in the West probably do so on some days, and this is probably why our GNP growth is so slow.

Happy laughter. But Mr Kawata, one of those fabulously intelligent Japanese with the memory of a computer, tries to cheer me up: 'Last year, real GNP in Sweden fell by 0.8 per cent. This year you will probably grow 3.5 per cent, despite another reduction in working hours; an extraordinarily fine result!' My heart feels warm and I recall my childhood: sometimes I was able to sketch a snowman who looked like a snowman, and then the teacher put a gold star in my workbook, and this is my feeling now.

The discussion then turns to the Kanamori-Shimomura controversy, the rate of development to 1985. Whom do you support?

'In our bank we share Dr Kanamori's general growth philosophy,' says Mr Kashiwagi.

Would you say you support his views 80 per cent or 40 per cent?

'I am more than fifty per cent convinced that Dr Kanamori will be proved right about Japan in 1985.'

We bow deeply to each other, and I walk out into the spring night. I have met banking realism, been introduced to the new values of the younger generation.

Back in my study, I sit down and read once more a few pages about the ambitions and values of the 1860's. The brain-power of the Japanese has been holding up rather well for ten decades, and I suspect that it will continue to do so in the decades to come.

CHAPTER SEVEN

Strategy for victory

*'The new age offers Japan a
choice: either to fade away or to
make a great leap forward.'*
MITI, 1971

The visionaries of Western countries, in parliaments and
ministries, keep on day after day, whittling a small stick — a
twelve-month stick, the one-year budget, and the chips fly in
all directions as they quarrel about the shape and proportions. 'Our national resources,' proclaim speakers with
confident voices, and take away, or add, a small shaving.

Japan, too, is the scene of discussions about the one-year
stick, but Japan's way of looking at her own future has
always been brutally large slashes into the future, the carving
of ten-year and fifteen-year chunks, and then a look at the
'accumulated total resources' — tomorrow's resources compared with yesterday's resources. What can we afford? What
do we want to do? Can we postpone any further a more just
distribution of resources, the fruits of growth? If in one year
we cannot make Japan into a country fit for human beings,
what are the prospects of succeeding in this over the next
fifteen years?

The Japanese began carving out the large chunks of the
future a century ago: first a strategy to avoid being
swallowed up by the West, later a strategy to catch up.

Now there is also a strategy for victory, a virtual
out-classing of all the industrial countries of Western
civilization: in productivity per employee, in annual GNP per
capita, in family income, and in public investments. This
strategy for victory in a number of sectors is an attempt to

sketch Japan's economic weight in the world by 1980 and 1985 and the accumulated efforts on the road to the targets.

The work programme: almost 1,000 pages in Japanese, three volumes being circulated at the top level within the ministries in Tokyo and within about one thousand of Japan's largest companies.

Chief author: Dr Hisao Kanamori, assisted by a dozen economists of the 'Nihon Keizai Kenkyu Centre' (Japan Economic Research Centre, JERC). The research took a year and a half, and the documents were presented in April and May of 1971, demanding an annual real growth up to 1985 of 9.9 per cent, while the twenty-year official programme of May, 1969, had suggested only 7.9 per cent.

The key question, or rather the lantern that Dr Kanamori preferred to hold up: how soon can Japan's economy be turned into a 'one-trillion-dollar economy,' one with annual production of goods and services worth one trillion dollars? (one trillion = one thousand billion; the official name of the Kanamori programme is: 'The outlook for a trillion dollar economy.') And what is needed to push the GNP up to and across that threshold?

When the question was first posed within the Kanamori Group, even the United States had not yet crossed the magic line – this was first achieved in 1971.

It took the US thirty years (1940-71) and three wars – World War II, 1940-45; the Korean War, 1950-53; and the intense phase of the Vietnam War, beginning in 1965 – to push the economy from the 100-billion-dollars-a-year level to the trillion level. Japan crossed the lower bar in 1965 and should, 'at the latest,' zip past the trillion level in 1984. This was Kanamori's conclusion in the spring of 1971, but in January of 1972 he gives me new figures showing that though he has now reduced the annual growth rate somewhat, the peak of one trillion will be conquered by 1981, due to a revaluation effect of 28.6 per cent (ie a change of the yen's value from 360 to 308 in December of 1971 and a further change, 'sometime in the 1970s,' to a parity of 280 yen per dollar. Therefore, I have converted Kanamori's 360-figures to the current 308-parity). This would mean – if Kanamori proves correct – that it will take Japan only eleven years

(1971-81) to take the stride between 200 billion and 1,000 billion dollars in annual GNP, while the US had to sweat at this task for 27 years (1944-71), all figures in nominal prices, and including the witchcraft of revaluation effects.

(An ecological side-thought: while it took the US about two hundred years to advance from zero to the first one trillion, America should reach the second trillion in about 1981, that is in eleven years.)

Before describing Kanamori's slashes into the future, where he is handling trillions like ordinary mortals handle apples, let me try to explain how much one trillion dollars actually is. The sum is equal to the world's combined GNP in the year 1955; it is one-third of the combined world GNP in 1970; it is 33 times as large as Sweden's GNP in 1970; about five times West Germany's GNP of the same year; eleven times as large as accumulated fixed investments by the EEC bloc in the year of 1968. Using ten-dollar bills, one could make a ten metre wide band and let it stretch all the way to the moon, four times. (It is the volume of such stratospherical figures that prompts me, whenever possible, to drag development discussions down to the per capita level).

Kanamori has split his growth programme into two phases: first, what Japan was able to achieve in the fifteen-year period of 1956-70; secondly, what Japan should be able to perform in the fifteen-year period up to 1985. *(see table next page)*

Kanamori's table means this, in my interpretation:

1. In the past fifteen years, we Japanese tried harder than any other people in the world; we carried the heaviest savings burden, the heaviest investment burden, worked more overtime hours than any other people

2. In the next fifteen years, we must try even harder: increase the savings ratio of GNP from 37 to 42 per cent, lower the ratio going to private consumption from 51.3 per cent in Fiscal 1970 to 49.3 per cent in Fiscal 1985, in nominal prices, and in constant prices make a reduction from 49 per cent to 42 per cent and this despite the fact that this ratio is already lower than in any other country

3. Because in the next fifteen years, we must increase our

Table 21: The Road From 1.5 to 13.6 Trillion Dollars

Accumulated 15-year-results; billions of dollars; exchange rate: 308; author's revision

	Period A 1956-70	Period B 1971-85	B:A (fold)	Period B structure in %
GNP (cumulative sums)	1,506	13,564	9·0	
Total savings	558	5,721	10·3	(100%)
(a) corporates	207	2,370	11·5	41·4%
(b) individuals	213	2,122	10·0	37·1%
(c) public (Gov't)	118	1,372	11·7	24%
Statistical errors	(9)	(−143)		
Total investments	558	5,721	10·3	(100%)
(a) corporates	297	2,889	9·7	50·5%
(b) individuals (including own homes)	125	1,359	10·9	23·7%
(c) public	133	1,401	10·5	24·5%
Net increase of overseas assets (= direct investment)	2·8	72·5	26	
Total consumption (private and public)	949	7,797	8·2	
Same, as % of GNP	63%	57·7%		

production nine-fold in nominal prices, in volume or constant prices four times our working results

4. And this despite the fact that between now and 1985, our labour force will grow by only *eight* per cent! And while cutting working hours, switching to a five-day week

5. Therefore, this is needed: ten-fold investments, more invested capital per employee than in any other country, higher productivity per employee per man-hour than in any other country; to be the world's most technologically advanced country

6. In order to be able to breathe in 1980, and live a more decent life: eleven-fold public fixed investments plus about 260 billion dollars to fight environmental destruction and pollution

7. In the past fifteen years, our sweat gave us an accumulated production of about one and a half trillion, as little as the US result for a single year, 1970, plus another fifty per cent. But in the next fifteen years

we shall produce the equivalent of 13.6 trillion dollars, that is fourteen times America's annual result in 1970, though our population is only half of America's. The sum of 13.6 trillion is 4.5 times as large as the combined world GNP in the year of 1970

8. In the past period, Widow Suzuki and Wage Earner Watanabe extended a helping hand to business and industry, which could not, or would not, cover the gap between their own savings and investments: 91 billion dollars. In the next period: about 500 billion dollars from the helping hand.

9. In the next fifteen years, private business must make fixed investments of 2.4 trillion dollars, because Japan will not be able to advance into any post-industrial era in this period. In order to afford the public investment programme, the economy must grow rapidly and thus business investment must also grow rapidly.

This sum of 2.4 trillion dollars is:

(a) Fifteen times larger than the US 1970 result in total fixed investments (162 billion dollars, including public investments)

(b) Almost twice as large as America's accumulated fifteen-year private sector investments in the 1956-70 period (1.3 trillion)

(c) Seven times all total fixed investments within the whole 20-nation OECD Group in the year of 1968 (factories, machinery, equipment, houses, railways etc).

'Well, it is a rather ambitious programme,' says Dr Kanamori, with the feeling of a former Oxford man for understatement and with faith in and knowledge of what his own people can perform. 'Do you take sugar in your tea?'

One of the rewards for the fifteen years of sweat will be these results in GNP per capita, in dollars, at the old rate of 360; any reader so inclined may add a revaluation effect of, for example, 28.6 per cent and perhaps deduct the same percentage to allow for the Nixon factor: (See table 22.)

Is Dr Kanamori an apostle of vengeance? Is he the high priest of revenge, the Goldfinger of macro-economics whom I have finally been able to track down in one of Tokyo's catacombs,

Table 22: A Super-rich Paradise?

	GNP per capita in 1985, dollars	Index (author's)
Suzuki-san	13,574	100
Americans	10,750	79
Europeans	5,748	42
Russians	3,746	28
S.E. Asians	258	2

a man who fanatically stares at the world map deep down in the basement, busy hiding secret documents of evidence that Japan is once again deadly determined to build a world empire — even if the price be growth to the last Japanese, just as other Japanese in the spring of 1945 were shouting: fight to the last Japanese?

The question is brutal, but I consider it essential that it be posed and an answer be found, as the European anti-growth lobby, for example, has a habit of regarding any Japanese optimist as a man with a scythe, ruthlessly cutting down his own people, and also because so many foreign analysts have started to regard defenders of a high economic growth rate for Japan as the outriders of a renewed militarism.

Yes, Dr. Kanamori *is* seeking revenge — a revenge for his own people in the battle against hopeless geophysical conditions: no raw materials, a cultivable area of only fiften per cent; a revenge for the public investment sector, a sector that was almost starved to death in the period when Japan was throwing practically all her resources into creating an industry that would be able to compete with US industry and be able to avoid the fate of their European counterparts — takeover by the US; he is seeking a revenge in the search for real quality of living, because Japan has so far lost the big battles in this struggle. And if Japan, as a by-product of these efforts, should happen to take a GNP per capita revenge against the United States . . . Well, that cannot be helped. What is wrong with trying to climb Mount Everest?

Secretive?

Dr Kanamori is so secretive that when he visits Moscow in October, 1971, he discloses in a lecture before eagerly listening Soviet statistical economists both Japan's growth strategy and this: 'We shall defeat the Americans in GNP per capita by 1982, at the latest!' Cheers from the Russians. (If we cannot lick the Yanks, let us hope the Japanese can do the job). In another lecture, in January, 1972, now addressing a guest group of the American Congress in Tokyo, Kanamori is just as secretive, saying roughly this: 'I am sorry, gentlemen, but we shall have defeated you per capita by 1980!' No cheers this time, only wrinkled foreheads, but some of those who listened may find it difficult in the future to keep alive the myth about 'those silent, sneaky Japanese.' Dr Kanamori is not planning any economic Pearl Harbor; he is saying, six to eight years in advance: this is our strategy, this is the timetable, this we believe we can achieve.

Growth to the last Japanese? 'I am the father of two children,' answers Dr Kanamori. 'Japan's 1980 environment will be better than the one we are now experiencing.'

An outrider of militarism? 'Never more than one per cent of the GNP, to defence, not one decimal more.'

The catacomb: a sunny room on the sixth floor of the Economic Planning Agency's new building in the Kasumiga-seki district, next door to the slum-like building that houses the Finance Ministry (Where they still turn a yen coin twice and rub it hard before letting go, though they controlled a 1970 tax flow of 36 billion dollars and will in 1985 be watching an annual tax river of about 340 billion dollars). The one who succeeds in finding Kanamori's catacomb discovers to his surprise that one gets answers to all questions, including his view of Japan's future market conquests in various regions of the world, in percentages and in dollars, and if Dr Kanamori happens to have some earth left on his hands, which means that he has been doing a bit of extra digging in his garden on the previous day and is thus particularly pleased, then one can even ask about the export coefficients and equations which have made Kanamori forecast 1985 annual exports of 150 billion dollars, six times the 1971 level.

His career: born in 1924; was 21 when the atom bombs fell; a law degree at Todai University in 1948; then five years at MITI followed by thirteen years at the Economic Planning Agency, 1953-66, including two years of studies at Oxford;

chief of EPA's domestic research department before being appointed, in 1967, chief economist of the Japan Economic Research Centre, probably the world's best forecasting institute; and since January of 1970 assistant chief of EPA's Economic Research Institute, under Professor Miyohei Shinohara, another pioneer in Japanese economic thought. Kanamori still directs some of JERC's tougher assignments, including a 'Japan and the world in 1980' study, presented in January of 1972, which I discuss further in later chapters.

'It was lucky that I did not study economics at the university — or I would never have been able to understand economics!' chuckles Dr Kanamori, and this opinion is shared by a number of other great economists, including Professor Osamu Shimomura, a director and head of the investment research department of the Japan Development Bank (Nippon Kaihatsu Ginko), and Dr Saburo Okita, for decades a key figure in Japan's economic planning at EPA, before founding JERC in 1964. These three economists, first of all Shimomura, in the mid-1950's, discovered that the economic textbooks, written mainly by Westerners, did not correspond to the reality of Japan. Soon, a crash, said visiting Western economists as they sat shivering in pure horror in their hotel rooms, thumbing through Japanese statistics. The crash did not come, only the recession years that must provide a breathing space from time to time, and the speed got even faster. All this violated common sense, said the Westerners, and the aged among Japan's own economists nodded.

It is worth noting that Shimomura is a former civil servant at the Finance Minstry (and was the economic brain of Prime Minister Hayato Ikeda, 1960-64); Okita is a former engineer and Kanamori has a law degree certificate somewhere — though in the end all of them had to go to the trouble of acquiring doctor's degrees in economics in order to be taken seriously.

When a new product is put on to the market, the 'product environment' should be right, all marketing people agree, and the environment for super-growth forecasts was far from suitable when the Kanamori-JERC trillion-dollar programme was published in the spring of 1971. Optimists had almost to hide in the bushes, but then came the Nixon shock and a reawakening of interest in fast growth. At the end of November, the trillion-dollar document was published as a Kanamori book, 'Japan's Economic Future,' a 275-page Japanese language extract, and Japan's ambitious people once again stretch out their longing hands: If we keep on trying hard, what will be the result?

At the end of March, 1972, the newspaper that had pushed the anti-supergrowth debate with particular emphasis, the *Asahi Shimbun,* noted in a feature article that 'an overwhelming majority' of Japan's economists are now looking at the future with 'great optimism' and the newspaper quotes, with apparent satisfaction, one forecast for 1985 as presented by the Kanamori Group:

'GNP per capita: largest in the world. A wage earner has an annual disposable income, after tax of 7.3 million yen (23,7000 dollars). He has bank assets of 16.3 million yen (53,000 dollars). He is devoting thirty per cent of his time to leisure activities. His working hours have shrunk to 28 per cent.'

It is here that the Kanamori Programme is unique: he has also dug into the future of the ordinary family's economy, the wage earner's economy, analyzed in detail future changes in the family's income tax burden, money alloted for rent, food, clothing, selective expenditures, savings and the likely development of house prices; he is looking back in five-year periods per 15-year span, and is looking forward in the same way. Kanamori believes in technology but he escapes falling into the nightmare technocratic marsh of, for example, Herman Kahn. He is trying to show how the material conditions of the individual and the family will change, in pace with Japan's economic growth, in terms both of private consumption, and of purchase of public sector goods and services. He is extrapolating as little as other Japanese economists (There is still a belief in the West that the Japanese 'just sit and let the growth lines keep on going straight, up to the sky.') Some of the new family income patterns may be seen in this book's Appendix of tables along with a numerical explanation of Kanamori's long-range strategy for victory.

Kānamori is a realist, and his launching pad is a set of basic assumptions that the fundamental character of the Japanese people will not change within the next thirteen years: the will to work, the eagerness to save, an unwillingness to pay high taxes. It is not a balanced state that Kanamori has sketched, ie a state with a reasonable balance between private and public consumption, between private and public investments, because even though Kanamori may personally prefer such a balanced state, he sees no desire among the people to pay for such a balance.

The same editorial writers who are one day demanding a welfare state on the Swedish model, complain the following day about the tax burden being already too high for ordinary wage earners. They maintain that as long as distribution of the tax burden is so unfair, with the self-employed, for example, able to make generous tax deductions, the wage earners cannot tolerate a higher tax burden. (When one objects that 'If you plan to wait for a completely just tax system, then you'll have to wait until year 2050, because no country has arrived at exact fairness, not even Sweden; it is the wage earners who must always carry most of the heavy burden,' — then the critics shake their heads, unhappily, in a dream).

Therefore, Kanamori expects only a modest increase in the total tax burden (now about 16 per cent of GNP compared to Sweden's more than 40 per cent — it is the national cake of total resources which must be made to increase rapidly; then public expenditure will also rise rapidly; jumps of 15 per cent per year for the total cake, leaps for 17-18 per cent for public expenditure. Nevertheless, Japan will continue reducing very quickly the tax burden of people on the lowest rungs of the income ladder. Income level where direct taxation starts for a family with two children (in dollars, per year, at the rate of 308, the figure for 1970 preliminary):

1960	940 dollars	1975	6,170 dollars
1965	1,525 dollars	1980	13,540 dollars
1970	2,825 dollars	1985	26,430 dollars

This is conservative economics, but Japan is a country run by conservatives, and even though the divided opposition can be expected to maintain the current trend of winning ever more city council and prefectural assembly elections, few analysts believe there will also be a revolt in the parliamentary elections in the decade of the 1970's.

Kanamori's main thought, found also in MITI's 1980 programme: an end to the era of wasting raw materials, a rush into the era of brain-intensive products. Away from industrial sectors with a low added value, entry into the high-technology sector and the so-called future industries.

Technology. Research and development expenditures are expected to grow fifty per cent faster than the GNP, advancing at an annual pace of 23 per cent, which would give accumulated fifteen-year R & D investments of about 400 billion dollars.

Capital. In 1970, the stock of all existing private sector fixed assets was valued at 283 billion dollars. The 1985 value: 1.8 trillion dollars. The nation's labour force will score a modest growth, from 52 to 56.5 million men and women, but they are to be given more equipment, and more up-to-date equipment, than in any other country.

Creative destruction. This will continue; out with anything that is obsolete. In 1985, hardly any machinery or equipment made in, for example, 1970 or 1972, will be left. The robots will have taken over in various sectors. In the West, business executives wet their lips as they drink a good wine: 'Nice vintage,' a fine age. Japan's economists, too, wet their lips as they study the 'vintage index' they have created with loving care to measure continuously the age of private equipment. The rule of thumb: fast increases in fixed private investments mean fast rejuvenation of equipment, including machine

Table 23: Average Age of Private Equipment

Number of years

	US	Japan	Japan in the future (Kanamori)	
1955	12·6	5·8	1975	6·15
1960	11·7	7·24	1980	6·18
1965	10·9	7·20	1985	6·35
1968	10·2	6·98		

tools. The United States has been out-classed in the age of private equipment too. *(See table 23.)*

Hence this complaint from US Commerce Secretary Peter G. Peterson in February, 1972: almost 70 per cent of Japan's machine tools are less than ten years old, compared to only 35 per cent in the US.

European and American assembly line and workshop workers are taller, heavier and stronger than their Japanese colleagues — but the Japanese is to an increasing extent being supplied with better tools, and is thus able to produce more per man-hour.

Housing. The housing shortage will 'definitely' be ended. About 7.5 per cent of the nation's total resources (GNP) will be reserved for private housing investments, compared to 6.6 per cent in the fiscal year that ended March 31, 1972. This would mean an accumulated sum of *one trillion dollars* between 1971 and 1985 — roughly eight times Great Britain's annual GNP. It would also mean a per capita investment of about 7,900 dollars, if we use as dividend a 1985 population of 126.6 million.

The Kanamori Group expects the housing stock to grow from 27 to 41 million units, the size of the newly constructed units to rise from a 1970 average of 70 square metres to 120 square metres in 1985. Also, one very dismal trend: building costs per unit will leap eight-fold, to about 60,000 dollars. The land price, too, is expected to keep on increasing at an annual average of 15 per cent, and this will keep the land price share of the total purchasing price at the current world-record level: over 60 per cent. The purchase price per unit: 'At present 4.69 times the average annual income, after fifteen years 5.53 times.' The use of industrially manufactured elements (pre-fabrication) will rise from 10 to 40 per cent, and one thing is certain: the Japanese will hunt all over the world for cost-reducing building technology, a hunt already launched.

Urbanization. There is no agrarian idyll to return to; thus a continued move of people into Japan's 578 towns and cities with more than 30,000 inhabitants, but at a somewhat slower pace. The urban population is expected to grow by seven percentage points, from 73 to 80, compared to a leap of 16 percentage points in the previous fifteen-year period. The number of urban residents: 67 million in 1965, 75 million in 1970 (meaning they squeezed the equivalent of Sweden's whole population into the cities over a five-year period), 84 million in 1975 and 97 million in 1985 — when Japan should have a total population of about 126 million. In general: 'another Sweden' put into the cities every five years, with tremendous pressure on these sectors, to mention just a few: housing, transportation, schools, waste disposal, water and air.

What makes the problem even more difficult is the fragmentation. In the 1960's Japan's population grew from 93.4 to 103.7 million, only eleven per cent, only 1.0 per cent per yeear. But the number of households grew 41 per cent, at an annual pace of 3.5 per cent, from 20.6 to 29.2 million. The young wife no longer wanted to live with her parents-in-law; young families revolted against the Confucian pattern of large families living together.

This fragmentation trend will continue, the sociologists agree, and thus the present cities must be smashed to pieces, the era of high-rise apartments begun. The current average for houses in all cities: below two storeys. Even in Tokyo's three most central districts (Chiyoda, Chuo and Minato), which house banking palaces, skyscrapers and Government buildings, the average height is as low as 3.22 storeys.

The battle with the US. If we prefer to believe that Japan will hit the one-trillion mark in 1981, as Kanamori says in his revised 1972-forecast, and look at the total fixed investments sketched in Table 20 of this chapter, a sum of 5.7 trillion yen, will that be in the neighbourhood of America's 1971-85 investment effort?

The answer is that the US would be out-invested even in the total accumulated sums.

My estimates of America's past and future, assuming no drastic change in her investment pattern: an accumulated US GNP of 9.6 trillion dollars in 1956-70, in nominal prices (8.6 trillion, in constant price, that is one trillion discounted as the 'air' of inflation, with most of this empty air in the 1966-70 period).

If we assume that Kanamori's guess of a US GNP in the

year 1985 of 2.8 trillion dollars is correct, we arrive at an accumulated US GNP of 26.9 trillion dollars between 1971 and 1985. That is roughly double Japan's GNP accumulation. If the US sticks to the current investment pattern (14.5 per cent of GNP for private sector investments, including housing, plus 3.2 per cent for public investments), we get 3.9 trillion dollars for the private sector investments and 0.9 trillion for the public sector, a total of 4.8 trillion dollars — which would be only 84 per cent of Japan's 1971-85 investment result.

These figures assume an annual nominal GNP growth rate of 7.2 per cent for the US, about half of Japan's. If the US were to succeed in maintaining that growth rate after 1985, and the Japanese pace after 1985 slowed down to 13.7 per cent, in nominal prices, then Japan's total GNP would overtake the US in the early 1990's.

Could this happen?

No one knows; very few with any sense at all are willing to look further ahead than 1985 or 1988.

'We Japanese must do our best,' the two young bank economists said in a previous chapter, expressing their belief in Dr Kanamori's Japan of 1985.

We do not know whether the efforts to 'do our best' will be good enough to realize Dr Kanamori's targets. But when he confirms that he himself regards the targets as 'rather ambitious' and asks if I should like to have sugar with my tea, I can only answer: yes, yes, I do indeed need sugar with my tea.

CHAPTER EIGHT

Japan's ten crises

*'At birth, we were put aboard a
train. This train is running
endlessly through a dark tunnel.
Sometimes there is a light far
away, a light of hope, but it
vanishes immediately.
Everything is black again. Where
are we heading? Has this tunnel
no exit?'*

Harumi Ogua, 24
Unknown Japanese poet

The Japanese are not so certain that the tunnel does have an exit, but the ruling Establishment and the thinkers who dominate the debate within Japan — including welfare economists — *believe* that they will be able to dig an exit, a work programme that will be described in the next chapter. The trend for the next few years: it will be even darker in the tunnel.

First, three reports from the world of theories:

Happiness index. Numerous attempts were made in Japan in 1971 and 1972 to measure both the plus and minus effects of economic growth, with the firm determination to start attaching to the annual GNP accounting also a table or indicators measuring 'NNW,' Net National Welfare, a concept first introduced by a welfare economist and one of 18 co-authors of the 'Kutabare GNP' ('To Hell with GNP') articles, Professor Naomi Maruo.

Among the first away from the starting line were the economists of the Sanwa Bank, who in 1972 published a 'happiness index' based on 33 indicators, divided into six groups: satisfaction with society, personal satisfaction, safety and a sense of security, working conditions, presence or absence of irritant factors and the feeling that life was worthwhile. Five countries were included, and Japan was ranked last. With Japan as index basis (100), the US was awarded 253 points, Britain 213, West Germany 190 and France 187.

Among the 33 indicators: wage levels, national income, crime and suicide rates, paved road surfaces, rises in the cost of living.

What made Japan rank so low — though the wage level is now comparable to Britain's and France's — was dissatisfaction with Society: lack of park space, inadequate drainage, sewage systems, shortage of public libraries and other public facilities and a great number of 'irritants' such as overcrowding and traffic congestion.

Social satisfaction, yes; fast wage increases, high TV density; but a five-fold rise in land prices in the last decade, a growing rate of neurosis and environmental disease, and consumer prices rising faster than in the other four countries. The conclusion of the privately owned bank: this index 'reinforces the arguments for a basic switch in policy to the building of a public welfare economy.'

A similar study was made by a group of professors, a 'welfare vision' group of advisors appointed by Domei, one of Japan's two leading trade union confederations. This group — Naomi Maruo, Tadao Yoshida, Hiroshi Kato — measured development in seven countries, using both economic and non-economic indicators, and arrived at this final 'welfare score': Sweden 2,699; America 2,426; Britain 2,285; West Germany 1,786; France 1,774; Italy 1,457 — and Japan ranked seventh, with 1,002 points.

The trend. Dr Hisao Kanamori and his group of associates at JERC did not merely suggest full-speed-ahead for investments in their 1985 programme; for example, a real annual growth rate in the 'stock' — or accumulation — of private fixed investments of 13.3 per cent in urban regions, and 11.9 per cent annual growth in public fixed investments. They also tried to measure the plus and minus facts of economic growth in the urban areas, in the past and in the future.

The plus account of sixteen indicators included city

budgets, number of hospital beds, telephones and students, and in the minus account, eleven indicators, including soot density, sulphur dioxide volume, land prices and traffic victims. The survey covered cities with a population of more than 50,000 persons, with 1965 as the base year (100), and constant prices for the monetary indicators. Simple averages are used, without trying to give different indicators different 'weights':

Table 24: Plus and Minus Points of Economic Growth
As measured in this index (1965 = 100)

	1955	1960	1965	1970	1975	1980	1985
Plus account	55	66	100	152	234	370	590
Minus account	39	60	100	148	223	339	510

Table 25: The Same Thing: But Now Annual Average Jumps in %

	1956-60	61-65	66-70	71-75	76-80	81-85
Plus account	5·4	8·5	8·8	9·0	9·6	9·8
Minus account	9·2	10·9	8·3	8·4	8·7	8·5

Note: A better terminology might be "account of benefits" and "account of distress" or "diseconomy".

The forecasters thus foresee an accelerating trend in the annual growth rate of the plus account, a declining trend for the minus indicators, with the exception of the 1971-80 period, which has a more favourable trend than the 1955-60 period but still hits harder than in the 1966-70 period. My comments: Japan's environmental diseases and other sicknesses of society emerged in full force in the 1966-70 period, and we know nothing about the tolerance level. Could it be that the minus account is already so overburdened that the people cannot endure any further deterioration?

It is very difficult, almost impossible, to reach agreement in giving different indicators various 'weights,' but an increase in the number of hospital beds, a plus item, is less impressive when one finds in the minus accounts increased pollution scores, making it necessary to put even more people into those beds.

The poison. The 1971 annual white paper of the Economic Planning Agency made an attempt to measure the 'guilt' or the relationship between different components of the GNP and sulphur dioxide pollution, and this over a five-year period, 1966-70. The question: which expenditure item is the main 'villain,' which has made the largest contribution to the increase in sulphur dioxide volume? In 1965 this exhaust volume showed an annual figure of 1.8 million tons, by 1970 it had grown to 3.4 million tons. The sectors listed below had made these contributions to the increase (in per cent):

1.	Private business fixed investments	32·7
2.	Private consumption	26·0
3.	Exports	21·6
4.	Inventory investments	11·4
5.	Public fixed investments	6·8
6.	Public consumption	1·5
		100

The wise Western reader: 'This is terrible; there can be only one conclusion: an annual increase of zero for investments. We must agree on a "stationary" society, be satisfied with what we have, be content simply with maintaining the value of present real fixed assets. The computers have told us that man — and his world — are otherwise heading for certain disaster.'

Sitting here in the Japanese environment, I can attempt an answer: It is all very well to sit in a rich European country — where everyone, everywhere, can spot public and private riches, fixed assets, created through decades and decades of accumulation — and conclude: we must come to a halt, we are content with what we have created so far.

The GNP measures only the annual flow of economic activities, says nothing about past accumulation. Nominally the Japanese is now well off, with an annual flow of half the Swede's or the American's level. But he is a poor man when it comes to measuring social riches, accumulated national wealth.

This is the per capita situation as to fixed assets, in dollars at the 1970 exchange rate, using 1968 statistics:

- Total fixed assets, both private and public: For Suzuki-san one-fifth of the American's, about half the West German's or the Briton's (28,300, 104,500, 54,400, 54,200 dollars respectively)
- Public fixed assets, excluding local communities but including private housing: 11,100 for Japan, 55,300 for the US, 24,300 for West Germany, 21,300 for Britain
- Housing: 6,100 for Japan, 36,900 for the US, 15,500 for West Germany, 15,500 for Britain
- Total fixed national wealth, excluding household goods and overseas assets but including inventory: Japan 286 billion dollars, the US 2,103 billion dollars, West Germany 316 billion dollars, Britain 300 billion dollars
- Relationship between this total possession and the annual GNP flow: Japan 2.02-fold, West Germany 2.39-fold, US 2.43-fold and Britain 3.41-fold.

So the question is not presented correctly if it is phrased in this way: why cannot the Japanese be satisfied with halting at an annual GNP per capita flow of 2,700 dollars (1972), half of the American's? It is more realistic to launch the question from the 'stock' pad: why isn't Suzuki-san content with *one-fifth* of the accumulated national wealth of the industrialized countries — including libraries, schools, housing, transportation, welfare facilities?

(In annual flow of manufacturing investments per capita, Suzuki-san has already surpassed the American, but as of 1968, these were the total fixed assets of corporations (buildings, machinery, equipment): United States 775 billion dollars, West Germany 159, Britain 132 and Japan 125 billion.)

The physical poverty of Japan's public sector (physical in the sense of fixed investments) was further worsened by two serious mistakes committed by every Sato cabinet since the first one was formed in November of 1964: firstly, the structure of public investment, secondly, the declining ratio for public investment in the total GNP.

The structure: The public investments of the Sato Era were mainly aimed at satisfying the needs of industry, and to a lesser extent the needs of the people. The industrial infrastructure received 46.1 per cent of the whole public investment pie in the six-year period of 1964-69 (fiscal years): for roads, harbours, railways. The social infrastructure had to be content with 16.9 per cent: public housing, public sanitation, health, welfare, schools. Plus six per cent for protecting the environment and another 31 per cent going to other items. The whole pie: 82.7 billion dollars, and here the people got 14 billion for their infrastructure, industry 38 billion.

The pace, the growing gap. Year after year, the Sato ministers let private business fixed investments roar along at a pace three times as fast as the annual growth of public investment. What brought Poet Ogura and the people of Japan into a darkening tunnel was the *unreined* economic growth, the widening gap between the shining beauty of factory equipment and the misery of society's human environment:

Table 26: The Mad Growth in Figures

Abbreviations: PI = public fixed investments;
PrivI = Private fixed investments, excluding housing

	In real prices (1965) Billions of dollars per year			Real prices As % of GNP		Annual increase in per cent Nominal prices		Real prices	
	GNP	PI	PrivI	PI	PrivI	PI	PrivI	PI	PrivI
1967	128·1	11·2	23·3	8·7	18·2	9·9	29·8	4·2	27·0
1968	146·6	12·8	29·7	8·7	20·3	16·2	27·9	14·7	27·4
1969	164·3	13·9	36·2	8·5	22·0	12·9	24·9	9·1	21·9
1970	182·8	15·3	42·4	8·3	23·2	14·5	21·1	8·3	17·1
And So — Suddenly — a New Trend:									
1970	186·7	16·3	42·5	8·8	22·8	21·1	14·6	15·6	11·7
1971	197·7	20·0	42·7	10·1	21·6	23·4	0·7	22·5	0·5
1972	214·5	24·8	44·9	11·5	20·9	26·1	6·1	23·8	5·1

Note: The 1970-1972 period is in fiscal years (FY).

As a percentage of total gross capital formation (including inventory investments) the public investment sector shrank from a 1963 figure of 26% to only 21·2% in 1969 — but was able to regain the 25% level in the recession year of 1971. (As compared to a public investment sector share in Great Britain of 40% and only 15-16% for West Germany. The West Germans *may* be able to endure such a low level, though I question the wisdom of such a low percentage.)

The 1970-72 fiscal period is a forecast by JERC (Japan Economic Research Centre; Nihon Keizai Kenkyu Centre) in March of 1972.

It is difficult to find a better example of 'tunnel-thinking' than the table above, illustrating the unrestrained economic growth.

Now all Japanese agree: a new course, a better society, with people and not machinery at the centre. But all work programmes collide with a number of handicaps: a land area that is too small, the world's highest land prices, too many landowners. The country must be remade but wide parts of the country are already poisoned and moving industries and improving the environment around the dwellings require the approval of at least *thirty million people* — people who own tiny parcels of land.

A few basic facts: Japan's total area is smaller than Sweden's, about 370,000 square kilometres. When one deducts the forests (68.7 per cent) and the cultivated area (18.8 per cent) there remains a 'working and living area' of only 12.5 per cent — only 46,000 sq km, the equivalent of Switzerland's total area.

This Japanese 'work and life' area is a bit larger than similarly defined areas in other countries — Britain's 39,800 sq km, West Germany's 34,700, Italy's 36,000 — but is only 2.3 per cent of America's work and life area. To fulfil MITI's 1980 ambition as outlined in May, 1971 — and confirmed as still valid in the spring of 1972 — of catching up with the six-nation EEC bloc in total GNP requires that Japan's small work and life area must be the scene of more hectic investment activity than in the whole EEC bloc, and ultimately also of larger industrial production and a larger transportation circus. A huge GNP, a gigantic annual flow of economic activity, must have corespondingly large transport activity — the shipping of both freight and people back and forth — and a correspondingly gigantic consumption of raw materials, water, energy.

Fate has put 105 million Japanese on a work and life area that is only a quarter of Sweden's similar area, and these 105 million are the world's most diligent people, a people who do not believe that their ambitions for an affluent future should be blocked by the small area, the limited elbow space.

But Japan is already spotting a number of ceilings, a number of emerging crises or smouldering sticks of dynamite.

Most analysts agree in naming the problems. This is my own ranking list:

1. The Japanese himself
2. The land problem
3. The lungs of the cities
4. Transportation
5. Environmental destruction
6. The car
7. Raw materials
8. Water volume
9. The world's attitude
10. TNP density (per area)

The first six problems revolve around the land problem and the basic characteristics of the Japanese: he is a farmer who happens to live in a city and he only puts his nose into the business of other people if he feels his own interests threatened. He is a go-go man, and thus prefers living in a city, but the idea of living in an apartment house is terrifying: he wants to live in a small, private, one-family house in the centre of the city and there keep his own little garden of 30-50 square metres. Therefore, the world's largest city is not a real city but a village society with two-storey houses and, here and there, some skyscrapers of 45 storeys. There are many small private patches of garden inside individual walled villa enclosures, but very few collective, public green zones.

When somebody wants to erect an eleven-storey apartment next to Suzuki-san's miniature villa, then he and his neighbours join forces: 'The new building will deprive us of sunshine for at least three hours per day, we are being deprived of a basic human right.' Neither Suzuki-san nor the press nor the politicians have discovered that the right to sunshine cannot apply to people who insist on residing in small private villas in the centre of the world's most heavily populated capital city. Thus millions and millions of people living in distant new apartment-block suburbs outside the cities have to commute to their offices and factories for 2-4 hours daily.

There are 29 million households, with about half the people living in miniature villas, i.e. one-family houses. The population of the so-called cities has climbed from 28 per cent in 1945 to 72 per cent in 1970.

The average area per villa lot: 252 square metres for the whole nation — only 123 square metres in the Tokyo region.

This sounds like a dream, a whole nation pottering around in tiny little gardens, a total villa society, but the reality is a nightmare: ten-ton trucks roaring full blast between the minuscule villas, with almost no pavements.

Japan's 579 'shi' — cities — are so many concrete deserts. The parks, the lungs of the city, are too few and too small. Park area per capita for the whole nation 2.7 square metres; in Tokyo only 1.1 — compared to New York's 19 and London's 10. Japan's Construction Ministry in 1971 announced an ambitious park expansion programme: the creation of 11,500 new parks, covering 21,000 hectares, up to 1977. The 1985 target is 10.7 square metres per capita. The cost: 65 billion dollars, because it will be very expensive to make Suzuki-san evacuate his tiny lot, at least 200-600 dollars per square metre.

The owners. In order to transform Japan's two-storey society into a functioning group of super-cities it is necessary to limit, somehow, Suzuki-san's right to utilize some of the functions of ownership, the functional right to be an obstacle; ie to apply Dr Gunnar Adler-Karlsson's definition of Swedish Social-Democratic thinking, 'functional socialism' (Roughly: keep the capitalists but reduce steadily the number of ownership functions that they may use freely). It is comparatively easy to make this theory work if one is dealing with a group of owners who make up perhaps one or two per cent of a nation's population. In Japan the number is just too great:

- Mountains, forests, farm areas, land in residential zones are owned by 29.5 million individuals plus 640,000 companies
- The number of people who own land in residential areas alone: 12.1 million individuals plus 490,000 companies.

Thus every third Japanese, perhaps every second household, owns a small piece of land (like money in the bank, but the value is growing faster than any bank interest) — and every third Japanese means that many votes and that much fear within Japan's political parties, the fear of violating ownership rights. Not all these owners live on the piece of land that they own: often the patch just stands there, increases in value 15-18 per cent annually, meaning that a piece of land now worth 20,000 dollars today will yield four times as much ten years from now.

Thus a great number of these owners must be dealt with, mainly by using the tax-payer's money in world history's greatest transfer of money to a group of property owners. These purchases should have been made in the 1950's when land was comparatively cheap (the ideal solution would, of course, have been to nationalize all city land in the autumn of 1945). The purchasing bill in the 1970's: probably as much as 500 billion dollars.

The car. There are 108 million motor vehicles in the US, cars, buses, trucks, and the American is desperate. Europe: 75 million cars. But for the US to be able to match Japan's car density per area, you have to squeeze into the US another couple of *billion* cars!

The dimensions of the poison blankets hovering over the cities of Japan are better understood if these factors are considered:

1. *The area:* America's work and life area is 41.7 times Japan's. But in total number of motor vehicles the US lead is only 5.4 times (108 million versus Japan's 1972 figures of 20.2 million and 1975 forecast of 28 million, meaning that in four years, the plan is to squeeze in another three 'automobile-Swedens')

2. *The roads:* America's network of roads is eight times as long as Japan's, but the paved sections are 19 times the Japanese figure (which is only 40 per cent of West Germany's)

3. *The dream:* A number of Japanese cities in 1971 proclaimed a 'car-free day per month.' The Japanese exclaimed, 'How nice, how nice,' and early in 1972 as many as sixty per cent of all respondents in a public opinion poll said they considered the car completely unnecessary. Then one lowers one's head from the clouds into a set of statistics, the new registration figures for the month of March, 1972: a new monthly record, another 357,000 cars on the roads, twelve per cent over the number of new registrations in the same month of the previous year.

Once again, the Japanese is his own worst enemy: one half of all households terrorizing and poisoning the other half — who have not yet got a car but who are working desperately towards getting one. Says a Japanese journalist friend: 'Two of my colleagues cursed all cars a year ago. Now they both ride around in their own cars, and you can no longer get a sensible word of lunchtime conversation out of them: they just talk about the automatic gearshift.'

All critics were basically correct in the environmental discussion, often savage, that shook Japan in 1971 and 1972, including all denunciations of the berserk plunge into equipment investment. Unfortunately, the debate went off the rails, leaving on the stage as environmental criminals only two groups, 'the Government' and 'Industry, big finance.' The two ruling cliques. It is a pity that the description is not accurate, because if it were, then it would be comparatively easy to solve all environmental problems.

It is the righteous citizens who injure and cripple one million people per year, who kill each other's children — with 2,000 children slaughtered on the roads every year, seventy per cent of them pedestrians. (Suzuki-san, such a nice fellow, becomes a madman when he sits behind the wheel.) The enraged citizens are the very ones who spoil and defoliate any green area they visit. Their hearts beat with respect and they meditate as they climb sacred Mt Fuji, the soul of Japan; but as they sit on the train en route home, the mountain slopes behind them are littered with garbage. In winter, tens of thousands of taxis stand still at night with their engines running, because the drivers do not want to have any trouble with the automatic shift when they resume driving thirty or fifty minutes later, and this right outside the windows of private apartment buildings; but the enraged citizens lack the civil courage needed to react and call the police. Every day, each Japanese has at least ten chances to act individually against environmental destruction: he is silent, he is passive, 'I do not want to make trouble.' It is much more simple to sign petitions of protest against the two recognized villains. As for all the small villains, spotted wherever one lets the eye wander — they are left alone, are allowed to continue their work of destruction.

Transportation. In two official statements in January of 1972, MITI Minister Kakuei Tanaka, one of the three top contenders for the premiership, confirmed that MITI is still aiming at an annual real growth of 'about 10 per cent' throughout the 1970's. Therefore, we need a completely different transporation system, said Tanaka. The government must now make a new road investment of 15 million yen for each new car put on the roads (at a purchase cost of half a million yen) — and despite this, the average speed of automobiles 'is now down to 9.2 kilometres per hour and is expected to be 8 kilometres at the end of this year.' This means increased transportation costs for industry, said the MITI chief, and thus something must be done. The freight-carrying capacity of the railways must be increased five-fold up to 1980, and the coastal shipping fleet expanded — if this is not done, with the roads having to do all the work, 'this would require 27 million trucks and 27 million drivers, and this is impossible.'

Therefore, another ministry, the Transportation Ministry, is requesting the tidy sum of 325 billion dollars for transportation investments up to 1985 — a sum twice as large as the dreamy figure announced in the spring of 1969. But in the countryside: more and more regional protests against super-speed trains flashing through their districts, neglecting to stop and leaving only noise behind. They protest, too, against MITI's plans to move factories from urban areas to thinly populated areas, the creation of completely new industrial zones out in the wilderness.

We have no choice, answers Mr Tanaka. He argues that Japan's real or fully exploited work and life area must be expanded: at present this fully exploited area occupies only 2.3 per cent of the nation's total area — that is two per cent for city areas and 0.3 per cent for factories — and he wants to advance for 2.3 per cent to '10-15 per cent' of the nation's total area. If the work and life area is not expanded, this would further boost land prices in the two per cent city area, and there would be no possibility of meeting industry's need for new land, the need for another 10,000 hectares per year.

This means, say the critics, that we spread the poison to larger and larger areas. We have no choice, answers MITI, and 'gradually, we shall detoxify the industrial structure, by directing industry into healthier work assignments.'

Congestion in Japan gets worse and worse: in the air, at sea, on the ground. The number of 'plane passengers will jump 10-fold up to 1985, airfreight will advance 50-fold. The 55 civilian airports are already stacked to capacity, and the manoeuvres of the steel birds trying to prevent collisions with other steel birds are, according to experts, 'pure acrobatics, a trapeze act,' with hundreds of hairs-breadth incidents every year. At sea, around the coasts: more and more collisions.

An advisory group attached to the Construction Ministry demanded in 1971 that the GNP share of the public investments be raised from the current level of eight per cent to seventeen per cent by 1985. This group said Japan would hit a number of 'ceilings' if she were to pursue policies aimed at a growth as close to her potential as possible, that is, almost eleven per cent. Among the ceilings: raw material needs, water volume, industrial waste, and the difficulty of recruiting a sufficient number of building workers able to meet the needs of both the private and public sectors.

Industry's waste and oil pollution: with an unchanged growth rate and the same industrial structure, an eight-fold figure in 1985 as compared to 1965. At present an industrial waste volume of one million tons a day. Even in 1965 it was equal to a 'carpet' with a pile of four millimetres if spread over all city areas; by 1975 this 'carpet' will be 13 millimetres high and, in 1985, 26 millimetres. Sulphur dioxide: a level of 1.7 million tons in 1965, about five million tons in 1975 and fourteen million tons in 1985 — 'above the limit, through the ceiling.' If Japan still keeps growing at her potential growth rate with no new industrial structure: 29 million tons in 1995, and in Year 2001 a level 23 times as high as in 1965.

Water volume: At present growth rates, Japan would need in Year 2001 about 550 billion tons of water, compared to 74 billion tons in 1965, making it necessary to raise the use of rain water from 18 per cent to 87 per cent — 'which is impossible,' hence a water shortage as early as in 1985. Even if 480 new water dams are built by 1985, at a cost of 23 billion dollars, there would still be a likely shortage of five billion tons in that year.

Raw materials: Japan would use up 92 per cent of all oil in the world in Year 2001, and in 1995 swallow as much as 77 per cent of all the iron ore in the world.

Therefore, a switch to public sector investments, please, said the group, suggesting that the Japan Development Bank, for decades a channel for money to industry, be converted to a 'Society Development Bank,' under orders to channel money to public sector needs.

There are plenty of discords in the futuristic music played by the competing orchestras — in evaluating both the future and the barriers. A power struggle is under way. The Construction Ministry is moving into a more central seat of power at the same pace as the public investment sector grows, because 70 per cent of the public works budget is channelled through this ministry. But MITI's strategists, who have for decades had the strongest bass voices, do not want to let go of the reins and the future, because MITI is sitting on the R & D funds, and the ministry says that the technology which has destroyed so much of the nation will also save the nation and lead the country to ever greater victories. Suzuki-san shakes his head, a little confused; he does not know what to believe, so he just goes on perfecting his golf shots with practice swings in his 30-square-metre garden lot, while his wife polishes the car with loving hands.

The thinkers of the Construction Ministry cannot be described as outrageously pessimistic. Their demand is that the annual real growth rate be lowered only one per cent below MITI's magic figure of 10.6 per cent.

The environment. Some 2,000 people were asked in the spring of 1971 how they looked at Japan's environment. The answers: 81 per cent said Tokyo's air and water pollution had reached 'Serious proportions,' but 37 per cent of the group felt, at the same time, that they did not have to worry about their health. About 65 per cent answered a firm yes when asked if they shared the Tokyo City Government's views that if the current trend is allowed to continue, all people in Tokyo will have to 'carry gas-masks in 10-15 years.'

The picture is not very consistent. As many as one-third of the respondents keep whistling, do not believe in the gas mask. In March 1972, more people would appear to have joined the ranks of the optimists, because the *Asahi Shimbun* notes that a 'pollution immunity' has emerged. In the press and on the radio, new announcements and new warnings that now the air pollution level is so high, twice as high as a year ago — 'This is terrible but we are no longer so easily shocked. People have started to build up a psychological resistance.'

The newspaper's 'Tensei Jingo' columnist warned:

When a real crisis arrives, people will no longer lend their ears to the warnings.

The following experiment was carried out by Louis Pasteur one hundred years ago. He put a small bird, A, in a sealed box. As time passed, the bird weakened because of lack of oxygen.

At a certain stage, he placed another bird, B, in the same box. Bird B died immediately. Bird A, which was weakened but which had become used to the bad environment, continued to live for a while longer after the death of Bird B.

Our fate may already be that of bird A in the sealed box. We are used to the bad environment and are still living — but it will be too late if we don't take steps *now* to purify the environment.

The newspaper's conclusion: the people's pollution immunity may already be heading for the next phase, 'pollution frigidity,' total inability to react, hence a need to lower the stridency and launch a more rational campaign to arrest public hazards.

There are some flashes of light in the dark tunnel. In April, 1972, Tokyo City's environment agency reported that the sulphur dioxide contents in the capital had dropped in the 1971 fiscal year to a level even lower than the target that had been set for Fiscal 1973. Other poisonous matter in the air had either stagnated at a high level or recorded a modest rise. This note of cheer was unexpected in view of a MITI warning in the autumn of 1971 that the volume of sulphur dioxide over the Kanto region industrial zone — including Tokyo — could be expected to be twice as high in 1975 as in 1968.

Officially, Tokyo City expects a better environment in 1980, through public environment expenditure in this decade of 6.8 billion dollars, an expenditure programme adopted in Jan. 1971.

Industry's contribution: Industrial production of environmental protection equipment rose by 79 per cent in 1971, to 1.1 billion dollars, and is expected to reach an annual level of 2.7 billion dollars in 1975. The share of total private business fixed investments now going to environmental equipment was reported to have doubled in 1971 — from 5.3 per cent in 1970 to 10.2 per cent in 1971.

The Government's contribution: a shame, a disgrace, a scandal. When the public Environment Agency was created in July of 1971, it got an annual budget of 14.6 million dollars — about one per cent of the equivalent US budget. There was an increase of 80 per cent in the 1972 budget, but this sum also is worthy only of contempt.

Big finance ('Zaikai'), the private economic power groups: 'Disturbed but not yet alarmed,' says a man who constantly meets with the dozen or so decision makers who control most of Japan's industrial economy. 'But here you can expect a change. Within 18 months, in the autumn of 1973, these strong men will push the environment protection button, and from then on things will go very fast.'

In critical situations, Japan often behaves like a boxer with too little ring experience, 'leads with the chin,' a kind of invitation to be hit. Japan was the international whipping boy at the United Nations environment conference in Stockholm in June of 1972, partly because Japan does deserve criticism, partly because it is comfortable to be able to point to a country where environmental destruction has advanced to an even more dangerous extent than in the delegate's own country. Now Japan is really leading with the chin, having invited the next UN environment conference to meet in Tokyo, and there are reasons to believe that Japan at that time intends to play a different role, because of a 1972 prediction that by the time of the conference Japan should be able to report a new and encouraging trend. Pessimists in the outside world probably have a different opinion. They would rather read Japan's conference invitation as a card carrying this text: 'You are hereby invited to attend the funeral of Japan. RSVP.'

Is the Japanese without a chance? Instead of happily waving his boxing glove — the 'boys-be-ambitious' signal —

should he perhaps give up, throw in the towel? Refrain from trying to re-make the country?

I initiated much of the gloomy international debate as to Japan's physical limitations by noting a few basic facts in *The Japanese Challenge:* that the superpower of Japan would be handicapped in competition with the US superpower by its small land area, and that Japan's growth as of 1969 had been producer-oriented, had first of all served the interests of the nation's producers, not the consuming public. I noted, too, that a new pattern of thinking was emerging, as of the summer of 1969, but nevertheless found it proper to pose this question: 'How much wealth can a country endure per square kilometre?' Now three years have passed, the annual flow of economic activities is even larger, and it would be logical to assume that I am now more alarmed than in 1969.

Answer from Bird A, who has by this time been sitting in the sealed box for another eighteen months: yes, any analyst who resides in Japan is now more concerned about environmental problems in general, that is in the whole world, as a result of the American MIT Group's computer pronouncements of where we are probably heading. But I no longer see any need to put Japan alone in the doom and gloom closet.

An economic journalist who wants to argue along a certain thought pattern, at a certain time, in a certain situation — he, like other debaters, researches statistical facts in support of his arguments. In 1969, I gave the GNP per square kilometre, that is the country's total production divided by its area, an idea that had first been developed by Japanese economists. I carried this thinking one step further: broke down also investment sums to a per area figure, and calculated the area pressure of certain industries — steel, for example, 'a square kilometre density 100 times as high as in the Soviet Union.' The result was a picture of Hell: 'The world's most satanic growth music in the world's smallest orchestra pit.'

Now the beat is even faster. If we — as was the case in my *Challenge* book — deduct from the total area only the forested regions, we arrrive at this current situation:

Table 27: Density Pressure Rose 52% in Three Years (1969-71)

GNP per square kilometre; total area minus forest area; in dollars

	1968	1970	1971	1980
Japan	1,449,700	1,990,200	2,204,500	8,074,000
US	136,100	153,400	164,900	304,400
Sweden	137,500	164,500		365,400

Note: My GNP per area figures for 1980 are based on Dr Kanamori's total GNP estimates, his forecast of January, 1972.

By deducting the forests (whose existence does not help city ants very much), we find that Japan exerted an economic pressure on her area, in comparison with the US, that was already 10.6 times as high in 1968 — that this 'pressure' had increased to a 12.9-fold difference in 1970 and can be expected to soar to 26.5-fold by 1980. In 1971 the pressure per area grew by 200,000 dollars in Japan, in the US, by only 10,000 dollars.

Almost any kind of economic activity affects that ecological system, particularly investments which in the case of Japan amount to almost 40 per cent of the GNP compared to a US ratio of 17 per cent, and particularly if one insists on creating a motorised society before conditions for such a society exist, including poison-free petrol, and pavements.

The calculations and reasoning in the table above seem to bear out the supposition that Suzuki-san has no chance, that Japan will be choked to death by her own superpower ambitions. Fortunately, or unfortunately, Japan is not the only country in the world with great ambitions for the material affluence of her people. Thus the table above is partly false: it is true only as long as one limits the discussion to a comparison between the geophysical conditions of two superpowers.

Take Holland: a nation with fragrant-smelling tulips, a small area. Switzerland: they are yodelling up in the mountains and down in the cities bankers thump batches of bank notes on their desks without disturbing the ecological system. West Germany: yes, it is smoky in the Ruhr but it is certainly better than in Japan. So one believes, but GNP statistics indicate a completely different picture.

In the following two tables I present two kinds of calculations: one for GNP per total land area, and secondly, an 'urban society' area figure that is left after deducting the following from the total areas: forests, cultivated areas, permanent meadows. The urban society's 'work and life' area is, as already noted, only 12.5 per cent of the nation's total area. In Britain it is 12.2 per cent — and in Britain an even higher percentage of the population lives in cities — while in West Germany it is 14.0 per cent.

Thus, we arrive at two lists of different rankings:

Table 28: Holland Leads in GNP per Total Area

GNP per sq. km per total area; 1970 figures; in dollars

1. Holland	1,039,100
2. Belgium	936·100
3. West Germany	854,200
4. Japan	622,900
5. Switzerland	593,100
6. Great Britain	540,000
7. Italy	330,00
Unranked:	
US	104,000
Sweden	82,100

In this case, the Japanese density pressure is 60 per cent of the Dutch figure, and 73 per cent of the West German figure.

But distant forests and farms and meadows do not provide any oxygen for the urban societies:

Table 29: West Germany Leads in GNP per 'Urban Society' Area

	Dollars per year	Based on this area (1,000 sq. km.)
1. West Germany	6,101,728	34·7
2. Japan	4,983,135	46·3
3. Great Britain	4,426,599	29·8
4. Holland	4,276,301	8·2
5. Belgium	3,600,630	7·9
6. Italy	2,775,415	36·1
7. Switzerland	2,492,115	9·8
Unranked:		
US	505,000	1,928
Sweden	196,800	171

In this latter case, Japan's density pressure is 82 per cent of West Germany's, which in its turn is 12 times higher than America's.

It is not the tulips that give the Netherlands a top ranking.

When looking at the GNP production structure for different countries, the contribution of various sectors, one may in the case of urban societies rather safely disregard the GNP contribution from the commerce sector, farming and forestry and the construction industry. If we look at the so-called secondary sector, industry, we find these contributions from industry to domestic gross national product (= GNP minus overseas net):

Table 30: Factories That Do Not Make Tulips

Secondary industry's share, in %, of GDP

	Japan	Holland	Belgium	UK	West Germany	US	Italy
1955	28·5	39·1	38·9	46·0	52·9	39·6	36·7
1960	36·3	40·3	38·4	45·6	54·4	37·0	35·5
1969 (or 1968)	39·2	42·2	38·5	43·5	54·4	35·8	36·4

Note: GDP = Gross Domestic Product, that is GNP minus overseas net.

Industrial pressure on the work and life area is thus highest in West Germany.

The solution for Japan is theoretically simple: detoxify the worst polluters, for example, the paper and pulp industry, steel, the chemical giants, preferably by moving as much as possible of these sectors out of the country — to nations with larger work and life zones: Canada or Australia; keep only the sectors with a very high added value, for example quality steel. By pulling out the poisoned teeth too quickly, one would destroy the bite of Japan's export industry. Thus the Japanese are planning for a step-by-step solution, structural changes.

Still, the risk is great that ten years later, a researcher may sit down and denounce my square kilometre tables as 'Bird-A tables,' and MITI's and Dr Kanamori's programmes for the future as 'Bird-A ambitions.'

The *real* birds may be wiser — they are escaping.

Three-quarters of Japan's 424 bird types are migrant birds, and more and more of these guest birds are chirping a warning to the people of Japan: we no longer want to visit your country.

About 150 of the migrant birds are so-called winter birds that fly in from the north, mainly from Siberia and Alaska, arrive in Japan in the autumn and stay until spring. Among these northern guests are wild geese and other members of the same family. In 1953, about 54,000 of them visited Japan; by 1971 the number had shrunk to about ten per cent or 5,160. In one year alone — in 1971 — the number of places in Japan visited by the wild geese dropped from 42 to 40, and the number of places visited by wild duck fell from 2,511 to 1,877.

The verdict of the guest birds managed to pierce the PPM immunity. The government budget for protection of birds and animals rose by 800 per cent in fiscal 1972 (to 380,000 dollars). But at the Environment Agency section assigned to keeping a protective watch over birds and other animals the staff is as small as eleven employees. The US figure: three thousand.

It will be a long time before the migrant birds start warbling that they believe in a future in Japan.

CHAPTER NINE

The revolution

'The sum of economic progress is the difference between what is created and what is destroyed.'
Nobutake Kiuchi
Japanese economist

The Japanese people dreamed in the spring of 1972 of a welfare state, a balance state. Bankers, industrialists and even Cabinet ministers rose and proclaimed: 'Now we shall build a welfare state.' What is going to happen instead is a fourth industrial revolution.

Japan's economic development can be divided into four phases or revolutionary changes:

1. **The Meiji Era, 1868-1912:** from a feudalistic society to a light-industry structure comparable to that of countries in the West; education for all; search for technology all over the world
2. **1930-40:** from light to heavy industry, to a heavy war-oriented industrial structure; cheap and shoddy sundries dominate exports, mainly textiles; but forty per cent of the labour force is still engaged in farming
3. **1951-70:** hunt for technology around the world; once again a switch from a light-industry structure to heavy industry but now a completely peace-oriented profile; only 0.4 per cent of industry's production value is defence-oriented; a quality revolution that brings Japan global export victories; the people enjoy the world's fastest growth in material affluence, catch up with and out-run West European countries in the possession of refrigerators, TV sets, washing machines, vacuum cleaners; now only 15 per cent left in the farm labour force — but suddenly the sky is poisonously yellow and

the people discover: we have built a strong industry, a competitive industry, but a weak society, a miserable social environment. We have built quality in our products but no real quality in our living conditions as human beings. We developed a rich enterprise environment, a poor human environment. All Japanese, including the ruling Establishment, agree with this analysis, and everybody joins in this demand: 'a new course.'

4. **1971-80**: a fourth industrial revolution; a break-through for Japan's own technology; the poisoned teeth of industry are pulled out or transplanted; a new structure in the exports pattern, with an ever heavier emphasis on research-intense products; the home market is opened to foreign manufactured goods — and the 'physical' welfare state emerges, a completely new physical environment for society, because in this decade Japan catches up with all countries, excluding Sweden, in accumulated public fixed investments per capita. In this decade, each new Cabinet is dominated by so-called 'ten-per-centers,' men who insist on a real annual GNP growth of at least 10 per cent. Before 1980, Japan becomes richest in the world in annual GNP flow per capita, and for each new year the Japanese is climbing faster and faster up the steps of the tables that are now of greater interest to him than the old GNP hysteria tables: tables measuring social indicators, welfare indicators, the genuine welfare development.

Mrs. Suzuki, the widow, who needs help from society in supporting her children, has one definition of what a welfare state should be: increased public consumption. The ruling Establishment has a different definition: increased public investments. A welfare state in balance should stand on two strong legs: 1. public consumption to help those who have been knocked out by the furiously spinning wheels of fast economic growth, and other similarly handicapped groups, and 2. public investments: playgrounds, schools, sports grounds, hospitals, sewerage, drainage, harbours, railways, airports, a safer traffic environment.

In the 1970's, Japan will grow into a limping welfare state, partly because the people do not want to pay for two strong legs, partly because the ruling power groups most of all want 'welfare investments' grounded in steel and cement, things you can touch, things that can be produced by private industry with money from the State.

Sweden is a Balance State, perhaps the only one — but the dilemma is that no economist will ever be able to say that 'there, exactly there' is the point of balance. There are at least two different scales, two different balance needles. One of the needles should, if one may wish to day-dream, give a warning bleep when the weight of the public sector has become so heavy that it threatens the force on the other side of the same scale, the country's international competitive power. Balance needle No. 2: no one can define the moment when the cup of tax tiredness becomes too full, when the citizen decides that he wants more money in his own pocket, when he stops smiling at the sight of more public libraries and playgrounds, when he feels that now, now he cannot endure even one decimal point more in his tax burden. Sweden's export development, above the world average, indicates that the Balance State has passed one of the scale tests — but the tax reform investigation commission appointed early in 1972 indicates as strongly that the citizen is fed up, that he can no longer endure what he considers 'over-balance.'

In Japan, references are often made to West Germany as a 'welfare state,' references of administration. In January of 1972, a Japanese newspaper noted that six million aged in West Germany, about 75 per cent of all aged, receive a monthly pension of 53,000 yen (172 dollars), while only 5 per cent of Japan's aged — a small group of 520,000 persons — get a state pension, and the sum is pitiful, 45 dollars.

Still, even West Germany is a limping welfare state, because the leg of public investment is weak — about 3.8 per cent of GNP compared to Sweden's 10.8 per cent, America's 3.2 per cent and Japan's current figure of 10 per cent. The United States, the Problem State, is limping on both legs: public consumption proves low when one deducts the military expenditure, and year after year the level of public investment as a ratio of the GNP remains glued at 3.2 per cent, though the cities are decaying and are in need of public investment: it is just as if Keynes never had lived.

I give in a separate table (*table* 31) in this chapter the GNE structure for a number of countries, in percentage and in dollars per capita, in an attempt to illustrate 'resources strategy,' the ambitions of a society and what this means at the per-person level. It is to me of minor importance if the GNP flow in a certain year is 100 or 80 billion dollars (one may arrive at the lower sum if one deducts the waste share, the negative and meaningless parts of the *Gross* National Product) but I feel as strongly that the present denunciations of GNP as a measuring-rod should not be allowed to snowball into 'GNP immunity,' or 'GNP-frigidity,' deceiving people into overlooking the relationship between the different components of GNP.*

Between 1951 and 1970, Japan built a strong industry, but a weak society. Up to 1980, Japan will get an even stronger industry, and in physical terms, a strong society.

The pulling power of the Technological Factor that must come if Japan is to experience the type of new industrial revolution was forecast by, for example, Dr Kanamori. Here

---

*Studies of this relationship are very rarely encouraged by bureaucrats in the West. A frightening example of this is the Swedish Supplementary Budget Bill document, presented in the spring of 1972, a document of 250 pages, with an appendix of 90 pages, and not even one page or table giving the GNE structure in per cent — only a deafening roar of millions of kronor. Citizen Svensson is assumed to be able to make his own structure analysis, if he is interested — and if he ever does, he will find this constant price development between 1964 and 1969 (in prices of 1959); the ratios of GNP of various components:

- Exports and other income from abroad rose from 26.6 per cent to 31 per cent
- Public consumption up from 17 to 18.5 per cent
- Public investments, excluding public housing investments, up from 7.8 to 8.6 per cent
- All kinds of housing investmens up from 5.3 to 5.4 per cent
- Private consumption fared very well, a slight decline from 57.25 per cent to 57.0 per cent

In Japan, however, there is a constant, daily debate on GNE structure. Even the daily newspapers, aimed at a wide readership, give detailed structure tables, which never happens in Sweden, not even when the budget is presented. In the Balance State of Sweden, Svensson is assumed not to be interested in structural shift information.

Table 31: Japan — The Limping Growth State

The structure of Gross National Expeditures in per cent ... and in dollars per capita; current prices

	The balanced state SWEDEN 1969	The limping welfare state WEST GERMANY 1969	The stagnation State GREAT BRITAIN 1969	The problem State USA 1972	A — The limping growth state JAPAN 1972	B — Japan in 1980 (MITI's vision: still limping growth state) %	B — Japan in 1980 $	SWEDEN	WEST GERMANY	GREAT BRITAIN (1972)	USA (1972)	JAPAN (1972)
	Too much public balance?	Low public investment	High private consumption	Low public investment consumption	Low public consumption							
GNP (1972 parities)							8460	3810	2862	2139	5400	2798
Total consumption	76·2	70·9	80·5	81·9	61·4	58·0	4907	2902	2029	1723	4422	1718
(a) private	53·1	55·3	62·7	62·8	52·6	48·9	4137	2021	1583	1342	3392	1472
(b) public	23·2	15·6	17·8	19·1	8·8	9·1	770	881	446	381	1030	246
Total effort	22·8	24·3	17·4	17·8	34·5	39·6	3350	869	695	371	965	965
(a) private gross fixed investment	8·7	15·3	6·0	10·6	17·2	17·5	1480	332	438	128	572	481
(b) private housing investment	3·3	5·2	3·3	4·1	6·8	11·3	956	126	149	70	220	190
(c) public investment	10·8	3·8	8·1	3·2	10·5	10·8	914	412	110	173	173	294
(of which public housing investment)	2·2	(?)	(?)	(?)	(ca 0·7)	(?)	(?)	84	(?)	(?)	(?)	ca 20)
To be added:												
(a) overseas net	−0·4	+2·4	+1·5	−0·02	+2·3	+0·7	+59	−15	+70	+33	−2	+65
(i.e. exports etc)	23·7	23·4	26·3	6·7	11·0	10·7	905	903	670	563	362	308
minus imports etc)	24·1	21·0	24·8	6·7	8·7	10·0	846	918	600	530	364	243
(b) inventory investment change	1·4	2·3	0·6	0·3	1·8	1·7	144	52	65	14	16	50

Note 1: Author's calculations, based on OECD's per capita sums for Sweden, West Germany, Britain, plus revaluation additions. Japan's per capita sum of 1972: a forecast by Japan Economic Research Centre, Tokyo, in March, 1972; the US 1972 figure is also a forecast, of Feb. 1972; MITI's 1980 view: estimates by author based on MITI's so-called secret document.

Worth noting: Japan's 1980 exports per capita would roughly equal Sweden's 1969 figure.

Note 2: In 1972, Suzuki-san's public consumption was only 65% of his British colleague's 1969 level — but in total growth effort, 2·6 times the British figure, and a four-fold difference in private gross fixed investments.

Also: right now a 'dead heat' in total investment per capita between the Americans and the Japanese. In 1973, Suzuki-san will definitely take over the lead, with an ever widening gap.

it may be worth noting that Japan's R & D expenditures are actually pursuing Kanamori's trend line of an annual rise of 23 per cent. At the end of April, 1972, it was announced that R & D expenditure by the nation's 1,631 leading corporations had climbed by 28 per cent in the fiscal year of 1971 (over the 1970 figure), with the number of researchers and assistants growing one single year by 12 per cent. Half of these corporations reported that they were also conducting 'environmental protection' research.

The poisonous teeth. MITI reports that this share of the companies' total equipment investments now goes to environmental protection investment:

Table 32: Soon A Quarter for the Paper and Pulp Industry

Environmental investment, ratio of total fixed investment

	Iron and steel	Electric power	Paper, pulp	Mining (not coal)
1970	6·1	11·6	6·5	9·5
1971	9·7	15·6	17·9	16·2
1972	12·4	17·1	23·9	18·6

The definition of 'environmental protection' investments is unpleasantly wide, and is so in all countries, but Japan's iron and steel industry — which normally shoulders a quarter of the nation's total environment investments — is expected to spend 272 million dollars on this item alone in the year 1972.

The electric power industry: it was announced in April 1972 that this sector will invest a total of 48 billion dollars up to 1980, and that 19 per cent — or 9.1 billion dollars — will go towards battling to reducing environmental destruction. (This programme, from the industry's cooperative council, said nuclear power will increase its share of output from 2 per cent in 1970 to 22 per cent in 1980, that total power capacity will grow at an annual rate of 10.5 per cent, consumption by 9.4 per cent, giving a 1980 capacity of 128.5 million kilowatts and a 1980 consumption of 637 billion kw-hours. The latter sum would be triple the EEC bloc figure for 1959.

Public investments. The American has already been defeated in the per capita table, and so has the West German, and even the Swede will be dethroned, pushed off his expensive world-champion chair.

In 1969, the West German spent only 110 dollars on public fixed investments per person, the Swede almost four times as much: 412 dollars. The intensity of Japan's tremendous leaps in this sector is best seen in a comparison with America's per capita figures.

Both countries are equally sick, both Japan's and America's cities must be re-built; the public transportation system is probably as deplorable in both countries, though America's social infra-structure is far better: sewerage, drainage, housing, sidewalks.

Table 33: America's Defeat in the Public Investment Sector

Fixed public investment, annual Results	Total, per year, billions of dollars, nominal price		Which results in these per capita sums		And in this index measuring the 'effort' (USA = 100)
	Japan	USA	Japan	USA	Japan
1955	1·8	9·9	20	60	33
1965	9·3	21·5	95	110	86
1970	20·1	31·2	194	152	128
1971	24·8	33·5	235	161	146
1972	31·3	36·6	294	175	168
1973	36·6	40·2	348	189	184

Note: Author's estimates. For Japan, the 1970-73 period is fiscal years; for the US all calendar years. My US estimates are based on the assumption that public investments remain at the level of 3·2% of GNP. Japan: my per capita estimates for 1971-73 are based on JERC's total figures at forecast in March, 1972, assuming that this sector in Japan would grow from 8.45% of GNP in 1970 to 9·45% in 1971 and 10·5% in 1972 (nominal prices; in real prices these ratios: 8·8—10·1—11·5%). For Fiscal 1973 I have assumed a sector investment increase of 17%, lower than the 1972 real increase of 23·8%, nominal jump of 26·1%. As for the US, I have assumed these total GNP figures for 1971-73, in billions of dollars: 1,047 — 1,145 — 1,256, with the 1973 figure, showing an increase of 9·7%, probably too high. (Japan's victory in the public investment sector came in 1969: 158 dollars for Japan, 146 for the Americans)

Why is the Japanese behaving so differently from the American, as seen so dramatically in the table above? One explanation is that 'welfare', including public investments, is an honourable word in Japan but is causing allergy in the United States. In a speech before the US Air Force Academy in June 1969, President Nixon told an attentive audience of pilots:

'I believe that America is not about to become a garrison state, or a welfare state, or a police state — because we will defend our values from those forces, external or internal, that would challenge or erode them.'

If the American pilots had the opportunity of listening to the 'eroding' and 'challenging' words spoken in the spring of 1972 by Japanese industrial leaders and even by Prime Minister Sato, they would probably urge Mr Kissinger to give rapid fulfilment to his promise to visit the allied nation where people have suddenly started to talk in such threatening terms: 'Now, yes *now* we shall build a welfare state.' Speakers who are particularly wise add a few words: '. . . similar to Sweden or Switzerland,' and that is not quite the same thing. American analysts based in Tokyo probably find strength in knowing that the road to hell has always been paved with good intentions, and as Japan's road is so very long — starting from scratch — there are good possibilities that the ultimate disaster, the welfare state, will yet be prevented. (But it is worth noting that 53 per cent of all respondents in a nation-wide public opinion poll demanded such a 'welfare state,' and only 9 per cent cared to nod their heads when shown an alternative card: 'a major economic power.')

Another reason for the frothing enthusiasm behind 'welfare investments' is that the Japanese are not dogmatic when they look at the GNP growth equation. When one component on one side of the equation, namely private business fixed investments, began staggering in 1970, then the rulers of Japan were not at all willing to repeat the mistake committed by the same Sato Cabinet in the recession year of 1965, when the Cabinet refrained from balancing the downturn in private equipment demand by expanding the public sector. Therefore, the 1965 recession became unnecessarily deep, and the journey through the valley in the fiscal years of 1970 and 1971 was far less painful. Japan's ruling groups are growth-oriented: they are more interested in growth as such than in where the growth takes place. If the growth carriage can no longer be pulled mainly by private sector investments, all right, then we must put in a new horse: public investments. But the question is, (and here Suzuki-san is very worried), when the exhausted and gasping horse of private equipment investment has recovered in 1973, will it then be allowed once again to set off at a maddening pace, or will there emerge a more balanced tandem-race, with the public horse now in the limelight?

There is no point of return. The Japanese people will no longer tolerate the public works horse being put out to grass once more. A key question, however, is how to supply this horse with hay. If the private sector, with pulling power from technology and structural change, should again advance very rapidly, then the financing of the expensive public investment programme can be done through the natural increase in tax income — but if the growth rate of the public sector proves slow, then the tax burden must be increased. (This increase looks inevitable, anyhow, in 1973: an addition of perhaps two percentage points above the current GNP percentage of 16.)

From the annual flow of public investments, we go over to Sweden's defeat in accumulated public investments. I draw this inevitable conclusion as a result of numerous interviews with Establishment decision-makers and opinion-moulders, including Professor Shimomura and Dr Kanamori, and from the GNE structure of MITI's so-called secret document.

Professor Shimomura. When I note that most Japanese economists envisage what to me looks like a limping welfare state, with weak public consumption and enormous public investments, then he asks me to remember that 'too many Japanese still think unambitiously, as a poor people, not realizing that all of us can now afford to start living more decently. In general, however, I see a cyclical development: the 1960's was a decade with emphasis on private equipment investment. The 1970's will be the decade of public investment, and the 1980's that of public consumption.'

He proceeds to give me some figures forecasting a strong advance for the whole public sector in the 1970's, so that this sector by 1975 will occupy a larger percentage of GNE than in West Germany or France.

Exerpts from the forecast (converted by the author from the professor's 360-yen-per-dollar habit to the current parity of 308; nominal prices):

Table 34: A Public Sector of 26·5% by 1980

Shimomura's view of the future; excerpts; billions of dollars and %

	GNP	Private consumption	Private fixed investment	Housing investment	THE PUBLIC SECTOR IN GNE Investment	Consumption	Total
1970 (prov)	234	(50·8%)	46·7 (20%) (7%)	(7%)	20 (8·6%)	16·6 (8·3%)	(16·9%)
1975	484				71 (14·8%)		
1980	818	(54·4%)	82·7 (10·1%)	(7%)	121 (15%)	94 (11·5%)	(26·5%)

When I object that even by 1980 the share of public consumption would still be as low as 11.5 per cent of GNP (compared to Sweden's 23 per cent in 1969 and West Germany's 15.6 per cent), the professor replies: 'There is a limit to what we can afford in the 1970's. I assume, however, that the welfare budget of the central Government will increase six times in this decade, with the same advance for public investment, while private consumption will have to be satisfied with a four-fold increase.'

It is a revolution in Japan's economy that Shimomura is sketching. (Among his star pupils in private session: Masayoshi Ohira, former MITI minister and foreign minister, one of the three top contenders for Sato's soon-to-be-cast-off mantle. 'Yes, Dr. Shimomura is my "sensei," my teacher,' Ohira confirms in a conversation with the author. 'We have no alternative: we must build a welfare state.')

I use the strong word 'revolution' for two reasons:
• No other industrial country has ever been able to carry a public investment burden of 15 per cent of GNP
• If Shimomura proves correct, Japan will have more 'over-balance' in her investment pattern in 1980 than even Sweden. In 1969, Sweden had an over-balance of 24 per cent (author's estimate, based on the following: public investments, including public housing = 10.3 per cent of GNP, compared to a ratio of 8.71 per cent for

private business fixed investments) while Shimomura's 1980 forecast means an over-balance of 48 per cent, that is 15 per cent compared to 10.1 per cent.

This would make Japan's investment pattern 'public goods-oriented.' If so, Japan would invest primarily to fill the needs of her own people, and only secondarily in consideration of the needs of export markets. Would the fury of Japan's creative genius then be mainly limited to the islands of Japan? Not quite. Shimomura believes in exports and other earnings abroad in 1980 of about 80 billion dollars, 'an annual growth rate roughly equal to the nominal GNP growth.'

Dr Kanamori. While Shimomura's forecast means a per capita sum for public investments of about 1,040 dollars in the year of 1980, Kanamori's ambitions are slightly lower: a 1980 figure of about 850 dollars and a 1985 figure of 1,800 dollars. Kanamori's and MITI's work programme amount to a new industrial revolution but they are not seeking a public goods-oriented investment pattern. Even so, Svensson is going to lose that crown, however hard he tries to keep it.

Some European economists consider their Japanese colleagues to be 'mechanical,' a little too stiff in their econometric thinking pattern. Personally, I hold the opposite view, and the dethroning of Svensson and Sweden is a good case history illustrating that a Japanese economist never gets lost, always finds a way out of the labyrinth. It was far from easy to topple Sweden — finance ministers such as Wigforss and Straeng, names that make my typewriter tremble, thought they had made certain that the crown would be secure.

A great number of economists participated in drafting Dr Kanamori's and JERC's 1985 trillion-dollar programme. One of them got the assignment of making accumulation sums for public investment in four countries, Japan, Great Britain, the US and Sweden, both for the seventeen-year period of 1951-67, and for the eighteen-year period of 1968-85. The generous assumption: that competing countries would be able to maintain in the future the growth rates scored in the first period: Japan 17.2 per cent, Sweden 11.2 per cent, Great Britain 10.5 and the United States 6.3 per cent. Even though this in Sweden's case would mean that public investments would jump from about 10 per cent to 17 per cent of GNP by 1985.

Step one. Total accumulation sums in the two periods and for the whole 35-year period up to 1985 (and at the old, 1971 exchange rates):

Table 35: Japan Will also Defeat the US in Cumulative Public Investment

Billions of dollars; nominal prices

	Period 1951-67	Period 1968-85	35-year period 1951-85
Japan	73.5	1,248	1,321
US	254	776	1,030
Great Britain	76	463	539
Sweden	21·7	169	191

Step two. That was encouraging, defeating the US, but here it is a matter of welfare investments, so to say, so let us go down to the per capita and divide with population figures for 1985. The soroban starts clicking, clicking, with this depressing result, in dollars, per person:

Table 36: But Wny Is That Swede at the Top?

Per capita; cumulative sum 1951-85 ; dollars

1. The Swede	25,685
2. Suzuki-san	12,700
3. The Briton	10,640
4. The American	3,990

Step three. Crisis. Hm! Hm! Even if we do revalue, we still cannot catch that Swede at the top. When we started the race in 1951, we had a per capita income of the Indian type. We have nevertheless been able to out-run the American, and have by 1985 lifted three times as much, per capita, but that Swede . . . Hm! The Brain Power Index of the economist proves up to this crucial test, however. What would be the total accumulated sum *per square metre*?! The soroban goes click-click-click again, and Sweden — whose total land area is twenty per cent larger than Japan's — has been able to lift only fifteen per cent of Japan's total sum (with 13 times as many people) — yes, Sweden goes crashing down to this brilliantly executed judo throw. Accumulated 35-year sums per country and per square metre, in dollars:

Table 37: The Ultimate Truth: Sweden is Only 12% as Good

Public fixed investments per square metre, in dollars; cumulative sum, 1951-85

1. Japan	3·57
2. Great Britain	2·21
3. Sweden	0·42
4· US	0·11

It is not known to me whether Swedish Finance Minister Straeng during his visit to Tokyo early in 1972 asked his ambassador to Japan, Gunnar Heckscher, (who just happened to be a former chairman of Sweden's Conservative Party) to protest in a formal note against this outrageous statistical crime of robbing Sweden of a world championship title for which the taxpayers have paid so dearly for decades.

(In principle, I believe that the Japanese economist was correct. It is a bit difficult to build public institutions and public libraries among the bears and wolves of Sweden's large forests, but the urban society of the future will be characterized not only by increased poison density per square kilometre but also by increased density of the fruits of public investment: easy and close access to public swimming-pools, etc etc).

Now, Sweden cannot maintain an annual growth rate of 11 per cent in the public investment sector. If we assume that by 1980 this sector's share of GNP has dropped from the current figure of 10.8 per cent to 9.5 per cent, and assume a Swedish total GNP per capita sum of 8,000 dollars in the year 1980, this would mean 760 dollars for Svensson, compared to Suzuki-san's 850 (Kanamori) or 1,040 dollars (Shimomura).

Thus a Japanese victory in annual flow of public investments in about 1977-78, and also an accumulated victory by 1985 — without any need to apply judo or square metre calculations.

The revolution. Japan's economic transformation in the 1970's will be dramatic, regardless of the investment pattern becoming public goods-oriented or undergoing only smaller changes as to GNE ratios. It will be a decade of sufferings and triumphs for the Japanese people whichever road is selected.

FOOTNOTE

Svensson may find some small consolation in the fact that he is doing better in competition with the Americans.

One of the myths of our times is that a 'passive welfare state,' with a high tax burden depriving the citizens of both job satisfaction and ability to take initiatives, etc etc, cannot grow as fast as a nation where private business interests are always given priority, where the 'low-productive' public sector is kept down to a reasonable level.

The Balance State is doing far better than one might suspect.

A comparison of the GNP per capita race between Svensson and Joe Brown, in nominal prices and at the new 1972 exchange rates:

Table 38: A Small Consolation for Sweden: She May Defeat the US

The GNP per capita race: Sweden vs the US; in dollars

	Sweden	US	Index (US = 100)
1950	918	1,870	49·1
1953	1,203	2,310	52·0
1955	1,354	2,430	55·7
1960	1,870	2,830	66·0
1965	2,859	3,580	79·9
1970	4,215	4,740	88·9

Note: Using OECD per capita sums up to 1965, plus revaluation effect.

The Swede is actually trying hard, perhaps not so hard as Avis in the race with Hertz, but at least about 30 per cent harder than Joe Brown. The ratio of fixed investments in GNP: 22-23 per cent for Sweden, 17-18 per cent for the US. This meant a fixed investment figure per capita in 1970 of 930-970 dollars for Svensson, compared to only 805 dollars for Joe Brown.

CHAPTER TEN

The Typhoon

> *'We seek an open world — open to ideas, open to the exchange of goods and people, a world in which no people, great or small, will live in angry isolation.*
> Richard M. Nixon
> Speech of inauguration, January, 1969

Suzuki-san, the average Japanese, is 32 years old, statistically. He was only a few years old when the Second World War ended, and thus he never learnt the military terminology. But in the spring of 1972, his worried eyes meet ever more warlike words in his own daily newspaper, because Japan's press reports in great detail anything that is said in the West about Japan: 'Formerly an economic submarine, now a threatening battleship . . . The Japanese invasion of our markets must be repulsed.' On the editorial pages, the Japanese writers explain that Japan has misbehaved, has been increasing her exports too rapidly, while being much too slow in opening her own market, confessions that could not have been imagined only two years ago. Suzuki-san sighs heavily: what will actually happen to Japan? Now they are angry at us in Europe, too; have we really behaved so brutally that all this criticism is justified? We are importing things, too, aren't we? — coffee, sugar, even furniture, and the TV set is full of imports, Perry Mason, Dean Martin, which-ever button one pushes out of seven channels, but in the country of Perry Mason they only talk of clubbing us over the head.

Just what is Japan's role in the world?

A discussion of this role must deal with Suzuki-san's role in the world, because Suzuki-san is Japan. It is Suzuki-san who is the engine in the growth machinery, it is his diligence and endurance that are behind Japan's global market victories and which will decide to what extent the ambitions for 1980 and 1985 will be realized, and thus it is worth scrutinizing Suzuki-san's role in the world of trade.

Is Suzuki-san a battleship? Are his ambitions too greedy compared to those of, for example, Svensson and Smith? What does he really want, is he so very different?

1. *Protectionism.* It has been melting like a snowball; now there are only islands of protectionism left, as in other countries. Few have written with such fury about Japan's own protective walls as this writer; therefore, it is a pleasure to note that Japan has managed to tear down far more barriers than I could ever have imagined in 1969 (*The Japanese Challenge*).

Import duties on manufactured products are still too high compared to the level of Sweden, but within two years, this hurdle too should be fully comparable to those of the most progressive free-trade nations;

2. *The Man.* Suzuki-san does not know any other language, never expects to be able to afford a trip abroad — though this will happen — and on Sunday, his only day off, he sits hour after hour watching foreign documentaries on his colour-TV. How green and pleasant it is in that country — they even have sidewalks — but if we keep on working and sweating we too should have it better in the future. Therefore, Suzuki-san (and other respondents in a large opinion poll) makes these crosses when facing the question: 'Do you think it a good thing that you were born in Japan?'

It was a good thing	86.8 per cent
It was not good	1.8 per cent
Cannot say either	9.4 per cent
Do not know, no answer	2.0 per cent

He is always dissatisfied with the Government. He is happy when Japan wins gold medals in the Olympic Games, but his state-consciousness, state-identification is very thin compared to his father's. He lives for his family, for his company, and for the future of his children. He plans to buy a car very soon so he can take his family for rides on Sundays. This will mean increased fuel imports, more congestion along the roads. Suzuki-san is exactly like us — just a bit more hard-working, more willing to work overtime, with a greater ability to endure difficult working conditions, and even if his children are humming Western pop melodies, they also spend more hours over their textbooks than children do in the West; even the children are trying harder. Because Suzuki-san and his family are Japanese. There has been a lot of interesting speculation over the past year that Japan's growth machinery must be supplied with new engines, so that the speed may slow down, but this will prove very difficult, because Japan, after all, is Suzuki-san — the man who enjoys working and working very hard.

3. *Growth.* Japan cannot be content with a GNP growth rate or export growth rate equal to that of Western rivals.

4. *Export ambitions.* Suzuki-san's appetite is less lusty than that of the Swede or the West German.

If Japan were to allow herself to be satisfied with a GNP growth equal to that of Sweden, the US, or West Germany, this would mean that Suzuki-san will remain forever at the present level: about 50 per cent of America's per capita level, about 55 per cent of the Swede's or the West German's. This would automatically mean:

(a) that Suzuki-san would stay at the twenty per cent level as to possession of physical national wealth ('the stock');

(b) that Suzuki-san could never catch up in real quality of living, because this quality costs more than in the West: land, for example, the need for sound-proofing, the width of sidewalks, because already back in 1950 the cost of such land was far higher in Japan;

(c) that Suzuki-san and his family will never be able to afford to catch up with the Swede in petrol imports per capita, or with the Swede's own demand that his nation's economy allow sufficiently large service expenditures in the balance of payments account so that his craving for visiting other countries can be satisifed.

In order to make the GNP as a whole grow faster than in the West, the components making up the GNP must also grow faster, for example exports, investments. But imports also must increase — and have been increasing — faster than in the West, because a rapidly growing economy results automatically in more rapid import leaps than in other nations (though Japan's past import pattern has been to a great extent the rule-of-thumb 'raw materials = 70 per cent'). Suzuki-san has been world champion in the pace of increasing both imports and exports.

This is the development in the 1961—70 period:

Table 39: Japan's Average Annual Imports Increase: 2·8 Times Britain's

Merchandise trade; customs statistics; annual increase in per cent

	Japan	US	West Germany	UK	France	Italy	Canada
Exports (fob)	17·1	7·7	about 11	6·7	10·1	13·8	11·1
Imports (cif)	15·9	10·2	10·8	5·7	11·7	12·6	9·6

Note: Thus Japan's global imports in the 1961-70 period rose at a pace 55% faster on average than US global imports.

All these countries, with the exception of the US and Britain, increased their exports considerably more than the world trade growth average of 9.3 per cent per year.

Japan is The Open Society, the kingdom for forecasters. New forecasts of future export growth are published continuously, covering the next 10—15 years, and these export ambitions are immediately published in the press. The outside reaction is always the same: Western businessmen desperately grasp their desks and exclaim: 'That cannot be endured . . . these are the targets of a lunatic . . .' One of the reasons why so many forecasts are written is that Japan has no raw materials, that Japan must secure her flow of raw materials by signing long-term contracts of 10—15 years; not because the Japanese necessarily enjoy signing such long-term deals but because they very often have no choice. The foreign mining company declares: 'No three-year contracts, thank you. We are willing to make these mining equipment investments only if you sign up for fifteen years.' This import must also be paid for, now and in 1987, and thus the need for long-range export targets.

Let us pause for a moment, to consider the 'lunacy' of mankind. Here are four case histories:

1. *Tokyo, spring of 1960:* A twenty-year vision is published by the Economic Planning Agency, thousands of pages long, after a year of work. While Japan's exports in 1958 amounted to only 2.9 billion dollars the 1970 figure is expected to be eight billion and about eleven billion in 1980, but in that year there will still be a trade balance deficit of 'one billion dollars.' The forecasters expected a GNP real growth of about seven per cent in the 1960's, only five per cent in the 1970's.

Smiles in the West. Too ambitious. We know what happened. In 1967 Japan exceeded the target set for 1980. The same proved true, however, for imports: in 1971 her imports were almost twice the figure that had been projected for 1980.

2. *Tokyo, March 1970:* After a year's work (and with working documents ready two months previously), Dr Hisao Kanamori and his JERC associates publish a study, 'Japan and the world,' in which the group forecasts this development in Japan's foreign trade — with the 1980 figure based on the assumption that the yen in that year will be worth about ten per cent more than the 1972 parity (280 vs 308 per dollar).

Table 40: The Road to Annual Imports of 75·5 Billion Dollars

Billions of Dollars

	1960	1970	1980
Japan's exports (fob)	4·1	19·3	92·2
Japan's imports (fob)	3·9	15·7	75·5
Annual exports increase in %		(16·9%)	(16·9%)
Annual imports increase in %		(15·0%)	(17·0%)

Note: The percentage jumps show the results of the previous ten-year average.

Once again, we had better hold on to our desks, and close our eyes to Japan's import sum in 1980.

3. *Stockholm, spring of 1950:* Economist Svensson drops into the office of his chief, The Minister: 'This year, our total exports and other earnings abroad amount to 213 dollars per capita. Eighteen years later, in 1968, the figure will be four times as large, 893 dollars. Our merchandise exports alone will rise from 173 to 700 dollars per capita. May I give these figures to the press?' The Chief: 'You are crazy, we are already ranked fifth in the world in GNP per capita, we must leave something also for other countries!' The Chief to his secretary, later: 'Make a note that we must get rid of that man, he is wasting ministerial time thinking about the future.'

4. *A chancellery in West Germany, spring of 1950:* Economist Schultze to his Chief: 'This year an exports, etc. inflow of 73 dollars, but we shall have increased this figure eight-fold by 1968, to 628 dollars.' The Chief: 'For Heaven's sake, do not tell the press.' To the secretary: 'Make a note, Schultze should get a rise, and book in my diary an appointment with him for eighteen years from now.'

The outcome? The economists were correct in their forecasts, and I personally interpret Dr. Kanamori's 1980 forecast as meaning: 'Let us see if the world will allow us to be almost as ambitious as Svensson and Schultze.'

These are my per capita estimates of annual merchandise exports, using the official parities of 1972 for past years also:

Table 41: Svensson, a Battleship in Pushing Exports

Merchandise exports, per capita, in dollars

	1950	1960	1970	1980	Annual increase in %, 1971-80
1. Svensson of Sweden	173	371	900	?	?
2. Schultze of Germany	50	275	630	?	
3. EEC (six nations)		175	475	1,260	11·0%
4. The Briton		190	375	?	?
5. The American		113	207	447	10·6%
6. Suzuki-san of Japan	10	51	218	710	15·9

Note: A great number of countries are ahead of Suzuki-san and roughly at the Swedish per capita level, for example, Switzerland, Holland, Belgium.

The percentage jumps show the country's annual increase rate, not the per capita increase. Rate of exchange: 1972 parities.

The 1980 sums and percentages have been calculated on the basis of Dr Kanamori's 1972 foreign trade forecasts.

If Svensson, the battleship, were to make his exports grow at an annual rate of about 7%, this would give him a 1980 figure of about 1,800 dollars. Suzuki-san's annual growth rate 1971-80 is exclusive of the 10% revaluation forecast by Dr Kanamori sometime in the 1970s.'

The discussion in 1971 and 1972 of Suzuki-san's surge into foreign markets started to assume the character of a world tribunal: he is in too much of a hurry, we must stop his galloping. But I am afraid that if there should happen to be a World Trade Moral Tribunal, and the wise men of this court were given the assignment of deciding what might be a 'fair' annual exports increase rate for the 1970's, then Svensson would be in deep trouble. The table above shows that his per capita exports are four times as large as Suzuki-san's. And Suzuki-san is only requesting the right to sell in 1980 about 79 per cent of Svensson's 1970 result.

To the World Tribunal:

The evidence against Svensson is overwhelming: in the year of 1970, he exported cars and car parts for 78 dollars compared to 21 dollars for Suzuki-san. He is exporting one car per 80 Swedes compared to a Japanese figure of one export car per 150 Japanese.

SVENSSON: Yes, but Suzuki-san is beating the US market to death!

THE JUDGE: Silence, Svensson; you are overwhelming the poor West German market with Swedish per capita exports of 105 dollars per year. Suzuki-san has restrained his export fury by selling to the richer US market for only 77 dollars in 1971. (A year when the Japanese bought US goods for 58 dollars per capita. That year, the American took 38 dollars out of his pocket to buy Japanese goods.)

SVENSSON: But Suzuki-san has such tremendous surpluses, eight billion dollars in merchandise trade surplus in 1971 — that is 77 dollars for Suzuki-san, probably a new world record.

THE JUDGE: Silence, Svensson; back in 1961 you had a current account surplus of 110 dollars.

SVENSSON: I have a car and a boat, and I have to import every drop of petrol, so I must be allowed to try a bit harder, sell more than others ...

THE JUDGE: Svensson buys four tons of oil per year, Suzuki-san only 1.9 tons, and he, too, wants a pleasure boat; his country's possession of pleasure boats is one thousandth of America's, and now Suzuki-san says he would like to shrink this gap to one hundredth. That sounds like a fair argument.

SVENSSON: Yes, but Suzuki-san is hurrying along too fast. In Dr Kanamori's forecast of March, 1972, it is disclosed that Japan intends to keep her annual export increase rate at a speed level 1.59 times faster than the world trade increase of 10.6 per cent, measured in dollars, not in volume. This is too much!

THE JUDGE: Svensson, the burden of evidence against you is too strong. In 1970 you raised you exports 19 per cent, and in 1971 — a year when world trade grew only five per cent — you had a brutal increase of 9 per cent, meaning your pressure on the world was 1.8 times as large.

SVENSSON: Your Honour, you do not understand the problematique. We have had it rather easy here in Europe, very friendly and cosy, and suddenly up pops Suzuki-san, after first knocking out the American market. He is a threat to the future of our children!

THE JUDGE: According to statistics, there is still a little life left in the American market. The 1971 import flood from Japan amounted to eight billion dollars, that is 0.7 per cent of America's GNP of 1,047 billion dollars. Even West Europe may survive: Japanese exports in the fiscal year that ended March 31, 1972, of 3.9 billion dollars, if spread among 389 million West Europeans, come to just 10 dollars per person.

(Svensson is sweating profusely, receives permission to get assistance from Schultze from Bonn and Pierre from Paris.)

PIERRE: Imports from Japan are climbing at an unbearably fast rate. As recently as in 1961, our per capita imports from Japan amounted to 38 cents, but had by 1970 exploded to an annual level of 3 dollars and 76 cents. And no

Japanese speaks French. I support Monsieur Svensson's view that Suzuki-san does not conduct 'orderly marketing,' with calm and peaceful marketing advances.

THE JUDGE: In the month of March, 1972, Japan's imports from France increased by 43.9 per cent over the same month of the previous year — is this a sign of orderly French marketing? In front of me I have a UPI telegram dated London, January 13, 1972: In it the Renault manager announces that this year Renault plans to increase its sales in Britain 'by 50 per cent, from 40,000 to 60,000 cars per year.' Is this calm marketing?

PIERRE, SVENSSON and SCHULTZE, in chorus: Yes, but *we* are after all members of the same club, *we* grew up together, and though we do over-sell a bit some years, things even out over a longer period. Suzuki-san's different; he never tells any funny stories when he comes visiting, he just works and works. That cannot be fair? He has now succeeded in conquering, yes, conquering, *two* per cent of the European automobile market, and that was *our* market; we were in complete agreement on the prices we should charge — and then, Suzuki-san rushes into our own back yard, *pushing down* the price level! Your Honour, this is outrageous, justice must be done.

THE JUDGE: When you Europeans sell the tail-end of your production in, for example, Latin America and in Africa, you charge prices to cover only the actual run-on costs, prices below what you charge in Europe. Now Suzuki-san has started to sell his tail-ends in Europe, applying your third-market rules in your own yard. This may be a departure from European gentlemen's agreements. Let us hear Witness Suzuki.

SUZUKI-SAN: Yes, I am guilty; in past years I was a real villain, I locked up my own cashbox, but now everybody is welcome to compete in our markets. I deeply apologize that Europe's consumers have had to pay such low prices for our products. I now promise to talk with Svensson and Pierre and Schultze, so that we can help arrange a price level that suits the consumers of Europe.

(Silence in the court room, deep sighs of relief.)

SUZUKI-SAN: Give me another chance. Our sales in Western Europe amount to 0.50715 per cent of West Europe's combined GNP of 769 billion dollars, and on behalf of the Japanese people, I apologize for the suffering that this half of one per cent has caused the businessmen of Western Europe.

(Everybody nods solemnly; yes, truly the continent has suffered.)

SUZUKI-SAN: But now I, too, want to build a welfare state, and I hope that you gentlemen won't be too unhappy if Japan should increase her annual exports to West Europe from 2.9 billion dollars in 1970 to 17.7 billion dollars in 1980?

(Whistles, boos.)

SUZUKI-SAN: That is an annual growth rate of only 19.7 per cent, according to Dr Kanamori's programme dated 1972. It sounds like a terribly large sum, but by 1980 Western Europe's combined annual GNP will be 1,924 billion dollars, so our share of the market will be only 0.91995 per cent, not even one per cent. And in 1980, the number of West Europeans will have grown to 426 million, meaning that the purchase bill for each of you will be only 41 dollars. All right?

SVENSSON: This is shocking. It is a *typhoon* that you are planning to unleash on us! Your Honour, show Suzuki-san to the door! Close all the windows before we drown!

SUZUKI-SAN: Yes, but there will also be a typhoon in the other direction. We shall increase our annual purchases from Western Europe from 1.7 to 11.7 billion dollars, an annual growth rate of 21.2 per cent. This means that in 1980, my capita purchases from you will be 101 dollars, compared to a sum of 17 dollars in 1970.

(An impressive silence. But still some uncertainty in the air.)

SVENSSON: You aren't lying, are you?

SUZUKI-SAN: You should recall what happened to our twenty-year import plan of 1960. We smashed that one in seven years.

SVENSSON: Ah, but those were different times.

SUZUKI-SAN: Gentleman, I plan to be in a hurry in the future, too.

(Silence. The European Club in a corner, members whispering to each other: Let us push him a bit more. He has slanted eyes, does not look like us, so how can we trust him one hundred per cent? And that poor Yankee, what will happen to him up to 1980 . . . Maybe he will be completely blotted out?

SVENSSON: Your Honour, we have decided to give Suzuki-san one more chance, but first . . .

THE JUDGE: You have misunderstood this tribunal, Svensson. *You* are also before the court; the question is whether you should be given another chance. Already in 1968 your ship exports per capita amounted to 32 dollars, compared to Japan's 10 dollars. It was in the fiscal year of 1971 that Suzuki-san first managed to catch up with your 1968 figure. You are an economic battleship, Mr Svensson. You are a greedy man, Mr Svensson. Right now you are at a level of 90 per cent of America's GNP per capita, so what are your ambitions? Do you intend to become No 1?

SVENSSON: I do not even know what GNP is — I thought it was a swear word. But Suzuki-san, what *do* you plan to do with the United States?

SCHULTZE: Your Honour, I want to emphasize the importance of that question, because the situation is truly desperate: if all of us in this chamber do not help arrange matters so that the US can once again enjoy annual merchandise trade surpluses of 6—8 billion dollars, this would mean that the US can no longer afford to buy up German and French and other European companies, cannot even afford more wars, a military deficit so to say. If this disaster were to materialize, then Mr Nixon will not be interested in saying, 'The cause of Berlin is our cause' — he may very well pull back all American troops. So, Suzuki-san, what do you plan to do to save Berlin and America's trade surplus? What does Dr Kanamori's 1980 programme say about this problem? Out with it now, Suzuki-san!

SUZUKI-SAN: We are all Berliners, Herr Schultze, and you can rest assured that Dr Kanamori's programme will not fail to meet your expectations in this matter, even if he does not mention Berlin by name. Our imports from the US will be increased from 4.6 billion dollars in 1970 to 21 billion dollars in 1980, an annual growth rate in the 1970's of 16.1 per cent compared to only 12.4 per cent in the 1960's. We, however, are going to lower the pace of our exports to America, from 18.4 per cent in the 1960's to only 16.1 per cent in the 1970's.

SCHULTZE: This means?

SUZUKI-SAN: ... that our exports to the US will climb from an annual level of about six billion in 1970 to 26.7 billion dollars in 1980. Unfortunately, our surplus in trade with the US will increase from 1.4 billion a year to 5.8 billion dollars a year by 1980.

SCHULTZE: Then Berlin would fall? Then West German companies would continue to be owned by West Germans?

SUZUKI-SAN: I am not at liberty to comment on that problem, but Dr Kanamori's forecast shows that the US will once again have a global surplus by 1980. On IMF accounting basis, the US will have 1980 merchandise exports worth 116.6 billion dollars, with imports at 1.2 billion dollars below that figure. In that year the US will also cash annual dividends of about 20 billion dollars from her overseas investments, and America's reserves of gold and foreign currency are at the comfortable level of 23 billion.

PIERRE, red in the face: Le défi, le défi! Le défi Americain! What will be the situation of the multi-national corporations by 1980?

SUZUKI-SAN: Here again we can rightly talk of a typhoon, Monsieur. Dr Kanamori's calculations are very exact on this point. He says the multi-national firms which in 1969 had an annual production overseas worth 230 billion dollars — more than Japan's annual GNP — will triple their production, and reach 690 billion dollars in the year of 1980, roughly 14 per cent of the combined GNP of all advanced, industrialized countries.

PIERRE: But will French companies be given the right to enter Japan and buy you up? We have had some difficulties in doing this in the past.

SUZUKI-SAN: Good news, a typhoon here too, the strongest one so far. The book value of foreign direct investments in Japan will increase 26-fold, advance from 0.4 billion dollars in 1968 to 10.5 billion in 1980.

SVENSSON: Now you sound like a sensible man, Mr. Suzuki. I shall advise the SKF President to pack his bags and book a flight to Tokyo. But let me question you on one point: your companies are entering under-developed countries, very aggressively, and you call this 'aid' — investments, credits and — not to put too fine a point on it — gifts. What will be the figure in 1980? You probably plan to become a gigantic exploiter?

SUZUKI-SAN: I should advise you not to make a per capita comparison, Herr Svensson. But our so-called economic co-operation or assistance programme will hit an annual figure of 12.4 billion dollars in 1980, which according to Dr Kanamori would be equal to a quarter of all contributions from all DAC countries.

SVENSSON: But you will remain a threat to monetary stability in 1980 too. You mentioned a while ago the fob-sums: 92.2 minus 75.5, that is a merchandise trade surplus in one single year of 16.7 billion dollars! Are you crazy? Does Nixon have to crash your stock exchange once more in order to make you come to your senses?

SUZUKI-SAN: We must, however, deduct a great number of deficit items before we arrive at a final figure, a total balance of payments situation, a final figure of zero — no surplus. In 1980 we shall have an annual deficit in our service account of six billion dollars, that is payments to your shipowners, your airlines, giving a transfer account minus of almost three billion dollars; an investment account outflow — long-term capital account — of eight billion dollars. Yes, the money will just fade away, just disappear.

SVENSSON: Now the truth is emerging; you are scheming to buy us! Hedberg was probably correct in 1969 when he predicted that you would put 100 billion dollars on that table.

SUZUKI-SAN: His estimate was probably a bit high. The value of our overseas investments will grow from 2.7 billion dollars in 1969 to 27.3 billion dollars in 1980, but I agree that the annual sum will be rather high in the year of 1980.

THE JUDGE: But your wage level is still low, Suzuki-san, and I should like to express a sharp warning: beware, the whole world is watching.

SUZUKI-SAN: Our wage level has already surpassed that of France, and I should be very grateful if Your Honour could take this opportunity of warning Svensson and Schultze as to their behaviour in 1980. In that year our industrial wages will be higher than in West Germany and Sweden, meaning that we may experience some problems in the form of an import flood from those low-wage countries, and in order to avoid friction in 1980, the Japanese people would be extremely grateful if Svensson and Schultze would start drafting now a programme for their orderly marketing in Japan in the year of 1980. We are a small country and we should not like you to make too large annual leaps in your exports at the end of this decade.

THE JUDGE: Case dismissed. Svensson, a self-confessed battleship, is hereby served a warning. He has been found to be too greedy. In the decade of the 1970's he should be content with an annual export growth rate of half of Suzuki-san's — whatever that rate turns out to be.

SUZUKI-SAN: I thank you, Your Honour. I'm sure Svensson will do all right. We promise to keep a high growth rate in the future, too.

CHAPTER ELEVEN

Hiroshima

'All I want is a fair advantage'
John Connally, 1971
US Finance Minister

*'At this point in our history, the
people are going to keep their
eyes on the ball; they will not —
and in a sense should not — care
how the game is played, but
whether or not it is won'*
David C. Anderson, 1971
Editorial writer, Wall Street
Journal

Japan experienced a 'Pearl Harbor in reverse' in 1971 — was slammed against the wall and forced into a more drastic revaluation than any other country. The picture in the spring of 1972: continued export successes for Japan, and great anxiety among Japan's trade analysts. Is the United States prepared to escalate the trade war against Japan — ultimately, to an 'economic Hiroshima?'

A second question, equally important: is Western Europe, Japan's only alternative, as eager to build a protective ring as was indicated early in 1972 when ever more European countries joined in demanding a slower Japanese advance?

The trend is discouraging. With each new month, the US protectionists put yet more ropes around the Japanese trading neck, and block more and more European products. It is thus worth discussing, at least briefly, two questions: how deep is Japan's penetration of the US market? How much does the flow of Japanese exports to the US mean to the total Japanese economy, particularly to Japan's industry?

In an earlier book, I named Japan as the world-champion

of protectionism. Her place has now been taken over by the
US. Between 1963 and 1971, the US increased the number of
products subject to import restrictions from 7 to 132, while
West Germany reduced hers from 87 to 63, Britain from 112
to 69 and Japan from 132 to 40. This is the stick of
dynamite confronting the Japanese economy: Japan's largest
trading partner is also the world's most diligent builder of
barriers.

The world may be able to tolerate eight million battleships
of the Svensson class, and perhaps sixty million cruisers of
Schultze's type, but 105 million energetic submarines
carrying slant-eyed Suzuki-san? Any common sense in the per
capita estimates of the previous chapter – aimed at
documenting the right of any citizen, regardless of where he
lives, to a certain export and import level – dies a quick
death when they collide with national realities, particularly
America's trading history.

Countries with a huge population are expected to be
passive foreign traders compared to the bee-hive activities of
small-population countries. The United States, too, followed
this pattern in the field of trading products (not capital): the
US has her own raw material riches, and it is daring enough
for businessmen in the state of Ohio to launch an attack on
the market of the state of California, in spite of their
common language. As a result, foreign markets such as those
of Japan or France never enter into the production cost
analysis of America's home-oriented firms. Thus, merchandise exports make up only four per cent of the US GNP (with
1971 figures of 44.1 versus 1,046 billion dollars), compared
to West Germany's figure of about 18 per cent, Japan's 11
and about 20 per cent for a number of West European
countries, including Sweden. This is the game as played:
American businessmen try hard within America's own
borders but always under-achieve, under-perform in
exporting US made products.

The penetration. US annual imports from Japan:

       1970: $5.9 billion = 0.6% of US GNP

       1971: $7.5 billion = 0.7%

US exports to Japan were an even less essential part of the
American economy (the US had a deficit of two billion

dollars in her Japanese trade in 1971); about the weight of a fly, with the exception of food exports (about a billion dollars) and aircraft exports, which showed this 1968-71 development, in millions of dollars: 87–131–249–341.

The broad picture: Japanese penetration has been insignificant, and this may explain why in any normal year the US press publishes a news and fact volume about Egypt ten times as large as that devoted to Japan. The depth of Japan's export knife-thrusts into the US economy is comparable to Sweden's slices into the West German GNP pie — about 0.5 per cent. West Germany's penetration of the Swedish economy is far deeper: about four per cent of Sweden's GNP, meaning that the West German 'pressure' on Sweden's markets is six times as strong as the Japanese pressure in the US. Svensson is not quite the villain he appeared to be in court: he buys for 176 dollars per capita from West Germany, sells for only 106 dollars, giving a merchandise deficit with West Germany of 70 dollars per Swede. The American's deficit in Japanese trade: about 10 dollars.

If a huge nation like West Germany can subject little Sweden to a four-per-cent-of-GNP penetration, then the US giant, the Gulliver, should surely be able to endure pinpricks of 0.7 per cent from a nation whose total economy is only one-fourth of America's? The answer, of course, is no, because we are dealing with the United States — a country awarded by God the eternal right to enjoy merchandise trade surpluses, experienced every year from the 1890's to 1971, a right that no one in the US expects to be affected by two realities: first, that the US has lost its competitive power in production of goods, secondly, that US businessmen do not care to make the efforts needed to boost exports; they are more interested in buying up foreign firms.

The answer is no because of a further factor: the crazy pattern of Japan's exports.

Japan offers for export at least 10,000 items. The pile of product catalogues would probably extend as far as Mars, if put on top of each other, but only 5-9 products make up the bulk of Japan's exports. A GATT study in the summer of 1971 noted that while West Germany has only four product groups which have reached a share of at least 33 per cent of all OECD exports for that particular commodity, Japan has nine such heavyweights: ships, radio and TV sets, tape-recorders, synthetic fibre cloth, motorcycles, toys and sports equipment, cameras, pottery.

In the first ten months of 1971, five products alone made up forty per cent of Japan's total exports to the US — steel, cars, motorcycles, TV sets, synthetic fibre-textiles. It is easy to get purple in the face and say how evil this is, but all the Japanese are doing is to sell what is easiest to sell, where their competitive power is particularly superior. They have now a new awareness: we must diversify the pressure, advance along a wider front with perhaps 100 star products instead of, as now, 5-9 big guns.

America's importance to Japan. About 30 per cent of Japan's total exports go to the US, but the relationship between this export value and Japan's total GNP has not changed very much:

> 1960: 2.6% of Japan's GNP
> 1971: 2.9% of Japan's GNP

This means that from the narrow GNP perspective, Japan's dependence on the US is roughly comparable to Sweden's dependence on West Germany. The value of Sweden's exports to West Germany is 12 per cent of total exports — and 2.5 per cent of Sweden's GNP. But Sweden, nevertheless, allows herself a risk of conflict by defeating West Germany at soccer from time to time.

The American, richest in the world in annual GNP flow, is not even the largest per capita-purchaser of Japanese goods. In 1971, the year when Nixon blitzed Japan's stock exchanges, the American was ranked only fourth as a per capita purchaser. My estimates, based on Japan's fob export values: the buying league is topped by Australia and Norway, each with 57 dollars per year, then the Canadian with 41 dollars, the American 38, the Swiss 34, and, for example, the Swede 16, the West German 11, the Briton 10, the Frenchman 4.

The Chinese could afford to buy for only 80 cents, the Russian for a dollar and a half, the Indian for 40 cents. China's annual total purchases from Japan of 578 million dollars – eight per cent of the US total, or a mere 2.4 per cent of Japan's total exports – indicate that if Japan should be forced to turn away from the US market, then China is no alternative.

When one avoids the trap of looking at GNP ratios in nominal prices, the truth begins to emerge:

- Japan's export dependency is already very substantial; in constant prices, Japan's exports and other overseas earnings have climbed from 11.1 per cent of GNP in 1967 to these fiscal year figures, in per cent:

	constant prices	nominal prices
1970	13.5	11.8
1971	14.8	12.4
1972	14.0	11.0

- This dependency will grow in the future. MITI's 1980 programme anticipates a constant-prices ratio in 1980 of 16.3 per cent (and annual exports, etc, of 72 billion dollars in constant price, 90 billion dollars in nominal price)
- Large sectors of Japan's machinery and manufacturing industries already have export shares of 25-40 per cent:
  Passenger cars: exported units only 8 per cent in 1961, but 22.5 per cent in 1969 – and 5?.1 per cent in 1971, with a slight ratio-drop early in 1972, to about 40 per cent for the first three months;
  TV sets: now 40; *ballbearings* 22 per cent in 1970; *generators:* 36 per cent; *steel:* export value 35 per cent; *cameras, ships:* more than 60 per cent
- For the whole 'machinery' sector: a current dependency of 20-25 per cent, which is less than Sweden's 50 per cent but growing very fast.

This means that Japan's real export dependency is far greater than claimed in the 'ten per cent of the GNP' songs, and thus Japan will have to follow the rules of international trading behaviour. The era of the kick-boxer is over.

The fact that Japan will from now on act with greater caution and responsibility should not allow anybody in the West to believe that Japan will also exert herself less, will not try so hard – on the contrary.

Japan's forecasters agree in general on the potential of Japanese exports in the future:

1. Dr Kanamori's 1972 *export*-fob forecast — of a 1980 figure of 92 billion dollars — means (my estimates) an accumulated fob export sum in the 1970's of *503 billion dollars* compared to 107 billion in the 1960's, a five-fold pressure as measured in nominal prices (and in the case of the 1980 figure slightly inflated by Kanamori's use of a future parity)

2. The same forecast foresees an accumulated *imports*-fob sum in the 1970's of *411 billion dollars* compared to only 89 billion in the 1960's, a 4.6-fold leap

3. Professor Hiroya Ueno in 1971: exports, etc, in 1985 of 176 billion and imports, etc, in 1985 of 155 billion dollars, meaning (my estimate) accumulated fifteen-year exports of 1,151 billion dollars — a *fifteen-fold* pressure compared to the 1953-67 period. And accumulated imports, etc, of about *one trillion dollars:*

Table 42: One Trillion Dollars — in Three Stages

Billions of Dollars

	Exports, etc	Imports, etc
1971-75	154	134
1976-80	324	280
1981-85	673	588

A few years ago there was every reason to start sweating at the sight of tables such as the one above, because at that time the Japanese displayed not an iota of interest in fair play: they were shooting at the world from behind a comfortable wall. Now the situation has changed. Now is the time for Western Europe's businessmen at least to throw into the wastepaper basket all 'trans-ocean' theories, the argument that it is so very difficult to export to distant lands — the hour has come to go in and start *fighting* on the Japanese home-front, the world's most rapidly expanding market.

But efforts are needed in order to achieve results comparable to Japan's export successes in Europe. Japan has at least one thousand experts familiar with the markets of Europe; could there be even one hundred businessmen in

Europe as competent in their knowledge about the Japanese market? An American businessman, Howard Van Zandt, for decades ITT's chief in Japan, claims that if US industrial leaders and salesmen took their hands out of their pockets, there would be an immediate annual increase in exports to Japan of at least half a billion dollars.

A British or Swedish or American businessman who is afraid of competition, who is afraid of any kind of change, should fear Japan and what will happen in the 1970's. But those who believe that changes also contain driving forces with positive values — they should welcome Japan's entry on the stage, both the competition and the huge Japanese market now being opened.

Dr Kanamori believes — and here he is supported by other forecasters, because Japan wants to lessen her dependency on the US and intensify her trade with Europe — that imports from Western Europe should climb at an annual rate of 21 per cent. If Sweden could keep that high a growth rate, it would mean accumulated Swedish exports to Japan in the 1970's of 2.4 billion dollars. A jump in annual values from 71 to 485 million dollars. Volvo, at present selling less than one thousand cars per year in Japan, should sell 20,000 in the year of 1980.

Japan's product exchange pattern is rather strange, to use a mild phrase. Exports of consumer durables (in 1971) of 5.7 billion dollars, imports of 424 million dollars. Ratio: 12-1. Exports of passenger cars for 1.8 billion dollars, imports of 54 million dollars. Ratio: 33-1. Exports of capital goods to industries in other countries for 7.5 billion dollars, imports of 2.3 billion dollars. Ratio: 3-1. Selling steel for 3.5 billion, buying for 112 million dollars. Ratio: 31-1. Selling ships for 1.8 billion, buying for 95 million dollars. Ratio: 19-1. (Customs statistics; exports cif, imports fob).

Are the Japanese really that good? So devastatingly superior? Not at all. Svensson, the battleship, should refrain from trying to sell crude steel to the Japanese, or supertankers or colour-TV sets, but there are virgin territories in field after field, particularly in the consumer goods sector.

The Japanese — the world's fastest learners — have not yet learned, for example, how to make a piece of furniture of an acceptable quality and at a competitive price. In 1980, that market alone will be worth at least eight billion dollars a year. Suzuki-san and his family are as peculiar as we in the West: they want to have possessions and gadgets at home that are different from what the neighbours have, and this even at a comparatively low income level. Visiting rather typical middle-class homes in Japan over the past year has become more and more like visiting a United Nations exhibition: 'This thing here is from West Germany, we found it at a boutique in Shinjuku; here is a piece from Italy; my husband has a tie made in France, and soon we shall buy a chair made in Sweden,' (at a cost three or four times as high as in Sweden).

Suzuki-san as a consumer is not a nationalist when he enters a department store or a food shop — if you believe that he is, then the larger but now silent majority at MITI will chuckle, because that group keeps hoping that the West will not try too hard in the markets of Japan. They have Mr Amaya's new golf manual in their hands — well, well, so this is how we are supposed to think in this New Era — but many of them get nasty headaches as they watch Mrs Suzuki getting a taste for French cheeses and Danish bacon, and running her fingers over German leather jackets or British cloth. But there is no way of arresting the trend. It is just a matter of finding out who has the most energy: Schultze or Smith, Svensson or Pierre.

The shipping lines. One item is often forgotten by European trade analysts as they study their country's fob export statistics, (sums that exclude freight costs, insurance, etc) — they ignore the huge sums that the Europeans have already earned in shipping, for example, Japanese cars to Europe, let alone helping to ship raw materials on the routes between Japan and her sources in Africa, Australia, South America. There may be some kind of Solomon-like justice in the fact that the number of 'invisible' billions for Europe will be so great in the 1970's, some compensation for the success of Suzuki-san's bosses in charging too little for the sweat of their wage-earners. In calendar year 1971, Japan exported exactly 1,429,534 passenger cars, for exactly 1,810,511,000 dollars. A unit price of 1,266 dollars plus 50 cents, answers my electronic calculator, so that there may be some consolation in knowing that Europe's shipowners charge almost 200 dollars for shipping a car, while the Japanese themselves have succeeded in reducing their own shipping costs to 20 dollars per car on the route between Japan and the US.

There will be a virtual rain of money over the shipowners of Hamburg, Gothenburg, London and Athens. Jackie does not have to worry. The flow of diamonds will be large; Mr Onassis will not get any poorer.

A document in my hand, not published previously, shows the way. It consists of a few pages from the Kanamori Group's trillion-dollar forecast.

A country's 'invisible' payments and receipts — in addition to the very visible commodity trade — is normally an accounting of five items: transportation-freight; insurance; travel; income from overseas investments, and 'others,' including transfers of, for example, foreign aid.

Let us first look at the figures showing the total balance of 'invisibles,' in annual sums, at the old conversion rate of 360 yen per dollar:

Table 43: Japan's Invisible Deficit: 94 Billion Dollars

Billions of Dollars

	1961	1965	1970	1975	1980	1985
Payments	1·5	2·6	6·3	13·5	25·0	44·5
Receipts	1·0	1·6	4·2	9·1	17·7	33·6
Result (−)	0·5	1·0	2·1	4·4	7·3	10·9

A few minutes with the calculator shows an accumulated deficit in Japan's invisible trade of 93.5 billion dollars between 1971 and 1985. If you add 16.88 per cent, you get the current parity.

The worst loss item is transportation and freight, mainly payments to foreign shipowners, to a much smaller extent payment for air cargo services:

Table 44: A Table for Jackie and Gothenburg

A Japanese Freight Deficit of $55 Billion
Billions of Dollars

	1961	1965	1970	1975	1980	1985
Payments	0·9	1·2	3·0	6·4	12·0	21·5
Receipts	0·4	0·7	1·7	3·8	7·8	15·0
Result (−)	0·5	0·5	1·3	2·6	4·2	6·5

Thus an accumulated freight deficit of 55 billion dollars between 1971 and 1985. If we limit our vision to this deficit figure alone and try to make a guesstimate of where this money will go — as compensation for over-exports of Japanese goods — some guidelines may be found in Japan's foreign trade freight statistics for the year of 1971. In this year, Japanese ships were able to carry a tonnage of 245 million tons, the foreign-owned shipping lines a bit more, 268 million tons. (Japan's total export cargo tonnage is rather small, about 53 million tons, or about one-ninth of the total import tonnage of 460 million tons, with foreign-owned vessels carrying 52 per cent of the total import tonnage, 42 per cent of Japan's total export tonnage).

Thus, foreign ships carry 268 million tons. This pie was cut in the following way in the year of 1971, in millions of tons, percentages within brackets:

Table 45: Japanese Goods — but in Whose Ships?

1. Liberia	88 (33%)	6. Sweden	6·4 (2·4)
2. Norway	40 (15)	7. West Germany	6·1 (2·3)
3. Britain	20 (7·6)	8. Denmark	6·0 (2·3)
4. Greece	15 (5·9)	Others:	
		USSR	8·3 (3·1)
5. Panama	11 (4·1)	US	0·8 (0·2)

Note: Most of the Soviet tonnage goes only between Japanese and Soviet ports.

The poor American seems to be getting another raw deal, but this is not the case: in New York, they cash billions coming from ships sailing under flags of convenience, the low-tax flags of Panama and Liberia.

If we stick merely to the deficit of 55 billion dollars, Britain's shipowners can look forward to a flow of 4.2 billion dollars, their German and Swedish colleagues to 1.2 billion dollars , and Norway — the world's busiest buyer of Japanese goods, mainly ships though Toyota has also cornered the taxicab market in Oslo — will be flooded with 8.2 billion dollars, a tidy sum for a country of only four million people. The assumption behind my estimates is that a ton of cargo yields equally as much, regardless of the nature of the cargo and the route. The aggressive Svensson-san at least — whose name in this case is probably Brostroem and who in 1971 decided to double what is already Sweden's largest merchant fleet — may safely be expected to put his eggs in the most profitable cargo baskets.

Between 1963 and 1971, Japan's import tonnage grew 3.3 times, her exports tonnage only 2.9 times. In Japan's terrible recession year of 1971, the import tonnage carried into Japan by foreign vessels grew by only 0.9 per cent — with millions of tons of ships laid up all over the world, and with foreign shipowners waking up in tears at least three times a night, and praying to the distant Shinto gods to give Japan supergrowth once again. Japan is the world's largest importer of raw materials, and the future of Japan is also to a very great extent the future of world shipowners.

The type of trade statistics which the world is using today and which is quoted in the daily press is dangerous — most of all to Suzuki-san. One example: In 1970, Svensson had a merchandise trade deficit with Japan of 8 dollars (exports, fob, of 8 dollars, imports, cif, of 16 dollars), just a little bit less than Joe Brown's 'loss' of 10 dollars. But then one looks at Sweden's net total shipping gain of two billion kronor in 1970, which makes 51 dollars per capita, and at least one-fifth, or ten dollars, originates from Swedish ships on the 'to-and-from Japan' routes. One may safely extend this reasoning to apply to New York's income from 'Panama' and 'Liberia' — Japanese money. In reality, when all kinds of transactions with Japan are included, the American has a per capita surplus, but this he will never be willing or able to understand.

It must be very tempting to wish that Japan would fade

away forever when, for example, Japanese exports of stainless steel advance in this aggressive manner and grab these chunks of the Swedish stainless steel market:

1968   0.5% (of a market then worth about $40 million)

1969   1.5%

1970   11.3%

1971   15% (with Japan's share now worth $6 million)

One is also deeply shocked when reading reports from London that Japan's ballbearing exports to Britain have increased 'by 500 per cent since 1967, doubling in 1971 alone.' The heart beats a little bit less nervously when one discovers that after all these aggressive leaps, Japan's share of Britain's ballbearing market value of about 100 million pounds is still only four per cent.

In the spring of 1972, more and more European countries, mainly the EEC nations, started acting in the US manner: calling for, and also getting, 'voluntary' Japanese agreements to limit the export volume for some products (and also bring about Japanese export price cartels). In some cases, these limitations may very well be necessary. In others, however, European consumers might be wise to check the situation from time to time, making sure that the price competition does not become too comfortable.

Before joining forces with the stranglers who sit in the US Congress, West European analysts should consider for at least a few minutes the losses that would come as a result of 'an economic Hiroshima' — an isolated Japan — and also the losses caused by not trying hard enough to sell on the Japanese market.

1. Let us consider as realistic Dr Kanamori's import forecast for the 1970's, an accumulated total of 411 billion dollars. If West Europe should remain content with its current share of the pie, 10.5 per cent in 1971, the accumulated share would be 43 billion dollars, and for West Germany, for example, 12.7 billion dollars (3.1 per cent of Japan's total cif import sum), for Britain 8.6 billion (2.1 per cent).

If so, the European countries should hurry along with

an average increase rate in Japan's imports of 17 per cent per year — but Dr Kanamori and his associates believe in a European pace of 21.2 per cent, compared to 16.1 per cent for the US which is believed to have less competitive power, to be less willing to try hard.

2. If West Europe should keep up the pace of 21 per cent, this would raise its share of Japan's imports to about 15 per cent, and give an accumulated sum for the decade of 57.1 billion dollars — an extra 14 billion dollars, to be pocketed by those nations which make the extra effort.

3. The figures I mention are not impossible; they are in accord with results already achieved and a consequence of the fact that *the Japanese market is now really opening up.*

In the 1960's, West Germany managed to boost her sales to Japan at an annual rate of 17.5 per cent (My estimate, based on Japan's cif import values: in 1960 = 123 million, in 1970 about 617 million dollars and in 1980 — with a pace of 21 per cent — about 4.2 billion dollars. An accumulated sum for West Germany of 3.3 billion dollars in the 1960's, a sum of 20 billion dollars in the 1970's. Thus Schultze has a choice: either to continue the present we-are-doing-all-right efforts that would give 12.7 billion dollars or launch a determined campaign that should give an additional seven billion dollars.

But watch out for Svensson, the battleship.

One example: In the 1960's, the Gadelius Corporation, with 1,000 employees in Japan, succeeded in raising its sales from Sweden to Japan at an annual pace of 17.3 per cent, almost double the world trade growth rate and above the European growth average. Gadelius handle 29 per cent of all Swedish exports to Japan, mainly equipment for Japanese industry, high-technology products.

The Japanese is very much like us. But he is different in one way: he can only function in one kind of environment, the environment of frankness. He puts his future cards on the table, he does not attempt to hide his ambitions — while Western businessmen and ministerial forecasters anxiously keep their cards very close to the chest: no one may look at my ambitions — what would happen if somebody had a sneak preview of my cards?

These are my cards *now*, says the Japanese. This is the hand of cards I plan to hold in 1980. Here are my specialization coefficients, here are my elasticity calculations. I plan to raise, for example, our annual exports of machinery from six billion dollars in 1969 to 57 billion dollars in 1980 — and I believe that you will succeed very well in my market — here are the estimates; I plan to try very hard in your market area, kindly come over and do the same in our market.

Suzuki-san has been a villain, yes. Now he is wearing, well, if not a halo, at least a suit as respectable as those of the progressive free-trade countries in the West.

He is extending a calloused and much too industrious hand, and wants to shake hands. West Europeans, who seldom refrain from boasting of how liberal they are in their trade compared to the Americans, should not reject that hand — shake it, gentlemen, and after that: don't lose a minute in trying to sell as much as possible to Suzuki-san and his wife. They are more eager to buy than you could ever imagine.

The alternative is to help US protectionists build an 'economic Hiroshima' — a wall isolating Suzuki-san from the world, and isolating us from him.

Susuki-san does not deserve that kind of a future — nor do we.

CHAPTER TWELVE

The Revenge

*'There is only one time — the
future'*
Erik Westerberg

At exactly eight o'clock on an October evening in 1973, the Emperor Hirohito will seat himself in his palace in Tokyo, his face in the direction of the Ise Shrine, 483 kilometres away. At that very moment the Sun Goddess, as symbolized by a mirror in a box, will be moved to a new home, a new box. This change of residence takes place every twenty years, and preparations for the latest change — the 60th — began in 1965, with a budget of 13.7 million dollars.

Japan, the world's most future-oriented country, still has deep roots in the past. The United States will not celebrate its 200th birthday until 1977 — the year before the 'eclipse' of the American — while Japan's imperial line is at least 1,600 years old and may, according to the myths, go back as far as 600 BC. The Sun Goddess is not only the highest deity in the Shinto pantheon — the State religion that was supposed to be obliterated in 1945, when the US occupation forces decreed a divorce between the State and Shintoism — it was her grandson, Ninigi, who descended from heaven to the island of Kyushu. His great-grandson, Jimmu, moved to Yamato in Nara Prefecture in 660 BC and nobly founded the Japanese state and the imperial line, 'which has continued unbroken up until the present,' the myths proclaim.

What will be the thoughts and message of the Emperor as he faces the deity of his forefathers, joining from afar in the ritual at the Ise Shrine? Will he be able to report that Japan's future is bright? That the recent years of heavy thunder up in the clouds over Japan are by no means evidence of any permanent 'confrontation' between this nation and the outside world but only a passing phenomenon? That the people will continue to work hard and endure, until all the mountain peaks have been conquered, but only by peaceful means?

Will the Emperor dare report that he himself is worried, that his people are worried? That his people have launched a desperate search for identity, are daily seeking clues as to who they are, what they are, and why they think as they do?

Let us hope that the Sun Goddess will flash back words of encouragement: the very fact that people are worried and are questioning their own values and actions is a sign of health, a sign of self-examination that will make Japan's future even brighter.

Not being an emperor, but only an economic journalist fighting a daily battle with a declining brainpower index, and with my face turned away both from mirrors and from my Japanese publisher, who is sitting on the sofa waiting for this last chapter, I find it impossible to evaluate the dimensions of the thunderclouds over Japan — mainly because more and more of the forces affecting Japan's destiny are located outside the borders of Japan.

Still, here is an attempt to summarize some of the signals in earlier chapters and perhaps add a few more:

A new heart. It was a shock to return again to Japan at the end of 1970 and find a different country: physically, Japan was the same but the discussions were different, the public probing of Japan's own actions and attitudes the most intense in the world. Japan, 'the one-eyed society' of 1969, suddenly opened both eyes, suddenly recognized the rights and interests of other countries. Sometimes these two eyes 'over-reacted' — week after week they were able only to criticize Japan, to see only the dark side of Japanese society. It was a public bloodbath where a number of popularly loved fictions were trampled to death, including the idea that a Japan for ever increasing in economic strength would just as steadily increase her share of the world's affection; the idea that hard work would be applauded in other nations; the idea that Japan's post-war economic transformation had been a success curve affecting a majority of the people — above all, nothing was left of the GNP hysteria, not a spark, though some people who had difficulty understanding the new rules of play tried hard to revive it.

Killing old beliefs is not a pleasant task. When the job is over there is a feeling of emptiness, loneliness, a vacuum. So the Japanese rushed to the bookshops, looking eagerly for new values and new concepts to put into the vacuum but most of all searching desperately for identity: we Japanese, what *are* we? A million people stormed the bookshops to buy copies of a book called 'The Japanese and the Jew,' (by an anonymous author who may turn out to be Japanese) a book pointing out a number of character similarities and differences. Then the Japanese sat on the trains — I'm sorry, stood squeezed like sardines on the trains — and read and read. Weekly magazines flooded foreign correspondents based in Tokyo with article requests: please write us your opinion of the Japanese; we should be very pleased if you would try to be as critical as possible. It was the greatest exhibition of national masochism ever seen in the world, and no one can tell the ultimate outcome. But my preliminary appraisal in May of 1972 is that Japan will emerge stronger and healthier.

Late in the autumn of 1971 one Japanese newspaper wrote:

> At no other time in the post-war period has Japan been made to stand naked in such a difficult position in international society as it is now.
>   . . . Where in international society is there a good place for Japan? Such a bitter anxiety exists among the people.

A nation with people as searching and eager as this to find a constructive role in the world will discover, I believe, a world that will say: 'Welcome back to the fold . . . There will be friction in the future, of course, because of your haste, but some way, somehow, we'll get along, we can co-exist.'

As a journalist I have walked through too many jungles, seen too many illusions die, seen too many political promises broken, seen too many faces and facts shot to pieces. So I take only one lump of sugar in my coffee and my optimism is never very deep. When I use the word 'friction,' I am as aware now as in 1969 that the result may very often turn out to be 'collision.'

Confrontation. I still believe, as I did in 1969, that the interests of Japan and the United States will be in collision with each other — and when I use the legal expression 'in collision with,' this choice of words is deliberate. An English-language journalist, not wanting his newspaper to be sued for libel, uses this expression when reporting that two ships have collided: if he should write that Ship A collided with Ship B, this might indicate that Ship A was the more active party in causing the crash; thus 'Ship A and Ship B were in collision in the Thames yesterday . . .' We do not know who will take the more active part in causing a collision, a clash, betweeen the economic interests of Japan and America, but I personally have a feeling of inevitability, because of two factors: 1. the pride of the United States, a nation more conscious of face than Japan, 2. the utter inability of the Japanese people to refrain from being ambitious, refrain from doing their best; and doing their best means upsetting the vested interests of other countries.

Joe Brown sees his cities collapsing. He may agree, when he has had one whisky too many, that the US has never been a truly affluent nation because if this had been so, then these two indicators would be different: (a) the rate of infant mortality is lower in twelve other industrial countries; (b) men in seventeen other nations live longer than the Americans do; and women live longer in ten other countries. Still, Joe Brown loves his fictions, as all of us do, and therefore, Japan must somehow try to defeat Joe Brown as gently as possible, without hurting Joe's feelings too much. The assignment is almost hopeless: to take away that piece of sugar from Joe Brown's mouth, the sweet taste of GNP per capita supremacy, and at the same time try to make him enjoy losing it. Can it be done?

Over the next fifteen years, Japan will create a trading empire never before seen in world history, will launch blitz operations not seen since the times of the Roman Empire. Japan may prefer to go slower — push the annual export growth rate down to the 15-16 per cent desired by the forecasters instead of the 25 per cent leap witnessed in 1971, and the 20 per cent jump scored in the first quarter of 1972 — but this will probably prove very difficult, because the engines of Japan's super-energy machinery cannot be re-cycled.

America's military defeat in Vietnam will be followed over the next 15 years by a series of economic defeats in the race with Japan: she will be dethroned as richest in the world in annual flow per capita, as the No 1 exporter, as the world's financial centre, with Japan's so-called foreign aid programme being double or triple America's sums, and with Japan gaining bigger and bigger market shares in Asia, Africa, South America, Europe — with US market shares steadily dwindling.

Can the Americans be expected to applaud these defeats? How hysterical will they become?

We do not know.

Suzuki-san is not seeking overseas 'revenge.' He does not want to 'conquer' larger market shares. He will just want to keep on trying as hard as possible, and then it is up to world politicians — and economic journalists — to scan the horizon for proper words to describe what is happening.

Suzuki-san, 32, very eager to buy that new car he saw in the window, does not want to 'defeat' anybody abroad — he just enjoys climbing mountains. Even if there should be no other competing climbers on that mountain, he would still swing his rope and do his best to get to the peak. Why? The answer of all mountaineers: 'because it is there.'

Militarism. A military revenge? 'Thirty years ago, we could not even defend an annual oil supply of three million tons. How could we ever defend three hundred million tons — impossible,' notes Professor Shimomura. He tells the author that though he wants to keep the military budget down to the present level of 0.8 per cent of GNP (a fifth of Sweden's GNP level), he wants to widen the definition of 'defence' and spend a total of 4.8 per cent on 'true defence.' His defence strategy plan: two per cent of GNP to fight pollution and environmental hazards, which would make the people of Japan happier, and so safer in a wider sense; another two per cent of GNP in help for under-developed nations, mainly Asia, because only by building prosperous neighbours can Japan maintain true peace, have a true defence.

The nations where people most often accuse Japan of 'signs of renewed militarism' are the world's most militaristic countries: China, the United States, the Soviet Union. America's defence budget is 29 times Japan's. Joe Brown is spending about 400 dollars a year on his generals, Svensson 150 dollars, which makes him fourth in military spending per capita while Suzuki-san spends only 25 dollars. Japan's new Fourth Defence Plan, originally scheduled to start in 1972, called for a five-year expenditure of 18.8 billion dollars, which would by the end of the Plan lift Suzuki-san's annual defence outlay to 57 dollars per year (38 per cent of Svensson's 1971 level), and *might* give Japan a navy as strong as Sweden's, though I doubt it. Experience has shown that almost any old lady in tennis shoes can walk in and take over a Japanese military installation. When Author Yukio Mishima and his followers invaded a defence barracks in 1970 (with Mishima's head ultimately to roll on the floor, cut off by one of his associates after his ritual suicide), the colonels of the barracks phoned the police for assistance: I say, could you kindly come and help us out? Please come and arrest these invaders!

There is evidence to the contrary — heavily dressed facts in Japan's own press, which has for the past year spotted more and more signs of 'a military-industrial complex.' They would be unable to sleep for months if they were to have a look at Sweden's similar apparatus. As a pacifist, I still sleep at night. More evidence is needed before I can join in with the more hysterical comments in the Japanese newspapers. I am very fond of Japanese journalists, partly because I consider them the world's best analysts whenever they are given the opportunity to analyse and comment freely, partly because they are the greatest pessimists the world has ever seen: give a Japanese journalist one hundred facts, 99 happy and one sad, and he will behave like a true rugby player; grab the sad fact and head for the try-line with it, looking for a touch-down. A few weeks ago, I met a journalist friend at one of the nation's three largest weekly economic magazines. Has your magazine written even one friendly word in the last year about economic growth? My friend thinks hard, tries to recall 52 issues, perhaps 1,000 articles, finally answers: 'No!' It is a triumphant denial, and I applaud the magazine's determination: one cannot make an omelette without breaking the sacred eggs of so-called objectivity; one cannot in a journalistic campaign aimed at persuading the nation to steer into a new course achieve the trick by balancing five A facts against five B facts.

The rope of satisfaction. Japan's newspapers spend more money on public opinion polls than any other country. Suzuki-san's attitudes to anything under the sun are measured constantly; six to eight alternative question cards are put in front of his eyes almost every day. For the past year Japan's press had been denouncing everything in Japanese society, giving the readers a detailed and daily diet of misery, unhappiness, suffering, death — and finally they put a question card under Suzuki-san's nose: 'Do you find life worth living?' A surprisingly large percentage answer that they intend to go on living, and some even answer that they are on the whole satisfied with life on this earth and in Japan. As I am vitally interested in the quality of the mountain climber's rope, his endurance, how much stamina the people of Japan possess, I jump at each new opinion poll and study the answers with a mixture of fascination and horror.

The Mainichi newspaper empire questions people twice a year, in December and April, and keeps repeating the question (as do the other newspapers): 'Are you satisfied with your daily life?' In April 1972, 61 per cent of the respondents expressed satisfaction — a drop from last December's 66 per cent.

'Do you expect better living conditions in the future?' Here 63 per cent answered yes, and no drop was reported, so I venture to assume that the number of people who believe in the future is rather stable. Suzuki-san is being bombarded with sad news, but he refuses to give up.

Another newspaper, the *Tokyo Shimbun*, throws even tougher questions: 'Do you want to escape from Japan, if possible, and live in another country?' In January 1972, these answers were given, in per cent:

Want to live in another country	7.1
Do not want to so much	15.5
Do not want to live in another country	75.1
Do not know; no answer	2.3

So a suicide probe: Do you find life worth living in your present circumstances?

Feel life worth living	62.1
Do not feel it worth living	14.0
Cannot say either	21.0
Do not know; no answer	2.9

Another newspaper, in the Sankei newspaper group, asks questions every second month as to countries most liked and disliked. In a poll of December, 1971, when the respondents were asked to list any three countries that they liked (with the total percentage thus exceeding 100, and rigging the deck in favour of the US, a country that is easy to remember), Switzerland won, with 28.7 per cent followed by the US, 22.9 per cent, Britain 21.5 per cent, France 20.8 per cent, West Germany 11.9, China 9.6, Italy 6.6, Sweden 4.1 (and with the two Koreas ranked 14th and 15th, with 0.5 and 0.3 per cent). The dislike list was topped by the Soviet Union, the US and China, in that order, with 32, 21 and 18 per cent respectively. The newspaper noted that the US was advancing, percentage-wise, on the dislike list — from 10 per cent in April of 1971 to 20.7 per cent in December. 'The younger the person the more likely to reply that he dislikes the United States.' Thus the people of the Pearl Harbor generation are now more likely to like the United States than the nation's youngsters.

After assuring its readers for more than a year that Japan was guilty of 'economic aggression' by pushing her exports too hard, the *Asahi* newspaper posed these questions in January of 1972:

'At present various things are being said about Japan. What do you think of these views? There is a view that Japan has caused a flood of its goods all over the world, oppressing foreign industries. Do you think so?' The answers, in per cent:

Oppressing	33
Do not think so	37
Other answers	4
No answer	26

(It is a bit difficult for me to imagine this question being asked in the country of Battleship Svensson.)

Japan has the world's most advanced quality press. The nation's largest newspapers are also the country's best quality newspapers, completely different from the case in Western countries. Suzuki-san shrugs at the sight of a sensational tabloid; he wants serious news presented seriously, and he gets an avalanche of sad news and is being buried up to his neck in it, but he always emerges, with a rather rueful smile, maybe, but still eager to go on living.

The growth rate. Whom are we to believe? Dr Kanamori? Dr Shimomura? Mr Amaya of MITI? Will Japan really be able to maintain a pace resulting in economic revenge?

'The people of Japan would be very unhappy if the leaders did not make sure that our real growth rate is at least 10 per cent per year,' says Prime Minister Eisaku Sato and looks at me with the kind of sincerity that only Mr Sato can display. As this is Japan, perhaps the only country where a foreign journalist can ask a chief of government a brutal question without being placed on any black list, and as I am a very modest man, ever reluctant to express my own opinions, I tell the Prime Minister, 'In my opinion, the worst mistake committed by you since you came into power seven and a half years ago was that you let the GNP ratio for public investments slide and slide. What do you think?' As this is Japan, Mr Sato does not even wrinkle an eyebrow. He replies: 'You are right, Mr Hedberg. It was a mistake, and I do regret it. I could give you some excuses but I shall not.' As this is Japan, the Prime Minister does not follow up this confession by declaring, for example, that 'as a consequence of this policy mistake, I take political responsibility and am handing in my resignation.' All the leaders of the ruling Liberal-Democratic Party, not only Mr Sato, gladly confessed in 1971 and 1972 that past policies had been wrong, that there must now be a new direction, but there was no attempt to jump off the bandwagon of power. Loyalty to the group is stronger than loyalty to any principle.

As I had treated Mr Sato rather brutally in my book, I had expected the Prime Minister to show a stern face at the beginning of the hour-long interview. He disarms me with hearty laughter and shoots from both hips: 'You'd better give me some of your royalties — I have been doing so much PR for your book!' (Which is true; the politicians of Japan, and other Japanese, yawn in disinterest if told of a book that flatters Japan; if told that it is a highly critical book, they jump for joy, exclaiming 'How interesting!' One day I was having lunch with four Japanese editors whom I had not met previously. When I said that my new book would be rather friendly to Japan, because Japan had changed so much, one of them exclaimed: 'Write a friendly book about Japan, and we'll cut you dead!' Another case story: in 1971, a young French journalist wrote a book in French called, 'Japan — model or monster.' The book was translated into Japanese and the publishers changed the title, dropping that 'model' nonsense, with the final title reading: 'Japan — monster of progress!' It became a best-seller. It is not so easy to imagine a bestseller in a Western country, in Britain, for example, titled 'Britain — monster of inertia,' or an American book titled, 'US — monster of capitalism.' The basic attitude of the Japanese: the writer may be wrong, but there may be some grain of truth, some ideas worth studying — while we in Western countries tend to escort any foreign critic to the door.)

Revenge, Mr Sato, some evil-tongued foreigners (meaning my own thoughts) claim that Japan lost the military war but is now aiming at an economic revenge, by becoming richest in the world. Is this idea completely wrong?

'That is a great mistake' answers Mr Sato.

About a week from now, you will be meeting President Nixon. If Mr Nixon should ask you when Japan intends to be No 1 in GNP per capita, what would your answer be?

The Prime Minister laughs merrily.

'I would answer: "Would you like that? Would you congratulate us, Mr Nixon?" '

But would *you* like this to happen, Mr Sato?

'I don't know whether it is a good idea or not, but I shall now discard the "priority to GNP" idea. "Kutabare GNP," to hell with GNP, that is today's password among Japanese.'

Following this statement, the Prime Minister proceeds to explain the need for a real growth of ten per cent — it's what the people want.

'But, Mr Hedberg, what do you think is the one thing I can be proud of during the seven years I have been Prime Minister?'

(Mr H looks puzzled, it is noted in the official transcript of the meeting.)

'It is the fact that Japan has been at peace, that I have constantly and truly maintained peace as Prime Minister. I think I can be proud of this.' ("Mr H nods strongly," the transcript notes).

Mr Sato recalls that before becoming Prime Minister, he wanted to make up his mind about Japan's major defence problem, (whether to acquire nuclear weapons or not), so he probed the thinking of President Charles de Gaulle of France and Harold Wilson of Great Britain. 'I asked de Gaulle: "Why is France acquiring nuclear arms?" He answered: "I love my country, France, more than anyone else does. And I don't want to put the safety of France in the hands of a President of another country. That is why we possess nuclear weapons." Mr Wilson, whom I met next, said "The trouble with the Conservative Cabinet was its passion for nuclear armament. The Labour Party is not going to do what is beyond its ability. We are going to establish a Government more faithful to NATO." The words of these two statesmen are still clearly etched in my mind.'

What did you decide, who was right?

'I think both of them were right. But when making a choice between these two alternatives, Japan selects Mr Wilson's idea of "a world in harmony," without the possession of nuclear arms. I have believed that this was the political direction for me to take and that this would lead to happiness for Japan. This Japanese policy will never change, not even in the future. Japan will never possess nuclear weapons, and Japan will protect herself by maintaining the US-Japan Security Treaty. This policy has helped bring Japan her present prosperity, and this policy will also help maintain world peace.'

The Prime Minister emphasizes that Japan 'will never let militarism revive. Japan's national policy is not to own nuclear arms, not to produce nuclear arms, and not to allow nuclear arms to be brought into the country' (by the US, for example).

The world has changed very much in the past thirty years, Mr Sato notes. 'This is the age of lunar travel, and exploring Space, Mars, Venus . . . Japan will achieve what history has never experienced before, a country that is economically powerful but not militarily powerful. I hope you will watch the economic race, encourage us, and cheer us on our way up! . . . The world has changed so much, and another attack like Japan's on Pearl Harbor is an impossibility . . . I am now beginning to sound like a buddha and to say what he might say, perhaps because my life is drawing closer to its end.'

At the end of our meeting, (with my book royalties still in my pocket) I tell Mr Sato that Japan has changed very much in the past year, 'and I believe I can now say that Japan has two eyes.'

The Prime Minister: 'Please say two eyes and not two faces!' It was a pleasure meeting Mr Sato, a man whose policies I have always disliked, a pleasure because the BPI of this 71-year-old is impressive; when he draws his sword, he does not have to search for words, he slashes very quickly.

The man who may succeed him, Masayoshi Ohira, is slower, more philosophical, more solid. He is closer to the people; knows better the dissatisfactions of the ordinary citizen.

'At this juncture, we Japanese have made up our minds to change policies — now we shall try to catch up with you in the West in creating a good environment, in building a welfare state!'

But let us assume, Mr Ohira, that you don't win the premiership, that one of your rivals — Takeo Fukuda or Kakuei Tanaka or Takeo Miki — walks off with the prize, what will happen then to the welfare policies you mention? What will happen to your vision of tomorrow's Japan?

'Any one of us four will have to realize this vision. The

energy of the Japanese people will push any Prime Minister, whoever he may be, to do what must be done, create a different Japan. My philosophy, Mr Hedberg, is "to do or not to do" — not whether "to be or not to be" the next Prime Minister.'

The Nixon Doctrine; perhaps an American pullout from Asia; who would move into the vacuum — Japan?

'Never! We have neither the power nor the desire to replace the US if any vacuum should develop. Look at Asia: chaotic conditions, with little prospect of change. Asia has never enjoyed blue skies or freedom or peace. Asia has been chaotic in the past, and I am afraid that it will be so also in the future, but it is up to the Asian countries themselves to maintain their own peace.

'How long will Asia remain chaotic? Only the Gods know but probably for a long, long period. Japan must pursue a peace-loving policy; we should be able to help Asian countries in economic planning, for example, but we absolutely do not want to play a dominant role in Asia. We have suffered tremendously in the past from our involvement in Asian affairs. Now it is our duty to give, not to take. We must give useful service, but we must expect no gain from our services. No Asian nation will ever be made dependent on Japan for peace and security. It is our duty to serve Asia, to co-exist.'

1980. Will you defeat the US in GNP per capita by 1980?

Mr Ohira does not swallow the bait. Though he is aware that Professor Shimomura makes this prediction, 'and Dr Shimomura is my sensei,' he himself finds it difficult to express a definite opinion about Japan's growth rate in the 1970's. 'The rise or fall of Japan's economy depends on Japan's own technological development in the future.'

Nuclear arms? 'Never.'

Trading policies? 'Japan must not be an egoistic power in the world. We must behave like a true international insider, not like an international outsider.'

The enormous public investments in the 1970's suggested by Professor Shimomura? 'If you are still in Japan in ten years' time — you'll be surprised!'

From two politicians, over to two economists, both of

them co-authors of the 'Kutabare GNP' (To Hell with GNP) articles, and both of them welfare economists; both of them playing leading roles in shaping Japanese economic opinion. What will be the growth rate?

Professor Naomi Maruo, 38: 'I believe it is possible and desirable to maintain over the five-year period of 1973-77 an annual real growth rate of nine per cent, provided, of course, that the Government increases its expenditure in general by 20 per cent a year, and welfare expenditure by 25 per cent a year.'

Isami Miyazaki, 48, councillor of the Economic Planning Agency, the chief architect of four annual economic white papers: 'A growth of seven per cent in 1972. For the next five-six years a rate of 9-10 per cent. Technology will not prove a ceiling in this period. We have caught up with the West technologically in some sectors, but further improvements can be made: agriculture, the distribution sector, spreading modern technology through medium-scale and small-sized industry. Even among the top firms there is room for improvement. But first of all, we must change the industrial structure, save the environment, switch the allocation of efforts to our domestic market; there is no longer any need to help our exporters. GNE structure? Private business fixed investment will see its share lowered to 15 per cent of GNP but this will still give us a real annual growth rate of ten per cent. We must create demand — and as for creating demand, we have been successful in the past — through fiscal measures, and do this in order to reach three objectives: first, to achieve a growth rate of ten per cent; secondly, to avoid over-expansion abroad; thirdly, to avoid a new revaluation.'

Why is a growth rate of, for example, five per cent impossible?

'Because that low rate would mean five things: waste of resources; disguised unemployment; excess capacity; low welfare and spreading social discontent.'

Thus even the 'To-Hell-With-GNP' thinkers believe in a real growth rate of 9-10 per cent up to 1977-78 — a period long enough to see Japan triumph in her hot pursuit of the United States up the GNP per capita mountain.

The forecasts of Mr Miyazaki and Professor Maruo, made in conversations with the author in April 1972, speak of no desire for revenge against anybody — they only echo their ambitions for a different and better Japan, for a nation where people enjoy true welfare.

May their dreams come true.

And may the world understand the true meaning of Japan's challenging boxing glove; no desire for vengeance, just a desire to live up to the fatherly advice of 1877, 'Boys, be ambitious' — one more step up the mountain, one more, here it is slippery but let us try one more step, one more; now the peak is near, very near; soon, soon, we shall have to find another mountain.

Epilogue

*'Perhaps things are not
so utterly hopeless.'*
J.K. Galbraith
The Affluent Society

It is May 1972, and I am once again sitting facing the typewriter, though I had not planned to do so. I felt that I could safely leave Suzuki-san where he was last seen, swinging his rope up the ever more demanding mountain. But something happened a few minutes ago, and I believe that I should add a few words about this event — a piece of paper that flew in through my window.

This window is located on the eighth floor of a building in the heart of Ohtemachi, Japan's financial centre, the blocks where bank and company strategists sit determined to keep up the furious pace of charge in the nation and this city, where I first arrived in 1953. Yes, both Japan and I have changed a lot in two decades: here I found my wife, here I matured, here I saw a poor people and a poor nation defeat poverty at a more rapid pace than anything ever achieved in world economic history. And here I met a people who will never find happiness. As I push aside that strange-looking piece of paper that flew in through the window, I suddenly remember the word 'happiness' and my memory is jogged. There they are: another three reminders of what should have been included in earlier chapters — 'happiness' and 'ocean — 108!' and 'social transfers up to Year 2005.' Yes, now I remember: I had been supposed to emphasize the fact that in the 1970's, Japan plans to spend 108 billion dollars on her ocean development programme, a hunt for riches on the ocean floor, an expenditure programme adopted in the spring of 1971. As for the Economic Planning Agency's recent attempt to estimate Japan's social transfers up to Year 2005, I think that can wait until the next book, if there is one. Happiness, however, might be worth a few lines, because happy peals of laughter are ringing in the street below, from young Japanese girls with swinging hips and a continuing willingness to obey the commands of men.

The curse of the Japanese is his belief that there is somewhere a Mountain of Happiness. While en route to that peak, he is unable to experience true satisfaction, true content. He is marked by constant dissatisfaction, but contrary to what is the case in the West, the Japanese variety may be described as 'creative dissatisfaction, creative unhappiness.' He will never be completely satisfied with the results of his own work; it is always possible, he thinks to try a bit harder, do even better. Today things are not so good, tomorrow things will be better. And tomorrow very often means fifteen years ahead. Suzuki-san has always been told to look ahead: in 1868 they told him, 'Think of 1888, build a strong Japan,' and when that date came, 'Think of 1910, build a strong Japan,' and so on and on. Thus Japan's soul is change, impermanency. Thus Japan suffers less from 'future shock' than any other people on earth. They have always lived in the future. They have always been willing to accept technological change, because without this willingness Japan would have been eaten up by the Western colonial powers. When Alvin Toffler's book with that title — putting forward the theory that too quick a rate of change causes future shocks — was published in Japan in 1971, it sold very well, because the Japanese are great readers. Toffler himself came visiting and travelled up and down the length of Japan, eagerly asking all the Japanese he met: How do you feel, does it hurt very much? 'Oh, yes,' answered the people, 'your theory is so interesting!' The people of Japan know more of 1985 and the roles they will play in that world than we in the West. As of 1972, the Japanese have decided to build a different kind of future from the one their rulers had envisaged only a few years ago, because the Japanese know that there are different futures, different roads, open to them, and now they think they are steering into a better road.

Happiness cannot be measured by an index, regardless of how hard we try. This reality of impossibility often becomes a comfortable excuse for not trying at all to evaluate the general *trend* of happiness and satisfaction in a country. Thus, is Japan more happy now than in the past?

As a new decade began, the 1970's, a new type of foreign analyst started arriving in Japan, visitors who knew nothing of yesterday's poverty, who hastened to their typewriters: 'Japan is a nightmare society. Japan's economic progress has been a complete failure. Judging from opinion polls, the Japanese people are the most unhappy, most maltreated people on this earth. People say that the Japan of 1950, before the Miracle, was much better — there were blue skies!'

I cannot agree with this verdict. The Japan of 1950 was certainly one hell of a nice country — for a small, small minority. With a national income per capita of 113 dollars per year, roughly at the level of India, Japan 1950 was a very nice country for 0.01 per cent of the people, a total of perhaps 80,000 persons, half of them foreigners, colonels, businessmen. The Japan of 1960 was perhaps a good country for 10 per cent of the people, and the Japan of May, 1972, may be good for perhaps 50 per cent of the people.

Mentally, we can return to the past and enjoy dreams of the good old days that were actually the bad old days.

Physically, we cannot return to the Japan of 1950, which was a desperately poor society; physically there is only one road open to us: *the future.*

To me, the Japan of 1991 — 19 years ahead — looks much more beautiful and romantic than when I look back 19 years, to 1953. Neither Suzuki-san, today's average Japanese, now 32 years old, nor this writer will look very romantic in 1991, but I believe that Japan 1991 will be a far better society than it is now, or ever has been.

The reason for my optimism is not the euphoric ramblings of the technocrats, that technology itself can do any job even if mankind remains passive. I base my optimism on what looks to me like the emergence of a new Japanese heart — new thought patterns, new value concepts, new and more solid dreams, far less hysteria in the pursuit of growth. The romantic glow that surrounded Japan's view of the future in the past decades has faded away, probably forever. Left are the realities of what the course toward the future means: sweat, hard work, triumphs, sufferings, and great risks — risks both outside and inside Japan.

Spring is waiting; because this has been a lost spring, lost in trying to sketch the mountain-climbing of a nation. But left on my desk is that piece of paper, carried by the wind into my room. It is a paper of strange quality. The writing is fully visible though it has an 'old' feeling. At the top there is one line reading 'Memory Notes,' and in the margin somebody has attached a computer tape, not punched but of a more advanced type, with words where I can read most letters: 'mistake . . . mistake . . . time   machine   in   wrong orbit . . . break . . .'

Could it be that somebody is playing a joke on me? No, the Japanese are much too busy working, much too busy hurrying into the future to play jokes in the middle of the day; the end of mankind is not supposed to be discussed during office hours, and thus it might be safe to assume that there is some sense, some meaning in the text that accompanied the 'break' order:

'When the Environment Crime Trials began in Tokyo in 1992, one of the most difficult issues — as was also the case in the Nurenberg Trials half a century earlier — was how far back the burden of guilt should be probed, as well as the individual's responsibility within Japanese companies, organizations, bureaucracy, all those groups dominated by collective thinking, group thinking, the established tradition of obeying a group decision.'

Excerpts from the text that followed, pieced together with great effort. The prosecuting lawyers were not in complete agreement as to the timing of the crimes:

- Had the crimes against the environment already begun in Japan in 1950, the year when Japan overtook the US in GNP per area, though the Japanese at that time produced only 1/14th of America's per capita output?
- Or did the crimes begin in 1972, when Japan had reached the half-as-good level of the US per capita output?
- Or did the burden of responsibility begin first in the last

quarter of 1978, when — as the newspapers of that day phrased it, 'Suzuki-san climbed past Joe Brown,' and when Japan was subjecting her area to an economic pressure 24 times as great as in the US?

- Or in 1985, when Japan overtook the US in accumulated affluence but the nation's leaders kept saying: there are other mountains to be conquered?

'One of the prosecutors expressed his belief that the guilt could be traced as far back as 1877, when an American school teacher made a challenging statement to the school generation of that day.'

The text also made a passing reference to the leadership of 1985: 'A conservative party, known as The Party of Let Us Save The Last Flower, in power through Japan's entire post-war history, and opposed by other parties which had also changed names, Let Us Save The Last Bird Party, etc.'

Apparently there were also lawyers for the defence, arguing that 'it should be kept in mind that as of 1972, Japan's per area production was still below that of countries such as Switzerland and West Germany — and no authoritative voices arguing for zero growth were heard in those countries either. Thus, the ruling establishment of Japan had no access to any generally accepted international norms in trying to evaluate either Japan's potential to survive, or Japan's optimal economic power potential.'

The text makes no reference to 'we Japanese,' mentioning only 'that country', or 'the people of that country.' It is not revealed how the trial ended, or when it ended, or the number of survivors or number of accused. The notes do not indicate whether any similar trials had been held before in any other country. It is also impossible to guess whether the Tokyo Environment Crime Trials were held under the auspices of the United Nations, or whether they were held at the initiative of the Japanese — or even whether there were any Japanese left who could take any initiatives. 'In winning, we almost died,' one sentence reads in the margin, but it is not clear whether the writer of that sentence was a Japanese or a Westerner, speaking on behalf of the Western world. The fact that at least one lawyer wanted to prosecute Teacher William C Clark, dead for almost a century, indicates that many — or most, or perhaps all — of those officially charged with environment crimes had already died; that it was only a matter of writing a historical parenthesis about a nation and a people which did not realize, until it was too late, that there must be a limit to the ambitions of man and nations.

Spring, spring — the season of hopes!

As I tear the message from the alleged 'time machine' into tiny, tiny pieces, and drop the pieces out of the window, a return gift to the sender, whoever he or it may be, of whatever era, I recall an earlier collision with a misplaced time machine.

I was sitting on a tree stump in the middle of the jungle in Laos. Beside me sat a Laotian corporal, a small man with a big, big American carbine. We were tired, exhausted; the whole unit had been marching for hours against enemy troops which were too clever to show themselves. This was in 1960, my first visit to Laos since an earlier war, in 1954, and I was eager to find out whether the role of the Laotians in the world had changed in any way, so I began a conversation with the corporal. Three years had passed since the first Sputnik had been launched into an orbit around the earth. Had he heard about that? No. Had he ever heard about Europe? No. But perhaps about the Soviet Union? 'Yes, that is where the Communists live.' What is a Communist? 'People who only want to fight.' I started talking about the Sputnik adventure. The corporal began to look more and more angry. 'Why do you make up such foolish stories? The earth is flat!'

I tried to explain that the earth really was round, or rather expressed myself a little more cautiously, because the corporal's carbine was big: my teachers had told me that the earth was round, and though sceptical for many years, I had finally come to share this belief. 'Then you were not so smart,' said the corporal.

It would be nice if all of us could sit on jungle tree stumps more often and be told the truth. Because truth is often a coin with two sides: it all depends on *where* you flip the coin. The same may prove to be true of our future: flip, you win; flip, you lose. Flip, we become prosecutors; flip, we become a historical parenthesis.

Appendix

Statistical Tables

Table 1. Japan has Already Defeated the United States

	year	Totals, billions of $ JAPAN	US	PER CAPITA in $ JAPAN	US
...in manufacturing industry investments per capita	1965	6.2	23.4	63	120
	1968	14.6	-	143	-
	1970	20.8	31.9	201	155
(Source: the author)					
...in gross fixed investments per capita when measured in constant 1965 prices (and excluding from the US figure US public investments, which amount to only 12% of all US fixed investments)	1952	5.9	57.2	69	363
	1960	16.9	68.9	180	381
	1965	31.7	90.1	323	463
	1967	41.9	93.5	418	470
	1968	51.1	98.8	501	491
	1970	68.6	99.8	662	486
(Source: the author)	real growth 61-70	15.2%	3.9%	14.1%	2.6%

...and in production of 9 out of 12 major products. (Industrial production volume per capita in 1970. (US = 100)

(Source: Japan's Economic Planning Agency)

	US	JAPAN	UK	FRANCE	W GERMANY	ITALY
Aluminium	100	49	21	44	46	13
Cement	100	163	90	169	191	184
Crude steel	100	155	88	81	132	56
Electric power	100	44	55	34	52	28
Newsprint	100	125	93	59	47	34
Passenger cars*	100	96	92	152	188	101
Plastics	100	127	62	67	190	81
Ships (1968)	100	3869	755	451	1073	448
Synthetic fibres	100	249	114	69	79	31
Synthetic rubber	100	62	45	57	50	28
Trucks, buses	100	249	99	70	64	31
TV sets (1968)	100	181	72	59	87	48
Number of items where country is outproducing the US		nine	two	three	five	three

Note: Table ignores US production strength in aircraft, bombs, pills, computers but also ignores strong Japanese sectors such as tape recorders, sewing machines, refrigerators, cameras, etc.

*Japan outdistanced the US also in passenger cars per capita in 1971.

Table 2. A Fine Revenge: The Japanese Will Defeat All Europeans in Hourly Pay

INDEX (Japan 100) 1960	1970	1980	(hourly wages in manufacturing industry)	A — Expressed in Dollars 1970	1980	B — Annual Change in % 61-70	71-80	Local Currency 1970	1980
753	322	121	United States	3.38	6.05	3.9	6.0	3.38	6.05
553	264	117	Canada	2.77	5.55-5.94	5.1	7.2	2.99	6.0
100	100	100	Japan	1.05	3.88-4.99	12.8	14.0	377	1398
373	210	97	Sweden	2.20	4.46-4.82	7.0	7.3	11.40	23.06
207	150	88	West Germany	1.58	3.80-4.38	8.1	9.2	5.77	13.9
253	115	48	Great Britain	1.21	2.32-2.41	6.4	6.7	121.1	231.7
140	78	32	France	0.82	1.77-1.91	8.1	8.0	4.55	9.82
123	81	43	Italy	0.85	2.05-2.17	8.6	8.5	531	1280
273	195	110	Denmark	2.05	5.09-5.51	10.3	9.5	15.4	38.2
247	138	62	Switzerland	1.45	2.66-3.07	7.1	6.2	6.36	11.61
147	110	65	Austria	1.15	2.86-3.26	10.3	9.5	30.0	74.4
	15	7	South Korea	0.16	0.37-	19.1	9.0	50	118
30	19	8	Taiwan	0.20	0.39-	9.5	6.8	8.14	15.72
40	13	4	India	0.14	0.21-	7.2	3.8	1.08	1.57

Note: In column A the 1970 figures are converted at the rate valid in May 1971; the second of the two 1980 figures anticipates a second revaluation in Japan and other countries. The first of the two 1980 figures: at the rate valid in May, 1971. Wage index: at 1980 rates.

(Source: Dr Hisao Kanamori and Japan Economic Research Center. Document of March, 1972: "Sakai no nakano Nihon Keizai, 1980 nen" = Japanese Economy in the World — 1980")

Table 3. But Japan Will Stay Ahead in the Productivity Race

1963 = 100	Wage Index (Nominal) 1961	1969	1980	Labour Productivity Index 1961	1969	1980	And Thus: Wage Productivity Index (= cost increase) 1961	1969	1980	annual growth in % 1970-80
Japan	82	204	853	92	199	679	89	103	125	1.8
US	94	130	246	92	117	153	102	111	161	3.4
West Germany	84	153	403	95	144	279	88	106	144	3.0
Great Britain	92	151	308	94	126	184	98	120	167	3.1

(Source: Dr Hisao Kanamori and Japan Economic Research Center. Document of March, 1972: "Sakai no nakano Nihon Keizai, 1980 nen" = Japanese Economy in the World — 1980")

Table 4. Japan Has Been Achieving Her Feats of Revenge
by the Most Hectic Investment Drive Ever Seen

Exchange rate: 320; add 3.9% for 1972 parity	"storm"		"lull"				"storm"					Accumulation		Structure in %
	1960	1961	1962	1963	1964	1965	1966	1967	1968	1969	1970	60-70	60-68	60-68
Gross domestic fixed asset formation	15.78	20.9	22.7	25.9	30.0	31.0	37.5	46.4	55.8	69.5	81.1	436	285	(100)
Housing	2.2	2.8	3.3	4.2	5.2	6.3	7.3	9.3	11.2	13.6	16.8	82	51.9	18.2
Other construction	6.3	8.7	9.3	10.4	11.7	11.6	14.7	17.6	20.8	-	-	-	111.2	39.0
Machinery, Equipment	6.0	7.9	8.5	9.9	11.5	11.5	13.7	16.7	20.2	bcd 55.9	bcd 64.3	bcd 354	105.9	37.2
Others	1.2	1.5	1.6	1.4	1.6	1.6	1.9	2.8	3.6	-	-	-	17.2	6.0
Agriculture, forestry, farming	0.9	1.2	1.2	1.4	1.4	1.7	2.0	2.4	3.3				15.6	5.5
Construction	0.5	0.8	0.9	1.0	1.0	1.2	1.6	2.2	2.5				11.6	4.1
Dwellings	2.2	2.8	3.4	4.1	5.0	6.3	7.2	9.1	10.8				50.9	17.9
Electricity, gas, water	1.4	1.6	1.7	1.8	1.7	2.1	2.4	2.3	2.8				17.8	6.2
Manufacturing Industry	5.2	6.9	5.9	6.5	7.3	6.0	7.2	11.1	14.1	17.5	20.2	107.8	70.2	24.6
Mining, quarrying	0.2	0.4	0.3	0.3	0.4	0.4	0.5	0.5	0.7				3.7	1.3
Transport, communication	1.7	2.3	2.6	3.1	3.4	4.0	4.6	5.2	6.1				32.9	11.5
Others	3.6	4.9	6.7	7.7	9.8	9.3	12.1	13.6	15.7				83.4	29.3
PUBLIC SECTOR														
Central government	0.5	0.6	0.9	1.0	1.2	1.3	1.4	1.5	1.7				10.1	3.5%
Other public bodies including transfers from central government	1.9	2.4	3.0	3.3	3.8	4.2	5.0	5.6	6.8	abc 15.8	abc 18.8		35.9	12.6%
Government corporations	1.5	2.1	2.7	3.2	3.2	3.9	4.6	5.3	5.8				32.1	11.3%

Note: Fiscal years, billions of $, nominal prices; annual results.

Manufacturing industry investment in 1969 and 1970: author's estimates.

Table 5. Japan's Investment Drive Gave These Rich Yields in Competitive Power
Average annual change in per cent (%)

	1955-1961	1962-1965	1966-1969	1966	1967	1968	1969	(1970, preliminary; author's estimate)
PRODUCTIVITY								
Manufacturing industry	8.8	5.5	14.7	13.0	16.5	14.3	15.0	13.9
Textiles	5.8	5.1	9.7	9.6	11.3	7.7	10.3	
Chemicals	10.4	9.9	16.3	15.0	18.9	15.1	16.1	
Iron and steel	9.0	9.4	18.6	20.1	23.0	10.9	20.6	
Machinery and transport equipment	11.7	8.4	19.3	16.0	22.8	20.2	18.4	
WAGES								
All manufacturing industry	8.0	11.8	14.4	12.2	12.6	15.6	17.3	15.7
Textiles	8.8	13.5	12.9	10.0	11.2	15.0	15.3	
Chemicals	7.2	10.2	13.6	11.3	12.6	13.4	17.1	
Iron and steel	7.5	10.2	15.0	12.2	16.8	13.8	17.1	
Machinery and transport equipment	6.6	11.3	15.0	14.2	12.7	16.2	17.1	
UNIT LABOUR COSTS								
All manufacturing	-0.7	6.0	-0.3	-0.7	-3.3	1.1	2.0	1.6
Textiles	2.8	8.0	4.8	0.4	-0.1	6.8	4.5	
Chemicals	-2.9	0.3	-2.3	-3.2	-5.3	-1.5	0.9	
Iron and steel	-1.4	0.7	-3.0	6.6	-5.0	2.6	-2.9	
Machinery and transport equipment	-4.6	2.7	-3.6	-1.6	-8.2	-3.3	-1.1	

(Source: Mainly GATT study of July, 1971, "Japan's economic expansion and foreign trade")

Table 5B. America's Competitive Power Withers Away at This Pace
Author's estimates based on index figures of Bank of Japan

	MANUFACTURING INDUSTRY, annual change in %						
US productivity	4.7	2.1	1.6	0.2	4.6	2.1	1.1
US wages	3.0	4.1	4.2	4.0	6.4	6.0	5.3
US unit labour costs	-1.6	3.0	2.6	4.0	1.6	3.7	4.2

	Average annual change in other countries, 1961-69		
	productivity	wages	unit labour costs
West Germany	6.0	8.1	2.0
Canada	4.3	5.1	0.8
France	6.4	8.1	1.6
Italy	3.2	6.4	3.2

Note: In the 1961-70 period, Japanese wages advanced at an annual pace of 12.2% (manufacturing), compared to 4.1% for US productivity growth: 11.1% for Japan, 3.1% for the US unit labour costs: 1.1% annually for Japan, and 1.0% for US, because the US had a good record in the first half of the 1960's.

Table 6. Can This Really Happen?
A Clinical View of the GNP per Capita Race Between Japan and the US

GNE (= GNP in dollars, per capita, nominal prices)	JAPAN						US			
	1960	1965	1970	1975	1980	1985	1970	1975	1980	1985
1 private consumption	290	572	1109	2128	4031	7528	3002	3936	5154	6675
2 public consumption	46	94	179	314	596	1145	922	1209	1583	2050
3 total domestic gross fixed investment	182	331	873	1729	3370	6505	812	1064	1387	1797
(a) public investment	38	93	181	390	822	1740	151	197	259	335
(b) private investment	101	154	450	877	1653	3054	500	654	856	1110
(c) private housing investment	21	59	151	306	612	1175	144	187	244	317
(d) inventory investment (change)	20	25	91	142	282	534	14	19	24	31
4 Overseas net	1	13	28	41	56	92	14	19	24	31
(a) exports, other income from abroad	58	114	-	508	927	1649	-	-	-	-
(b) minus imports, other payments abroad	57	101	-	467	871	1557	-	-	-	-
= Gross National Expenditure per capita	518	1011	2189	4197	8062	15270	4754	6233	8161	10570

TOTAL GNP, billions of $

	1960	1970	1980	1985
WORLD	1449	2970	6586	10077
US	508	990	1961	2776
USSR	205	399	779	1098
West Europe		723		2381
JAPAN	48	222	938	1856

Rate: 320

(Source: Author's per capita estimates based on total GNP figures forecast in Dr Hisao Kanamori's and JERC's document of April, 1971: "The outlook for a trillion dollar economy". Per capita estimates were made at a floating rate of 320 yen per $. To get 308 parity: add 3.9%.
By 1980 there would be a 2-1 lead for Japan in private fixed investment per capita.)

Table 7. Japan's Future Weight in the World
As forecast by Dr Hisao Kanamori in 1972
All figures in billions of dollars

(a) as an economic power

	1960	1970	1980
World GNP	1390	3044	7643
Japan's GNP	43	196	957
(% of world)	3.1%	6.4%	12.5%

(b) as a trading nation

	1960	1970	1980
World trade	128	311	850
Japan's exports	4.1	19.3	92.2
(% of world)	3.2%	6.2%	10.2%

(c) as a major importer

Japan's imports (fob) by regions, from

	1970	1980
West Europe	1.7	11.7
US	4.6	21.0
USSR	0.5	4.6
China	0.2	1.2

(d) with a revolution in Japan's import pattern

Japan's imports by commodity

	1970	1980
Machinery	2.3	16.9
Chemicals	1.0	5.1
Food	2.6	8.4
Textiles	1.0	1.2
Metal ores, scrap	2.7	7.0
Other raw material	3.0	11.3
Mineral fuels	3.9	16.7
Other manufactured products	2.4	22.3

(e) with a great leap in machinery imports

Ratio of machinery in Japan's total imports

1955	5.7
1960	9.7
1965	9.3
1970	12.2
1980	19.0

(f) and in imports of other manufactured products

Per cent of total imports:

1955	1.7
1960	6.5
1970	12.8
1980	25.1

(g) and, hopefully, trade of other countries will advance strongly

	1970	1980	annual change in % 61-70	71-80
World exports fob:			9.3%	10.6%
US	42.6	117	7.6	10.6
EEC	89	251	11.5	11.0
USSR	13	40	13.7	12.0
China	2	5.6	-0.1	10.8
Japan	19.3	92.2	16.9	16.9
World imports				
US	39	115	10.1	11.5
EEC	85	241	11.7	11.0
USSR	11	40	7.0	13.7
China	2.2	5.8	1.4	10.2

(h) but, but, there will be some merchandise trade balance difficulties for some regions

Annual trade balance surplus (IMF formula)

	1970	1980
Japan	3.6	16.8
USA	3.7	1.2
EEC (6 nations)	3.4	10.2
EFTA	-4.1	-10.9
USSR	1.7	-

(i) and Japan's trade strategy will be to aim for those sectors where world trade is growing fastest — double her share of world trade in machinery and equipment — as seen in the table below (all figures in %)

NOTE: the figures in these tables are excerpts from a January, 1972, lecture by Dr Kanamori and from JERC's 99-page "Japan and the world" study of the same month

years	Growth rate of world trade 60-69	70-80	Growth rate of Japanese exports 60-69	70-80	Trade elasticity of Japanese exports 60-69	70-80	Japan's share of world trade 1960	1969	1980
Machinery, equipment	12.1	14.1	23.3	22.4	1.93	1.59	3.4	8.0	17.3
Other manufactures	9.7	11.3	13.4	11.9	1.38	1.05	7.3	9.8	10.4
Chemical goods	11.1	12.8	22.0	18.3	1.98	1.43	2.3	5.3	9.4
Beverages, food	5.8	5.7	8.7	7.6	1.50	1.33	1.2	1.5	1.9
Raw Materials	3.8	6.0	7.4	2.1	1.95	0.35	0.7	1.0	0.7
Mineral fuel	7.8	9.2	12.7	3.4	1.63	0.37	0.1	0.2	0.1
Total	8.8	10.9	16.5	17.3	1.88	1.59	3.2	5.9	10.8

Table 8. The Economy of the Susuki-San Family — The Day When He has a Monthly Surplus of $239

| | 1955 | 1960 | 1965 | 1970 | 1975 | 1980 | 1985 | annual growth rate in % | | | | | |
								56-60	61-65	66-70	71-75	76-80	81-85
Per month: disposable family income (after tax), nominal prices, wage-earner households	76	105	186	324	604	1083	1908	6.7	12.1	11.7	13.3	12.4	12.0
Per month: family living expenditure	71	96	154	267	498	891	1569	6.3	9.9	11.6	13.2	12.3	12.0
Per year and in constant price: family's living expenditure, city households	1312	1588	1944	2660	3690	4934	6705	3.9	4.1	6.4	6.8	6.2	6.0
Food	643	724	776	913	1109	1359	1639	2.4	1.4	3.3	4.0	4.1	3.8
Home	84	135	196	327	509	733	1033	10.0	7.7	10.7	9.3	7.6	7.1
of which furniture, other home assets, including cars	22	57	99	210	354	531	771	20.8	11.7	16.3	11.0	8.4	7.7
Fuel, electricity	57	65	90	129	188	260	357	2.7	6.5	7.6	7.8	6.7	6.5
Clothing	127	181	232	334	480	660	899	7.3	5.1	7.5	7.5	6.5	6.4
Miscellaneous	400	482	649	952	1402	1985	2777	3.7	6.1	7.9	8.0	7.2	6.9
Health, cosmetics	10	33	49	76	121	180	258	25.8	8.5	9.1	10.0	8.1	7.4
Transportation, travel	20	28	49	77	136	211	317	6.8	11.6	9.3	12.1	9.2	8.4
Education	45	56	72	86	128	177	251	4.6	5.1	3.4	8.4	6.7	7.2
Reading matter, leisure	92	108	134	177	246	337	450	3.3	4.6	5.7	6.7	6.5	5.9
Basic expenditure	839	929	1008	1183	1440	1773	2211	2.0	1.7	3.2	4.0	4.2	4.6
Selective expenditure	473	660	936	1477	2249	3224	4495	6.9	7.3	9.6	8.8	7.5	6.9
Social expenditure	118	150	221	317	490	705	1007	4.9	8.0	7.5	9.1	7.5	7.4
Purchase of goods	954	1145	1331	1750	2345	3092	4032	3.7	3.0	5.6	6.0	5.7	5.4
Purchase of services	357	443	613	910	1345	1905	2674	4.4	6.7	8.2	8.1	7.2	7.0
Breakdown in percent:													
Basic expenditure	64.0	58.5	51.8	44.5	39.0	35.5	33.0						
Selective expenditure	36.0	41.5	48.2	55.5	61.0	64.5	67.0						
Social expenditure	9.0	9.5	11.4	11.9	13.3	14.1	15.0						
Purchase of services	27.2	27.9	31.5	34.2	36.5	38.1	39.9						
Food expenditure	49.0	45.6	39.9	34.3	30.1	27.2	24.4						
Miscellaneous expenditure	30.6	30.3	33.4	35.8	38.0	39.7	41.4						

(Source: JERC's trillion-dollar-economy forecast; converted by the author at rate of 320 per $)

Table 9. A 1985 Tax Free Family Income of $25,000

Income	1955	1960	1965	1970	1975	1980	1985	Annual growth rate in %					
								56-60	61-65	66-70	71-75	76-80	81-85
Level where direct income tax begins for family with two children, in dollars, per year	-	906	1469	2719	5938	13031	25438	-	10.1	13.1	16.9	17.0	14.3
Government current expenditure (billions)	2.8	4.4	9.5	18.1	36.1	71.8	143	9.5	16.4	13.8	14.7	14.7	14.7
Government fixed investments	2.1	3.9	9.8	19.8	43.0	98.9	219	12.9	20.2	15.1	16.8	18.1	17.2
Government transfers to individuals	1.1	-	4.5	9.7	20.8	44.7	95.9	(1956-70: 15.6%. 1971-85: 16.5% per year)					
Direct tax income	1.1	1.5	4.2	9.4	21.9	51.3	119.8	6.4	22.4	17.5	18.5	18.5	18.5
Corporate tax	0.8	2.2	3.8	9.3	19.1	38.7	76.5	24.8	11.7	19.5	15.4	15.1	14.6
Indirect tax	2.4	4.5	7.8	17.1	34.7	69.1	135.1	13.5	11.8	17.0	15.2	14.8	14.3
Tax burden in % of GNP	15.4	15.5	15.5	15.9	16.5	17.2							
Tax burden index	92.5	-	101	100	103	107.5	113						
Public expenditure:													
Defence	0.3	-	1.0	1.9	4.8	9.7	19.2			13.7	19.9	15.2	14.6
(share of GNP in %)	(1.1)	-	(1.0)	(0.8)	(1.0)	(1.0)	(1.0)						
Education	1.2	-	4.0	9.1	16.7	31.9	49.5			17.5	12.8	13.8	9.2
(share of GNP in %)	(4.2)	-	(4.0)	(4.0)	(3.5)	(3.3)	(2.6)						
Social security	0.9	-	4.3	10.3	24.7	58.2	130.8			19.1	19.2	18.7	17.6
(share of GNP in %)	(3.3)	-	(4.2)	(4.5)	(5.2)	(6.0)	(6.8)						
Housing investment by Government	0.1	-	0.4	1.5	3.7	9.6	24.3			29.6	20.0	20.9	20.4
(share of GNP in %)	(0.4)						(1.3)						
Roads, traffic investment	0.2	-	1.8	7.4	13.2	27.2	51.2			32.0	12.4	15.5	13.5
(share of GNP in %)	(0.6)	-	(1.8)	(3.2)	(2.8)	(2.8)	(2.7)						

(Source: **JERC**'s trillion-dollar-forecast; author's excerpts (billions of dollars, rate 320)

Table 10. Japan's Strategy for Victory — a Numerical Explanation

a) this is what Japan wants to achieve
o   an accumulated GNP in 1971-85 of 13.6 trillion dollars
o   compared to only 1.5 trillion in the 1956-70 period

b) A desperate shortage of labour — but the quality of labour will improve

	annual change in per cent					
	1956 -60	1961 -65	1966 -70	1971 -75	1976 -80	1981 -85
Total population	0.9	1.0	1.1	1.2	1.1	0.9
of which in productive age	1.9	2.2	1.4	0.8	0.8	0.8
total labour force	1.5	1.2	1.7	0.8	0.5	0.4
length of working hours	0.8	-1.0	-0.1	-1.0	-0.7	-0.4
quality of improvement (through lengthier education)	0.3	0.2	0.4	0.4	0.3	0.3
same, but because of sex change, age change of labour force	0.3	0.3	0.3	0.3	0.2	0.1
change in labour force-input after considering quality boost	2.9	0.7	2.3	0.5	0.3	0.4

c) an ageing labour force; which means higher costs

age distribution of labour force, in per cent

age in years	1965	1970	1975	1980	1985
15-19	8	6	5	4	4
20-29	27	28	26	21	19
30-39	25	24	24	26	26
40-54	15	27	30	33	33
Over 55 years	15	15	15	16	18

d) therefore, accelerated fixed investments per employee

(annual change in per cent)

	56- 60	61- 65	66- 70	71- 75	76- 80	81- 85
Real GNP growth	9.1	9.7	12.5	10.1	9.9	9.9
Labour force growth rate	1.5	1.2	1.7	0.8	0.5	0.4
Private capital stock	7.9	11.2	13.2	14.1	13.0	12.3
Investment per employee ("capital equipment ratio")	6.2	9.8	11.3	13.2	12.5	11.8
Capital coefficient	-1.1	1.4	0.7	3.5	2.8	2.2
Labour productivity	7.4	8.3	10.6	9.3	9.4	9.5

e) – and, therefore, accelerated R & D investments
A 25-fold jump between 1969 and 1985 (for details, see Chapter six, Brain Power Index)

f) – because technology is a key factor among the five hidden causes of growth

	57-70	71-85
Capital	43	54
Labour	9	3
Work hours	-1	-4
Rate of operation	2	-
Technological progress ("innovation")	45	47
	(100)	(100)

g) this is the mechanical, monetary explanation of Japan's GNP growth

	PAST PERIOD 1956-70		FUTURE 1971-85	
	increase in billion $	sector contribution (in %)	increase in billion of $	contribution in %
Private consumption	100.1	49.3	827.6	49.1
Public consumption	15.3	7.6	124.8	7.4
Private housing investments	15.5	7.7	131.2	7.8
Public fixed investments	17.6	8.6	199.4	11.8
Private business fixed investments	44.6	22.0	336.2	19.9
Private inventory investments	7.4	3.7	57.7	3.4
Exports, etc	23.8	11.8	180.8	10.7
Imports, etc	21.7	10.7	170.3	10.1
GNE (=GNP)	202.7	(100)	1687	(100)

Note: All tables based on JERC's trillion-dollar-economy forecast.

Table g): author's exchange rate, floating rate of 320 yen per dollar

Table 11. Susuki-San Suffered as Public Investment Mainly Helped Industry

Public investments, billions of dollars, nominal prices (exchange rate: 320)	Totals fiscal years 1964-69	Share in %
Social infrastructure	13.44	16.9
Public housing investment	(3.75)	(4.7)
Public sanitation	(3.1)	(3.9)
Health, welfare	(1.68)	(2.1)
Schools	(4.90)	(6.2)
Industrial infrastructure	36.69	46.1
Roads	(17.33)	(21.8)
Harbours	(2.06)	(2.6)
Railways	(8.76)	(11.0)
Environment protection	4.80	6.0
Other public investment	24.64	31.0
Grand total	79.58	100

(Source Mitsubishi Bank Review, November, 1971)

Table 12. Thus Susuki-San is Very Poor When Compared to Citizens of Other Countries

Accumulated value in billions of dollars (1968) (in 1968 prices)	Japan	US	West Germany	Great Britain
Total fixed assets	237	1,886	300	252
Corporate assets	125	775	159	132
Society's social infrastructure	112	1,112	141	120
of which dwellings	(62)	(743)	(90)	(83)
Inventory	49	217	16	48
Total stock (= total accumulated richness)	287	2,103	316	300
THE PER CAPITA PICTURE ($)				
Total per capita, in dollars	2,830	10,450	5,440	5,420
Social infrastructure, per capita	1,110	5,530	2,430	2,180
Dwellings, per capita	610	3,690	1,550	1,500
Total stock in ratio to GNP (fold)	2.02	2.43	2.39	3.41

Table 13. What is Sweden Doing at the Top of the Heap?

A private and unofficial JERC estimate of GNP per capita in 1980
(forecast date: January, 1972); in dollars per year

The world's 30 richest peoples in 1980

GNP PER CAPITA IN $	1970 (partly estimated)	1980	Country's growth rate in total GNP, in per cent (%)	
			1969-75	1976-80
1 Sweden	3760	9479	8.8	10.2
2 Canada	3733	9217	10.6	9.9
3 Japan	1895	8225	14.5	13.4
4 West Germany	3167	8221	12.0	8.3
5 US	4739	8217	7.6	6.0
6 Netherlands	2487	8126	14.3	12.6
7 Denmark	3057	7748	8.9	11.3
8 Belgium-Luxemburg	2596	6876	9.3	10.2
9 Iceland	2095	6429	14.8	14.8
10 Libya	1883	6395	18.0	15.5
11 Norway	2745	6360	9.9	9.3
12 Switzerland	3248	6072	6.5	8.1
13 France	2611	5850	6.2	9.1
14 Australia	2637	5469	9.6	9.0
15 Bulgaria	1897	5303	9.2	10.2
16 Kuwait	4318	5012	11.2	9.5
17 Hungary	2340	4953	5.3	7.5
18 Austria	1850	4745	9.9	9.0
19 East Germany	2155	4552	4.2	8.2
20 Czechoslovakia	2207	4300	4.6	7.0
21 Soviet Union	1842	4251	7.8	8.2
22 Poland	1892	4185	5.6	9.4
23 Finland	2105	4085	7.4	8.6
24 Great Britain	2155	3850	5.8	7.7
25 Italy	1648	3603	7.5	9.5
26 New Zealand	1934	2997	4.3	7.6
27 Greece	1054	2976	11.4	11.9
28 Israel	1746	2892	8.2	8.1
29 Romania	1210	2860	8.6	9.6
30 Ireland	1276	2475	7.2	10.0

Note: Author finds it very unlikely that Sweden's growth rate will be that good, in view of Sweden's
official growth forecast for the 1971-75 period. But as the figures above are in nominal prices,
both Sweden and Canada may be able to "out-inflate" Japan. The forecast for France contra-
dicts the opinion of European economists, who predict a higher growth rate for France in the
1970s than for any other European country. The growth rates are based on dollar-base figures,
including for some countries both revaluation and devaluation effects, including changes expected
in the 1970s.

Table 14. JERC's Trillion-Dollar-Economy Forecast; 1971

	1955	1960	1965	1970	1975	1980	1985	56-60	61-65	66-70	71-75	76-80	81-85
								annual change in %					
Population (millions)	89.3	93.4	98.3	103.8	110.2	116.4	126.6	0.9	1.0	1.1	1.2	1.1	0.9
Productive age population	54.7	60.0	66.9	71.8	74.9	77.7	81.1	1.9	2.2	1.4	0.8	0.8	0.8
Labour force	41.9	45.1	47.9	52.1	54.2	55.4	56.5	1.5	1.2	1.7	0.8	0.5	0.4
Primary sector	16.5	14.5	12.1	10.0	7.3	5.8	4.5						
Secondary sector	9.9	12.4	15.0	18.0	20.1	21.4	22.5	4.7	3.9	3.7	2.3	1.2	1.0
of which Mining	0.5	0.5	0.4	0.2	0.2	0.2	0.1						
Construction	1.8	2.4	3.1	4.0	4.5	5.1	5.8	5.5	5.5	5.2	2.5	2.6	2.5
Manufacturing Industry	7.6	9.5	11.6	13.8	15.5	16.1	16.6	4.7	4.0	3.6	2.2	0.9	0.6
Tertiary sector	14.8	17.7	20.3	24.6	26.2	27.6	28.9	3.7	2.8	3.9	1.2	1.1	0.9

Wages, prices

	1955	1960	1965	1970	1975	1980	1985	56-60	61-65	66-70	71-75	76-80	81-85
Annual income per employee, in dollars at exchange rate 320	668	913	1650	3145	5813	11380	22095	6.4	12.6	13.8	13.1	14.4	14.2
Consumer price index (1965 = 100)	68	75	100	133	177	236	315	1.8	6.3	5.5	5.9	6.0	5.9
Wholesale price index	96	98	100	112	120	128	136	0.5	0.5	2.2	1.5	1.3	1.2
same, industrial goods	100	101	100	110	115	120	126	0.1	-0.1	1.9	0.9	0.9	0.9

Productivity investments

	1955	1960	1965	1970	1975	1980	1985	56-60	61-65	66-70	71-75	76-80	81-85
Annual labour productivity per person (dollars)	998	1425	2125	3515	5473	8579	13492	7.4	8.3	10.6	9.3	9.4	9.5
Private capital stock (billion $)	59	86	146	273	525	968	1727	7.9	11.2	13.2	14.1	13.0	12.3
Public capital stock	36	47	76	131	230	406	723	5.5	10.2	11.4	11.9	12.0	12.3
Household savings of disposable income (%)	13.9	17.4	17.0	21.9	21.1	21.1	21.1						

GNP development
nominal prices, fiscal years
(billions of $; rate 320) GNP

	1955	1960	1965	1970	1975	1980	1985	56-60	61-65	66-70	71-75	76-80	81-85
GNP	27.7	50.6	102	230	478	969	1917	12.8	15.0	17.7	15.7	15.2	14.6
Private consumption	17.6	28.3	58	118	243	485	945	9.9	15.3	15.3	15.6	14.9	14.3
Public consumption	2.8	4.4	9.5	18.1	36.1	71.8	143	9.6	16.4	13.8	14.8	14.8	14.8
Private housing investment	0.8	2.1	5.9	16.3	35	74	148	20.0	25.5	23.5	18.0	16.0	14.9
Private business fixed investment	3.0	9.9	15.7	47.8	100	199	384	22.7	9.6	24.9	16.0	14.8	14.0
Public fixed investment	1.7	3.8	9.4	19.3	45	99	219	16.9	19.9	15.3	18.3	17.2	17.2
Exports, etc	3.2	5.6	11.5	27	58	111	208	11.7	15.4	18.7	16.4	14.0	13.3
Imports, etc	2.9	5.6	10.2	25	54	104	195	13.6	12.8	19.3	16.7	14.3	13.3

Share of GNE in per cent

	1955	1960	1965	1970	1975	1980	1985
Private consumption	64	56	57	51	51	50	49
Public consumption	10.2	8.8	9.3	7.9	7.5	7.4	7.5
Private housing investment	2.9	4.1	5.8	7.1	7.3	7.6	7.7
Private business fixed investment	11	20	15	21	21	21	20
Public fixed investment	6.3	7.5	9.2	8.4	9.3	10.2	11.4
Exports, etc	12	11	11	12	12	12	11
Imports, etc	11	11	10	11	11	11	10

GNP at constant prices
(1965 price level)

	1955	1960	1965	1970	1975	1980	1985	56-60	61-65	66-70	71-75	76-80	81-85
GNP	41.1	63.6	101	182	294	471	755	9.1	9.7	12.5	10.1	9.9	9.9
Private consumption	25.7	37.3	57.0	90	140	212	317	7.8	8.8	9.6	9.3	8.6	8.4
Public consumption	5.7	6.6	9.3	12.2	16	21	29	2.9	7.1	5.5	5.4	6.0	6.4
Private housing investment	1.3	2.6	5.8	11.6	18	27	40	14.5	17.4	14.8	8.7	8.8	8.2
Private business investment	3.7	10.3	15.6	42.2	76	132	227	22.6	8.7	20.0	12.5	11.7	11.4
Public fixed investment	2.3	4.5	9.4	15.6	29	52	95	13.8	16.0	10.7	12.9	12.4	13.1
Exports, etc	3.2	5.7	11.5	24.5	48	87	153	14.8	14.9	24.0	14.6	12.5	12.0
Imports, etc	2.6	5.6	10.2	22.6	46	84	150	16.9	12.5	16.2	15.2	13.0	12.3

Share of GNE in per cent

	1955	1960	1965	1970	1975	1980	1985
Private consumption	63	59	56	50	48	45	42
Public consumption	14	10	9	7	5	5	3.8
Private housing investment	3	4	6	6	6	6	5.3
Private business investment	9	16	16	23	26	28	30
Public fixed investment	6	7	9	9	10	11	12.6
Exports, etc	8	9	11	14	17	19	20.3
Imports, etc	6	9	10	12	16	18	19.9

Table 15a. Japan's Corporate Business Sector Will be Borrowing
Twice as Much Money in 1975 as in 1971

Sector financing by economic sector, in billions of $ (showing how Susuki-San's bank savings will continue to finance business investments)	A forecast by the Nomura Institute in March, 1972					
	1971	1972	1973	1974	1975	1976
Corporate Business Sector	-11.4	-9.3	-13.3	-16.4	-25.0	-36.3
Household Sector	27.1	29.3	32.0	37.7	45.9	55.5
Public Sector	-4.9	-11.0	-15.2	-20.4	-24.6	-25.9
Rest of the world	-6.5	-5.9	-5.2	-4.8	-4.5	-4.6
Public Bond Issues	7.3	14.9	19.8	26.0	31.3	32.4

Note: A diminished role for foreign banks

Table 15b. Japan's Merchandise Exports in 1976: about 48 billion dollars

(Nomura forecasts, 1972)	1970	1973	1976	Annual increase in %, 1971-76
Exports, etc	28	33.8	51.6	10.7
Imports, etc	25.1	29.2	47.1	11.1
Merchandise exports, fob	23.3	30.5	47.9	15.8
Merchandise imports, fob	18	22.0	36.8	15.6
Trade balance	(4.5)	8.5	11.1	
Current balance	(2.4)	5.1	4.6	
Basic balance	(1.1)	3.0	0.8	
GNP, nominal	238	337	540	14.7
Real GNP (1965 price)	187	226	312	8.9
Public fixed investments	20	37	63	21.0
Private business fixed investments	48	54	102	13.5
Private housing investments	16	22	37	15.4
Per capita (dollars):				
national income	1,640		4,813	
financial assets	1,840		5,236	
social security cost	32		249	
Working hours per week	44.5		41.7	
Ratio of paved roads, in %	17.2		42.3	
Industrial production (1965 = 100)	220	258	386	9.8

Note: Nomura believes in greatly increased imports in the latter half of the six-year period of 1971-76. Imports, fob, are expected to rise at an annual rate of 12.6% in the first half, and at a rate of 18.7% in the latter half.
Industrial production: a modest annual pace of 8.1% per year in the 1971-73 period, and 14.4% per year in the latter half — a lull-and-typhoon pattern.

Author's rate of exchange: the 1972 official parity of 308 yen per dollar for all figures above, with the exception of foreign trade balance figures

Table 16a. World GNP and Export Development; steady decline in weight of US

(1972 forecast by Dr Kanamori; JERC)	GNP billions of dollars			Merchandise exports billions of dollars			Population in millions		
	1960	1970	1980	1960	1970	1980	1960	1970	1980
Japan	43	196	957	4	19	92	93	104	116
North America	548	1056	2166	26	59	162	199	228	261
United States	511	977	1933	20	43	117	181	206	235
Western Europe	327	769	1924	52	138	369	351	389	426
(EEC (six nations)	187	471	1251	30	89	252	170	186	199
Eastern Europe	232	563	1531	13	31	80	310	346	382
Soviet Union	160	406	1155	6	13	40	214	243	271
China	60	75	230	2	2	6	647	774	911
Under-developed countries	166	324	700	28	54	124	1169	1522	2020
South East Asia	60	103	236	8	14	36	748	974	1284
Australia, New Zealand, and South Africa	26	56	136	4	8	18	29	36	45
WORLD, total	1401	3038	7643	128	311	850	2797	3396	4160

Note: Soviet GNP above assumes a rouble revaluation against $

	Share of World GNP in per cent			Share of world merchandise exports (%)			Share of world population in per cent		
	1960	1970	1980	1960	1970	1980	1960	1970	1980
Japan	3.1	6.4	12.5	3.2	6.2	10.8	3.3	3.0	2.8
North America	39.1	34.7	28.3	20.3	19.1	19.0	7.1	6.7	6.3
United States	36.5	32.1	25.3	15.9	13.7	13.7	6.5	6.1	5.7
Western Europe	23.3	25.3	25.2	46.2	44.4	43.5	12.6	11.5	10.2
EEC (six nations)	13.3	15.5	16.4	23.2	28.4	29.6	6.1	5.5	4.8
Eastern Europe	16.5	18.5	20.0	10.1	9.8	9.4	11.1	10.2	9.2
Soviet Union	11.4	13.3	15.1	4.3	4.1	4.7	7.7	7.1	6.5
China	4.3	2.6	3.0	1.5	0.7	0.5	23.1	22.8	21.9
Under-developed countries	11.8	10.3	9.2	21.6	17.4	14.6	41.8	44.8	48.5
South East Asia	4.3	3.4	3.1	6.0	4.6	4.3	26.7	28.7	30.9
Australia, New Zealand and South Africa	1.9	1.8	1.8	3.1	2.6	2.1	1.0	1.0	1.1
WORLD, total	(100)	(100)	(100)	(100)	(100)	(100)	(100)	(100)	(100)

Table 16b. World's Top 15 Nations in GNP in 1980; Japan Has Surpassed the Soviet Union

(1972 forecast by JERC; Japan 1980 at assumed 1980 rate; 208 ¥ per $)
(In billions of dollars, nominal prices)

1 USA	1,933	6 Great Britain	220	11 Poland	90
2 Japan	957	7 Canada	218	12 Mexico	83
3 Soviet Union	677	8 Italy	197	13 India	79
4 West Germany	445	9 Netherlands	118	14 Australia	77
5 France	299	10 Brazil	98	15 Sweden	75

Note: The growth of France has been underestimated; should be equal to West Germany

Table 17. Japan's New Export Strategy: Intensify the Structural Revolution, Reduce Share of Light-Industry Products to Half of Current Level

(1972 forecast by Dr Kanamori; JERC)	Billions of dollars				Share, in per cent				Annual average growth in per cent			
	1960	1965	1970	1980	1960	1965	1970	1980	1956-1960	1961-1965	1966-1970	1971-1980
Japan's total merchandise exports, (fob, customs statistics)	4	8.5	19.3	92.2	(100)	(100)	(100)	(100)	15.1	15.8	18.0	16.9
Heavy and chemical industry	1.8	5.2	14.0	79.6	43	63	72	86.3	18.2	25.0	21.7	19.0
Chemical products	0.2	0.5	1.2	6.8	4.2	6.5	6.4	7.4	12.4	26.4	17.7	18.6
Metals	0.6	1.7	3.8	12.1	13	20	19.7	13.1	7.8	25.0	17.2	12.2
of which iron, steel	0.4	1.3	2.8	8.1	9	15	15	8.8	8.4	27.2	17.1	11.1
Machinery	1.0	3.0	8.9	60.6	25	35	46	65.8	30.8	24.2	24.5	21.0
a) general machinery	0.2	0.6	2.0	17.3	5.6	7.4	10.4	18.8	15.9	25.4	26.4	23.9
b) electrical machinery	0.3	0.9	2.9	18.9	6.8	10	14.8	20.5	54.4	24.3	27.0	20.8
c) transportation equipment	0.4	1.2	3.4	20.6	10.7	14.7	17.8	22.4	29.5	23.4	22.5	19.6
d) precision machinery	0.1	0.2	0.6	3.8	2.4	2.9	3.3	4.2	20.0	20.3	21.0	19.9
Light industry products	2.0	2.7	4.3	11.0	48	32	22.4	11.9	12.7	6.9	9.6	9.8
a) textiles	1.2	1.6	2.4	4.6	30	19	12.5	5.0	10.3	5.3	8.8	6.8
b) non-metal minerals	0.1	0.3	0.4	1.2	3.6	3.1	1.9	1.3	11.2	12.8	7.0	12.4
c) other light industry goods	0.6	0.9	1.6	5.2	15	10	8.1	5.6	19.2	8.7	11.7	12.7
Foodstuffs	0.3	0.3	0.6	1.3	6	4	3.4	1.4	14.5	5.1	13.5	7.1
Raw materials, fuel	0.1	0.1	0.2	0.3	1.6	1.5	1.0	0.4	11.1	14.0	9.4	5.7

Table 18. Japan's New Import Pattern in 1980; Eight-fold Leap in Machinery Imports

(1972 forecast by Dr Kanamori; JERC)	Billions of dollars				Share of total imports in per cent				Annual average increase in per cent			
	1960	1965	1970	1980	1960	1965	1970	1980	1956-1960	1961-1965	1966-1970	1971-1980
Japan's total merchandise imports, (cif, customs statistics)	4.5	8.2	18.9	88.9	100	100	100	100	12.7	12.7	18.3	16.8
Raw materials	2.2	3.2	6.7	19.5	49.2	39.4	35.4	21.9	11.8	7.8	15.7	11.3
a) for textile industry	0.8	0.8	1.0	1.2	17.0	10.4	5.1	1.3	5.4	2.1	2.6	2.0
b) metals	0.7	1.0	2.7	7.0	15.0	12.5	14.3	7.9	29.3	8.7	21.4	10.0
c) other raw materials	0.8	1.4	3.0	11.3	17.2	16.6	16.0	12.7	9.5	11.8	17.4	14.1
Mineral fuels (oil)	0.7	1.6	3.9	16.7	16.5	19.9	20.7	18.8	20.8	17.0	19.2	15.6
Chemical products	0.3	0.4	1.0	5.1	5.9	5.0	5.3	5.7	18.3	9.0	19.6	17.6
Machinery	0.4	0.8	2.3	16.9	9.7	9.3	12.2	19.0	25.0	11.8	24.8	22.1
a) general machinery	0.3	0.5	1.3	9.0	6.3	5.5	6.7	10.2	22.9	9.9	22.8	21.5
b) electrical machinery	0.03	0.1	0.5	3.0	0.8	1.4	2.5	3.3	14.9	26.7	33.9	20.0
c) transport equipment	0.09	0.2	0.4	3.7	1.9	1.9	2.2	4.2	30.5	12.1	21.4	24.2
d) precision machinery	0.03	0.04	0.2	1.2	0.7	0.5	0.8	1.4	26.2	6.5	28.0	23.3
Other products	0.3	0.7	2.4	22.3	6.5	8.4	12.8	25.1	48.2	18.4	28.8	24.5
a) iron and steel	0.09	0.1	0.3	1.0	2.0	1.7	1.5	1.1	54.3	9.9	14.4	14.0
b) textiles	0.02	0.06	0.3	3.9	0.4	0.7	1.7	4.3	11.5	24.5	40.7	25.7
c) non-ferrous metals	0.1	0.2	0.9	8.0	2.3	3.0	5.0	9.0	37.7	18.9	30.8	23.8
Foodstuffs	0.5	1.5	2.6	8.4	12.2	18.0	13.6	9.5	12.6	21.8	11.8	12.6

Table 19. Japan's New Export Structure Will be a Result of This New 1980 Pattern in Japan's Domestic Production

(1972 forecast by Dr Kanamori; JERC)	Billions of dollars				Sector's share of total				Annual average growth in per cent			
	1960	1965	1969	1980	1960	1965	1969	1980	1956-1960	1961-1965	1966-1969	1970-1980
Agriculture, forestry, fishing	7.7	12.1	17.8	41.4	8.2	6.6	5.1	2.5	3.6	9.5	8.0	8.0
Mining	1.2	1.5	2.2	5.1	1.3	0.8	0.6	0.3	8.9	4.8	8.9	8.0
Manufacturing industry	45.6	85.9	169.7	781.7	49.0	46.7	48.6	47.3	17.7	13.5	18.6	14.9
a) food industry	5.4	10.5	17.9	48.7	11.9	12.2	10.6	6.2	9.5	14.2	14.3	9.5
b) textiles	4.9	7.4	11.0	26.9	10.8	8.6	6.5	3.4	9.7	8.4	10.4	8.5
c) paper, pulp	1.7	3.2	5.4	19.7	3.7	3.7	3.2	2.5	16.2	13.2	14.1	12.5
d) chemical	4.2	8.1	14.1	62.3	9.3	9.4	8.3	8.0	14.6	13.8	14.9	14.5
e) oil, coal products	1.2	2.7	4.9	18.9	2.6	3.2	2.9	2.4	21.7	18.3	15.8	12.9
f) ceramics, stone	1.5	3.0	6.0	26.7	3.4	3.5	3.5	3.4	18.3	14.4	18.6	14.6
g) primary metals	6.7	11.0	22.4	94.8	14.6	12.8	13.2	12.1	9.7	10.5	19.3	14.0
h) metal products	1.8	3.9	8.6	39.4	3.9	4.6	5.1	5.0	22.8	17.4	21.9	14.8
i) general machinery	3.5	6.5	15.8	97.8	7.8	7.5	9.3	12.5	31.2	12.8	25.1	18.0
j) electrical machinery	3.8	6.5	17.3	100.2	8.3	7.6	10.2	12.9	38.6	11.5	27.6	17.3
k) transport machinery	3.8	8.2	18.0	100.3	8.3	9.5	10.6	12.8	26.7	16.6	21.8	16.9
l) precision machinery	0.5	1.1	2.2	12.9	1.1	1.3	1.3	1.7	24.4	17.1	19.3	17.3
m) other manufactured products	6.5	13.8	26.0	133.0	14.3	16.0	15.3	17.0	14.6	16.0	17.3	16.0
Construction	8.4	18.4	36.2	213.2	9.1	10.0	10.4	12.9	20.5	16.9	18.3	17.5
Transportation, communication utilities	7.5	15.0	25.6	108.4	8.0	8.1	7.4	6.6	13.4	14.9	14.4	14.0
Commerce, service	22.7	50.7	97.4	498.4	24.4	27.6	27.9	30.2	14.1	17.4	17.7	16.0
TOTAL (note: production value; not added value)	93.1	183.6	348.8	1651.2	100	100	100	100	14.9	14.5	17.4	15.2
GNP (which is an added value calculation; here at the "old" exchange rate of 360 yen per dollar, for all years; nominal)	45	88	166	744					12.7	14.5	17.1	14.6

Table 20a. Japan's Foreign Trade in 1980 with Different Regions

(1972 forecast by Dr Kanamori, JERC)	North America	EEC	EFTA	West Europe	Latin America	ANS	Asia	Africa	Communist countries	Other countries	Totals
Japan's imports (fob) from various regions											
1960	1.2	0.2	0.2	0.5	0.3	0.03	1.4	0.3	0.07	0.04	4.0
1970	6.6	1.3	1.1	2.9	1.0	1.0	5.4	1.1	1.0	0.2	19.0
1980	29.8	9.1	5.7	17.7	3.2	5.2	23.8	4.1	7.9	0.6	92.2
Japan's imports from various regions											
1960	1.7	0.2	0.1	0.4	0.2	0.4	1.1	0.07	0.1	0.005	3.9
1970	5.4	1.0	0.7	1.7	1.0	1.6	4.5	0.6	0.8	0.1	15.7
1980	23.7	6.8	4.7	11.7	3.0	7.2	19.4	3.0	7.3	0.2	75.5
The regions will take this share, in %, of Japan's total export value											
1960	30.4	4.3	5.7	11.7	6.8	5.6	35.7	7.2	1.8	0.9	100.0
1970	34.1	6.7	5.5	15.1	5.1	5.5	28.0	5.5	5.4	1.1	100.0
1980	32.4	9.9	6.2	19.2	3.5	5.6	25.8	4.4	8.6	0.6	100.0
And the regions are expected to take this share, in %, of Japan's total import value											
1960	42.7	5.4	3.5	9.3	6.2	9.6	27.4	1.9	2.8	0.1	100.0
1970	34.5	6.3	4.7	10.9	6.5	10.4	28.4	4.0	4.9	0.8	100.0
1980	31.4	9.0	6.2	15.5	4.0	9.5	25.8	4.0	9.7	0.2	100.0

Note: ANS: Australia, New Zealand, South Africa.
EEC: The six-nation area of 1972

Table 20b. Japan's Future Market Conquests; She is Seeking to Double Her Share in Western Europe

(1972 forecast by Dr Kanamori; JERC)	Japan's share of country's or region's total imports (%)				Annual average increase in % in Japan's export value	
	1960	1965	1970	1980	1961–1970	1971–1980
United States	7.5	12.0	15.5	23.3	18.4	16.1
Western Europe	0.9	1.3	2.0	4.7	19.9	19.7
Asia	11.4	14.3	20.7	33.1	14.1	16.0
Latin America	3.5	4.4	6.6	12.4	13.7	12.5
Communist countries	0.5	2.2	3.4	9.3	30.6	22.3
Soviet Union	1.1	2.1	3.1	10.4	19.0	28.0
China	0.2	14.1	26.0	40.3	19.0	15.1
Oceania, South Africa	5.0	8.0	12.1	28.0	16.8	17.0
Africa	4.5	8.2	9.0	15.5	14.0	14.2
Total: Japan's share of total world imports	3.2	4.5	6.2	10.9		

Note: "We'd better not miss the bus," proclaimed Japan's businessmen when President Nixon announced his new China policy in July, 1971 — but the Japanese were already enjoying the best front-seat in the bus, despite the lack of official relations with China. Japan's share: one-quarter of China's total imports, and Europeans and Americans had better hurry if they want to prevent Japan from taking more than the 40 per cent share forecast for 1980.

The Kanamori Group expects Japan's exports to China to rise from 572 million dollars in 1970 to 2.3 billion dollars in 1980. To the Soviet Union: a rise from 341 million dollars in 1970 to about 4.1 billion (still only 4.5 per cent of Japan's total exports in 1980).

Table 20c. Japan's Export Forecasts Assume This Growth in World Trade

	Annual value of world trade, billions of $	THE GROWTH OF WORLD TRADE	
		Period	% per year
1900	10.1	1900-1930	3.2
1930	26.3	1931-1950	4.3
1950	61.2	1951-1960	7.6
1960	127.9	1961-1970	9.3
1970	311.3	1966-1970	10.8
1980	850.0	1971-80	10.6

Table 20d. Japan's Export Leaps, 1969-1971

(Fiscal years; the 1971 fiscal year ended March 31, 1972. Source: MITI, 1972)	(Millions of dollars)			Annual increase in %	
	1969	1970	1971	1970	1971
TOTAL	17,587	21,216	26,561	20.6	24.9
Machinery products	6,628	8,524	11,632	26.6	35.4
Motor vehicles	1,211	1,756	3,074	45.0	75.0
Ships	1,314	1,531	1,953	16.5	29.5
TV, tape-recorders	801	1,000	1,265	24.8	26.6
Radio sets	481	552	634	14.8	14.8
Cameras	137	154	241	12.9	56.0
Metals	3,395	4,217	4,957	24.2	17.5
of which iron, steel	2,670	3,320	4,025	24.4	21.2
Sundries	1,756	2,002	2,285	14.0	14.1
Textiles	2,352	2,541	2,921	8.0	14.9
synthetic textiles	581	692	816	19.2	17.9
garments	412	429	441	4.1	2.6
cotton goods	242	213	233	-12	9.0
Chemical products	1,223	1,424	1,687	16.4	18.5
Food stuffs	480	553	618	15.3	11.7

Table 20e. Japan's Exports to the US, 1969-1971

(Fiscal years)	(Millions of dollars)			Annual increase in %	
	1969	1970	1971	1970	1971
TOTAL	5,543	6,716	8,458	21.2	25.9
Machinery products	2,533	3,273	4,731	29.2	44.5
Motor vehicles	419	737	1,514	75.7	105.4
TV, tape-recorders	545	634	736	16.3	16.1
Radio sets	284	320	365	12.6	14.2
Cameras	56	55	93	-3	69.7
Ships	4	5	6		
Sundries	722	800	856	10.4	7.3
Metal products	1,230	1,504	1,600	22.3	6.3
of which steel	876	1,094	1,161	24.9	6.1
Chemical products	165	203	231	23.4	13.5
Textiles	560	606	681	8.0	12.5
synthetic textiles	64	93	118	44.1	27.4
Light industry products	1,480	1,579	1,728		
Heavy chemical products	3,928	4,981	6,560		

Table 21. "We Shall Catch the United States and Outrun EEC in our"
Export Share for Research-Intense Products"

		Share of total export value			Annual increase in %	
		1964	1969	1980	1965-69	1970-80
Japan's development	R & D products	15.5	19.1	29.0	24.5	21.7
	a) chemical products	5.8	6.3	7.4	21.4	18.9
	b) electrical equipment	9.6	12.5	20.5	25.7	22.6
	c) aircraft	0.1	0.3	1.1	55.0	32.7
US development	R & D products	18.5	22.8	29.1	11.7	13.5
	a) chemical	9.0	9.1	10.7	7.3	12.6
	b) electrical	6.3	7.2	8.2	10.1	12.2
	c) aircraft	3.2	6.5	10.2	17.2	15.7
EEC development	R & D products	16.2	18.5	21.0	13.2	12.8
	a) chemical	9.0	10.7	12.4	14.3	13.0
	b) electrical	6.3	7.0	7.6	12.4	12.4
	c) aircraft	0.9	0.8	1.0	7.5	13.0

Note: 1972 forecast by the Kanamori Group.   EEC = six-nation area.

Table 22. This Table Shows it is not Pure Luck that is
Behind the Changes in Japan's Exports Pattern

		Labour-intense products	Raw material-intense products	Technology-intensive products	Totals
Export structure	1955	58.9	22.3	18.6	100
	1960	55.1	14.9	29.6	100
	1965	36.5	21.3	41.6	100
	1970	27.7	18.9	52.7	100
	1980	15.3	11.5	73.2	100
Annual average increase in %	1956-1960	6.4	6.8	26.1	15.0
	1961-1965	7.1	23.7	24.1	15.8
	1966-1970	11.3	15.2	23.7	18.0
	1971-1980	10.2	11.2	20.8	16.9
GNP elasticity	1956-1960	0.36	0.38	1.47	0.85
	1961-1965	0.53	1.76	1.79	1.17
	1966-1970	0.61	0.82	1.27	0.97
	1971-1980	0.72	0.79	1.46	1.19
Exported share	1955	10.5	12.0	7.3	10.0
	1960	10.9	6.7	7.5	8.9
	1965	8.1	10.8	11.6	9.9
	1969	7.0	8.7	12.1	9.4
	1980	4.4	6.4	14.0	9.2

Table 23a. A Table Guiding Japan in Her Switch from 'The Era of Raw Material Waste' to 'The Era of Knowledge Industries'

	Labour intensity degree	Raw material consumption degree	Technology intensity degree
Total	139	6.99	1.00
Food stuffs	366	0.97	0.14
Raw materials, fuel	33	80.53	0.29
Textiles	196	0.58	0.36
Minerals, not of metal	139	27.94	0.76
Other light-industry products	316	2.56	0.47
Iron, steel	49	11.98	0.49
Non-ferrous metals	78	28.56	0.76
Metal products	131	2.02	0.44
Chemical products	100	8.87	2.72
General machinery products	107	1.02	0.98
Electric equipment	119	1.20	2.28
Transportation machinery	119	0.54	0.98
Precision machinery	133	0.97	1.69

(Source: Kanamori; JERC, 1972)

Table 23b. But Japan's Raw Material Purchases Still Will Become Enormous

		1960	1965	1969	1980
a) Japan's share of world trade in these raw materials, in %	Oil	5.7	9.3	12.2	19.6
	Iron ore	11.6	21.7	35.1	53.6
	Bauxite	6.0	6.9	12.3	20.7
	Copper	6.6	9.2	19.7	38.2
b) Japan's import volume, in millions of ton	Oil	25	76	146	560
	Iron ore	15	39	83	217
	Copper	0.2	0.3	0.6	1.8
	Bauxite	0.3	0.5	1.2	4.1

(Source: Kanamori Group, 1972)

Table 24. Japan's Future Trade Balance with Different Countries, Regions

o Big deficit for the US o Huge surpluses for the sheiks	Billions of dollars per year	
	1970	1980
North America	1.2	6.2
United States	1.4	5.8
Western Europe	1.3	6.0
EEC, six nations	0.3	2.3
EFTA	0.4	1.0
Australia, New Zealand and South Africa	-0.6	-2.0
Latin America	0	0.2
Asia	1.0	4.3
South East Asia	2.5	18.8
Middle East	-1.6	-4.5
Africa	0.5	1.0
Communist countries	0.3	0.6
Soviet Union	-0.1	-0.4
China	0.3	0.5
Other countries	0.1	0.4

Table 25. Dr Kanamori's Indian Rope Trick: a Surplus of $16 Billion Turns into Zero

(1972 forecast by Kanamori, JERC) Japan's balance of payments	Millions of dollars per year			
	1961	1965	1970	1980
Trade balance	-558	1,901	3,963	16,674
exports, fob	4,149	8,332	18,969	92,184
imports, fob	4,707	6,431	15,006	75,510
Services	-383	-884	-1,785	-5,965
receipts	1,016	1,563	4,009	22,766
expenditures	1,399	2,447	5,794	28,731
Transfers	-41	-85	-208	-2,738
(Government grants)	-105	-96	-179	-2,326
Current account	-982	932	1,970	7,971
Long-term capital movements	-11	-415	-1,591	-7,971
Assets	-312	-446	-2,031	-14,704
Liabilities	301	31	440	6,733
Direct Japanese investments abroad	-94	-77	-335	-4,500
Basic balance	-993	517	379	0
Total balance	-952	405	1,374	0
Reserve of gold, foreign currencies	1,666	2,152	4,839	15,100

Table 26. Japan Wants to Conquer One-fourth of the US Import Market — But in Some Sectors as Much as 50 or 60 Per Cent

(1972 forecast by Kanamori, JERC)	US annual imports from Japan (billions of $)			Japan's share of total US imports (in per cent)			Annual increase (in per cent)	
	1964	1969	1980	1964	1969	1980	65-69	70-80
Total	1.8	4.9	26.8	9.5	14.2	23.2	22.8	16.4
Heavy industrial products	0.9	3.4	23.2	16.9	21.2	29.5	29.7	19.2
a) chemical products	0.04	0.1	1.4	5.4	9.8	26.6	26.1	24.6
b) metal products	0.4	1.1	3.5	19.1	26.6	30.9	21.9	11.4
of which iron, steel	0.3	0.8	2.7	35.0	42.4	45.6	22.8	12.0
c) machinery products	0.5	2.2	18.2	18.3	20.4	29.3	35.5	21.3
general machinery	0.1	0.3	4.2	8.2	12.4	26.5	35.5	26.5
electric equipment	0.2	0.9	6.5	48.2	45.8	50.3	33.4	19.7
motor vehicles	0.1	0.5	5.4	8.3	9.8	18.8	48.9	24.7
precision machinery	0.1	0.4	1.4	30.2	51.7	62.8	29.1	11.4
Light industry products	0.7	1.3	3.3	18.7	18.0	19.3	13.4	8.9
textiles	0.3	0.5	1.3	25.5	25.4	21.9	13.3	8.4
products not of metal	0.1	0.2	0.3	18.3	16.1	14.0	10.6	6.8
other products	0.3	0.6	1.6	15.0	14.5	19.0	14.4	9.7
Foodstuffs	0.1	0.1	0.2	2.4	2.5	3.0	6.6	5.9
Raw materials	0.04	0.04	0.06	0.8	0.6	0.5	-	3.5

Table 27. But Japan is Offering the US a Chance to Win Equally Large Chunks of Japan's Import Market

(1972 forecast by Kanamori, JERC)	Japan's annual imports from the US (billions of $)			US share of Japan's total imports (in per cent)			Annual increase (in per cent)	
	1964	1969	1980	1964	1969	1980	65-69	70-80
Total	2.3	4.1	24.2	29.4	27.2	27.2	11.9	17.5
Foodstuffs	0.4	0.6	1.9	30.2	30.4	23.4	9.2	10.5
Drinks, tobacco	0.03	0.1	0.1	57.6	61.6	30.1	9.2	7.1
Raw materials	0.9	1.2	4.0	28.4	22.6	24.0	6.9	11.4
Mineral fuel	0.2	0.5	1.4	14.1	15.0	8.2	18.3	10.5
Animal and vegetable oils, fat	0.03	0.03	0.1	70.2	54.7	39.3	1.2	4.5
Chemical products	0.2	0.3	2.1	47.8	43.0	41.2	9.0	18.1
Manufactured goods classified chiefly by materials (leathers, etc)	0.1	0.3	3.5	14.0	15.5	20.3	25.2	27.1
Machinery products	0.4	0.9	9.8	50.7	60.1	60.0	16.6	24.3
general machinery	0.3	0.5	6.0	50.7	54.5	62.3	13.7	24.7
electric equipment	0.1	0.2	1.1	67.5	71.1	65.8	23.3	15.8
transportation machinery	0.1	0.2	2.8	38.3	69.3	70.0	20.9	29.5
Miscellaneous	0.1	0.2	1.3	51.3	46.5	19.6	20.9	18.3

Table 28. The 1980 Strength of the Multinational Companies

(Accumulated direct investments abroad by various countries; in billions of dollars)	1966	1969	1980	1980 share in per cent	Annual increase in per cent 67-69	Annual increase in per cent 70-80	Sum's share of country's GNP 1969	Sum's share of country's GNP 1980	Per capita sum of direct investments abroad, in dollars 1969	Per capita sum of direct investments abroad, in dollars 1980
United States	54.7	70.8	209.3	60.6	9.0	10.3	7.5	10.8	348	890
Great Britain	16.0	18.7	25.8	7.5	5.2	3.0	20.0	11.7	336	434
France	4.0	4.8	8.6	2.5	6.1	5.5	3.2	2.9	95	156
West Germany	2.5	4.8	35.8	10.4	24.4	20.0	2.9	8.0	79	586
Canada	3.2	3.8	5.9	1.7	5.5	4	5.2	2.7	180	232
Japan	1.0	2.7	27.3	7.9	31.4	23.5	1.6	2.9	26	235
Total, for six countries	89.6	116.2	345.1	100.0	9.1	10.4	6.3	7.0	187	-

Table 29. Japanese Companies are Expected to Make These Direct Investments Abroad

	Billions of dollars 1969	Billions of dollars 1980	Share in per cent 1969	Share in per cent 1980	And this is where Japan will put the money (millions of $)	millions of $ 1969	millions of $ 1980
A Natural resources-oriented investments (mainly mining)	1.1	13.9	40.7	50.8	North America	700	4,400
					Europe	300	2,300
					South East Asia	600	5,500
B Labour or market-oriented (mainly manufacturing)	0.6	7.1	23.1	26.2	Middle, N. East	300	3,800
					Latin America	500	4,900
C Others (mainly finance and services)	1.0	6.3	36.2	23.0	Africa	100	1,500
					Communist countries	-	1,500
					Oceania (mainly Australia)	200	3,400
Total	2.7	27.3	(100)	(100)		2,700	27,300

(Source: tables 28-29; Kanamori Group; MITI)

Table 30. Japan's 'Aid' Flow in 1980

	1965	1970	1980	Annual increase in % 1961-1970	Annual increase in % 1971-1980
I Government assistance	285	458	4,391	17.6	25.2
1) Bilateral	235	372	3,222	14.6	24.1
a) grants, etc	105	121	2,326	6.0	34.3
b) loans	130	250	896	24.8	13.6
2) Multilateral	51	87	1,169	22.5	29.7
II Other Government programmes	200	694	1,829	-	10.2
III Private flow	140	672	6,220	10.5	25.0
a) direct investments	69	265	4,292	10.4	32.3
b) export credits	72	387	1,742	8.9	16.3
Total	625	1,824	12,440		

(Source: Kanamori, 1972)

Table 31. Japan's Flow of 'Economic Aid' in 1980;
Susuki-san's Thrust Twice as Large as Mr Brown's

Sixteen DAC countries; millions of dollars	Country's total assistance flow		Annual increase in %		Of which this sum is Government assistance		Annual increase in % in Government assistance		Total 'assistance' in 1980 per capita, per year, in $
	1970	1980	61-70	71-80	1970	1980	61-70	71-80	
1 United States	5,971	13,530	4.6	8.5	3,218	8,698	1.5	10.4	58
2 Japan	1,824	12,440	22.3	21.2	1,152	6,220	23.2	18.4	107
3 West Germany	1,487	5,656	9.0	14.3	731	3,393	7.6	16.6	102
4 France	1,807	3,884	3.4	8.0	977	1,974	1.4	7.3	70
5 Great Britain	1,281	2,064	3.8	4.9	455	940	1.1	7.5	35
6 Italy	729	1,876	9.4	9.9	171	855	5.0	17.5	32
7 Canada	626	1,865	15.7	11.5	402	1,399	18.3	13.3	74
8 Netherlands	445	1,586	6.3	13.6	199	938	18.7	16.8	110
9 Australia	384	840	20.6	8.2	209	546	13.5	10.1	55
10 Sweden	229	811	17.2	13.5	117	405	32.5	13.2	95
11 Belgium	308	725	5.4	8.9	120	377	1.7	12.1	71
12 Switzerland	135	299	-1.5	8.3	24	128	19.7	18.2	43
13 Norway	67	295	21.0	16.0	37	147	13.0	15.8	69
14 Denmark	97	285	9.8	11.5	56	165	24.9	11.4	54
15 Austria	96	258	32.0	10.4	19	148	-	22.8	33
16 Portugal	65	99	5.8	4.3	35	71	-1.1	7.3	10
Total	15,552	46,517	6.7	11.7	7,948	26,404	4.9	12.8	-

Note: Total "assistance" includes all kinds of financial flows, including export credits, direct investments, loans, etc)

Table 32. The Resurrection of the US in 1980; Can She Afford to Triple Her Direct Investments?

US balance of payments; 1972 forecast by Kanamori, JERC	Billion dollars per year				Annual increase in per cent			
	1960	1965	1970	1980	61-65	66-70	61-70	71-80
1　Trade balance	4.9	4.9	2.1	1.2				
exports	19.7	26.4	42.0	116.6	6.1	9.7	7.9	10.7
imports	14.7	21.5	39.9	115.4	7.8	13.1	10.4	11.2
2　Military transactions including defence expenditure	-2.8	-2.1	-3.4	-3.0				
	-3.1	-2.9	-4.9	-				
3　Services, net	2.0	4.3	4.8	21.5				
of which income from direct overseas investments, net	2.8	5.3	6.2	25.5	13.3	3.3	11.3	15.1
Result of 1, 2, 3	4.1	7.1	3.6	19.7				
Transfers, net	-2.3	-2.8	-3.1	-6.6				
Government grants	-1.7	-1.8	-1.8	-3.4				
Current accounts	1.8	4.3	0.4	13.1				
Long-term capital movements	-3.0	-6.0	-3.5	-13.1				
Assets	-3.6	-6.1	-7.4	-22.2	11.1	3.8	7.3	11.6
of which direct investments	-1.7	-3.5	-4.4	-13.1	15.6	5.1	10.2	11.5
Liabilities	0.6	0.1	3.9	9.1			19.7	8.8
of which foreign direct investments within the US	0.1	0.1	1.0	2.6			19.8	10.3
Basic balance	-1.2	-1.8	-3.0	0				
Official reserve balance	-3.4	-1.3	-9.8	0				
Liquidity balance	-3.7	-1.3	-4.7	0				
Gold, foreign currency reserves	19.4	15.5	14.5	23.0				

Table 33. In What Branches Will Foreign Firms Invest in Japan up to 1980?

(accumulated values, millions of $)	1955	1960	1968	1980	Sector share in % 1968	1980	Annual increase 1961-68	1969-80
Machinery industry	4	19	91	3,139	22	30	21.9	34.0
Metal production	2	5	36	523	8.7	5.0	27.0	25.0
Chemical industry	5	29	106	2,616	25.8	25.0	17.5	31.0
Textile industry	1	1	2	52	0.6	0.5	16.9	28.0
Oil industry	14	24	106	2,093	25.8	20.0	20.3	27.0
Other manufacturing	1	11	35	1,046	8.6	10.0	15.8	33.0
Other sectors	2	2	35	994	8.5	9.5	39.7	30.0
Totals	29	91	411	10,464	(100.0)	(100.0)	20.8	32.0

Note: Out of an accumulated sum of 10.4 billion dollars by 1980, US firms are expected to pump in a total of 7.3 billion, West European firms 2.1 billion, other nations about one billion dollars. The US share was 69.1 per cent in 1968; is expected to be at 70.0 per cent in 1980.

(Source: Kanamori Group)

Table 34. Total GNP sums of Japan and the United States

(Billions of dollars, nominal prices)	Japan 1972	US 1972	Japan's 1972 level in % of US level	Japan in 1980 (MITI)
TOTAL CONSUMPTION	182.8	937.8	19.5	571.0
a) private	156.6	719.1	21.8	481.4
b) public	26.2	218.7	12.0	89.6
TOTAL EFFORT	102.7	203.8	50.4	389.8
a) private business fixed investment	51.1	121.4	42.1	172.3
b) private housing investment	20.3	46.9	43.3	111.2
c) public fixed investment	31.3	36.6	85.5	106.3
TO BE ADDED				
a) overseas net	6.8	-0.4	-	6.9
(ie exports, etc	32.7	76.3	42.8	105.3
minus imports, etc)	25.9	76.7	33.8	98.4
b) inventory change	5.4	3.4	-	16.7
Total gross national product	297.7	1,145	26.0	984.4

Note: For Japan, fiscal year, for US calendar year; a forecast in March of 1972 by JERC. Author's exchange rate: official parity of 308 yen per dollar, also in the case of MITI's 1980 forecast, which is a part of MITI's so-called secret document (third chapter). Thus, MITI expects Japan's total fixed investments to be roughly twice as large as America's 1972 results.

What these GNP totals mean on a per capita level, see author's estimates in Chapter table 30 A (Chapter: The Revolution).

Table 35. Japan's Difficult Decision in October, 1972: to Aim for Revenge —
or a Four-day Week in 1980?

The answer of this table: whatever happens, a revenge pace of eight per cent!

Economic Planning Agency's program of alternatives, March, 1972; constant prices of 1965. The alternatives are being studied prior to the adoption of a new five-year plan, expected to be finalized in October, 1972.	Economic Result in Billions of Dollars								
	If continues present policies			Alternative One		Alternative Two		Alternative Three	
	1970	1975	1980	1975	1980	1975	1980	1975	1980
GROSS NATIONAL PRODUCT	186	311	525	298	458	301	470	283	400
Public consumption	12.7	17.5	24.0	17.2	21.8	17.2	22.4	16.2	19.2
Public fixed investments	15.9	31.5	52.9	36.4	64.3	32.8	55.2	32.8	48.7
Public transfers to individuals	8.1	14.6	26.3	16.6	31.8	19.5	40.3	21.8	44.2
Private consumption	90.9	155	259	150	231	153	242	146	212
Private business fixed investment	43	67	113	57	79	64	88	52	62
Exports etc	25	44	87	42	77	42	77	40	69
"Stock" or accumulation A. Government fixed capital stock (a result of fixed public investment)	121	219	395	228	440	221	405	223	398
B. Private fixed capital stock (a result of private business fixed investment)	245	446	785	432	677	438	707	424	621

(author's conversion rate: 308 yen per dollar)	Real Annual Growth in Per Cent per Year							
	Present policies		Alternative One		Alternative Two		Alternative Three	
	71-75	76-80	71-75	76-80	71-75	76-80	71-75	76-80
GROSS NATIONAL PRODUCT	10.9	11.1	10.0	9.0	10.1	9.3	8.8	7.2
Public consumption	6.5	6.6	6.1	5.0	6.3	5.4	5.0	3.2
Public fixed investments	14.6	11.0	18.1	11.9	15.5	11.1	15.6	8.2
Public transfers to individuals	12.6	12.7	16.0	13.6	19.4	15.8	22.1	15.2
Private consumption	11.3	10.8	10.6	9.0	11.0	9.6	10.0	7.7
Private business fixed investment	9.2	11.0	5.8	6.5	7.0	7.8	3.9	3.7
Exports etc	11.7	14.5	10.6	13.0	10.6	13.0	9.5	11.7
"Stock" or accumulation A. Government fixed capital stock (a result of fixed public investment)	12.6	12.5	13.5	14.1	12.8	12.9	13.1	12.3
B. Private fixed capital stock (a result of private business fixed investment)	12.8	12.0	12.1	9.4	12.4	10.1	11.7	7.9

Note: The alternatives are based on three basic assumptions: a) the relationship between Government fixed capital stock and private fixed capital stock; b) Government transfers to individuals, mainly welfare expenditures; and c) working hours.

Work hours: A continuation of present policies would mean an annual reduction of only 0.5 per cent per year. Alternatives One and Two both suggest a cut of 1.6 per cent per year and two days off by 1980, and by that time also four weeks leave per year. Alternative Three suggests a slash of 3.5 per cent per year which would result in three days off per week by 1980, and an annual leave of three weeks.

Transfers: Now only 4.3 per cent of GNP. Alternative One suggests 5.6 per cent by 1975, 6.9 per cent by 1980. Alternative Two: 6.4 per cent in 1975, 8.6 per cent by 1980 — ie would reach Britain's current level. Alternative Three: 7.6 per cent by 1975 and as much as 11 per cent by 1980, ie more than either Britain or West Germany.

Investment pattern: The ratio of public fixed capital stock to the private one has been 50 per cent in the past. One suggests 54 per cent by 1975, 60 per cent by 1980. Two 51 and 58 per cent respectively, and Three 54 per cent and 65 per cent respectively, with great impact on exports growth rate.

One emphasizes public investments, Two social welfare expenditures, Three a combination of both.